14 95

Hannah Arendt

Key Contemporary Thinkers

Hannah Arendt

Politics, History and Citizenship

Phillip Hansen

Stanford University Press
Stanford, California
1993

Stanford University Press
Stanford, California
© 1993 Phillip Hansen
Originating publisher: Polity Press, Cambridge
  in association with Blackwell Publishers, Oxford
First published in the U.S.A. by
  Stanford University Press, 1993
Printed in Great Britain
Cloth ISBN 0-8047-2145-9
Paper ISBN 0-8047-2146-7
LC 92-64252
This book is printed on acid-free paper.

Contents

For Jan and Michael

Acknowledgements

For their support, kindness and assistance throughout the period during which this book was written, I am deeply grateful to Harold Chorney, Dave Gullickson, Murray Knutilla, Eugene Szach, Maureen Woods, Brian Caterino, Paul Browne, Michelle Weinroth, Ken Reshaur, Davis Daycock, Paul Breines, Alvin Finkel and John Keane.

The political science department at the University of Regina, my 'home' for the past ten years, has offered unflagging encouragement and support for my work. My experiences there have been the happiest of my academic career. I want to thank all of my colleagues, and in particular Lorne Brown and Joe Roberts. I wish as well to acknowledge the financial support provided by the President's Fund of the University of Regina.

Years ago, Meyer Brownstone, then at the University of Toronto, came to my aid, personally and professionally. I have not had occasion to thank him publicly for kindnesses I have never forgotten, and I welcome the opportunity to do so now.

The late C. B. Macpherson played a major role in the preparation of the doctoral dissertation which served as a basis for this work. He is missed very much by those of us who were fortunate to have encountered at first hand his powerful intellect and his kind and gentle ways.

For more than twenty years, as a teacher, mentor and friend, Alkis Kontos has shared with me his powerful insights into political philosophy and life in general. I hope this study at least partially repays him for the faith he has shown in me.

The people at Polity Press have been a joy to work with, particularly my editor, John Thompson, Gill Motley, Debbie Seymour, Pam Thomas and Jennifer Speake. No author could wish a better publisher. The readers for both Polity Press and Stanford University Press, my American co-publisher, provided many helpful criticisms and comments which greatly strengthened the manuscript.

Leanne Overend prepared the different drafts of the manuscript with skill, intelligence and good humour, qualities which she possesses in abundance. Aydon Charlton carefully copy-edited the penultimate version of the manuscript with a keen eye for both grammatical errors and stylistic excesses.

Alicja Muszynski painstakingly read the entire text and offered many extremely valuable insights and criticisms. I doubt I have addressed satisfactorily all of her concerns. But her influence on the book, and on me, has been very great, far greater than she might imagine.

Finally, there are two people who have meant so much to me over the last ten years. I want to thank Jan Joel for her forbearance, and much more; and my son, Michael Joel-Hansen, whose arrival while this book was being written brought home to me in a particularly powerful and personal way the importance Hannah Arendt ascribes to birth as a new beginning. This book is dedicated to them.

Phillip Hansen
January 1993

Introduction

There is considerable uncertainty these days about what politics means in contemporary society. Recent developments, ranging from the collapse of Soviet hegemony in Eastern Europe to the movement for reform in the Soviet Union itself, the end of the Cold War and the restructuring of the world economy under the auspices of transnational capital, have called into question many of the fundamental assumptions about political life that have taken root over the last five decades.

Primary among these assumptions has been the equation of politics with the state or government. Whether in the form of the national security state, exercising and preserving its sovereignty in a hostile Hobbesian world, or the welfare state, buttressing economic enterprise with some measure of social redistribution at home, the organized institutions of power and coercion have been the objects of the desires and aspirations, hopes and fears, of individuals and groups seeking to use this power for the achievement of their goals. Even those new social movements ostensibly seeking to defend an 'autonomous' civil society from the supposed encroachments of the state have defined themselves in relation to this power, if only to ensure that it serves to restrict its own reach. Similarly, regardless of its rhetorical claims, the neo-conservative attack on the state is an effort to use state power in different ways, not to roll back the state as such.

In other words, the state and the relation which groups and individuals bear to it have been central to the construction of social identities. Even as social movements have challenged what they view as illegitimately imposed identities, these movements have sought to inscribe new, more meaningful and authentic ones into the power and authority relations of the state itself. This dilemma of supposedly anti-statist movements which remain implicated in the exercise of state power is unavoidable – there can be no 'withering away of the state' nor an autonomous civil society without the supportive structures of state power as critical elements of its very make-up.

Yet the criticisms of state power as an alien force undermining ties of solidarity *and* possibilities for individual autonomy in support of the aims and purposes of unaccountable social interests are powerful and persuasive.[1] Given this dilemma, what may be hoped for in respect to politics and political action in the current era? Beyond the provision of a basic framework of order, what might such political action accomplish? Do notions such as 'community', 'solidarity', 'public life' and even 'democracy' any longer illuminate for us the demands of human living together?

The current problems and prospects of politics have triggered an outpouring of studies concerned with these issues, a veritable renaissance in political theory. Feminism, post-Marxism, post-modernism, new forms of contract theory, communications theory, even a new 'communitarianism' – all testify to the significance of recent developments for serious reflection on the demands of public life.

However, in spite of these creative efforts to rethink the nature and limits of politics, there remains a gnawing doubt that we have become fully clear about the central concerns of collective life. A fuller understanding of the nature of the state or a self-reflexive sense of the inevitable partiality of our beliefs and values have not, for all their intellectual elegance, helped much to stem the operation of powerful social, political and economic forces which confront people as blind and uncontrollable fate. According to the French social theorist Claude Lefort, what is needed to grasp our current situation is neither political science nor political sociology, which is all that the most nuanced theory of the state and state-dependent social identities can amount to, but political philosophy. By this he means a form of inquiry concerned not with the institutions and practices of *politics*, but rather with the *political*: the constituting power by and through which a society represents itself to itself as a unity, a coherent social space rendered intelligible by means of distinctions between the real and imaginary, the true and the untrue, the good and the bad. Only when such distinctions are deeply embedded in the processes by which individual and social identities are formed is it then possible to deal with the 'real' world as an array of particular social facts and institutions such as the state or the economy.[2] Political science unreflectively presupposes the instituting work of the political without confronting it; the political is thereby concealed as a world-constituting activity. To retrieve it we must, according to Lefort, pose the questions with which political philosophy, going back to the Greeks, has historically begun: what is the form of society and what is the nature of the difference between different forms?

But if the questions themselves go back to the Greeks, our means of reflecting upon them cannot. Lefort's notion of a constituting power implies that, unlike the Greeks, we can no longer be 'innocent' about our own role in establishing the terms by which we understand ourselves. Reflecting the historical growth of human power over nature, Lefort's position suggests that we cannot assume, with Plato, that our categories are 'natural', given to us by an objective order of being. The old questions must be raised in a new way which both acknowledges our capacity to transform our world and, without relying on by now incredible metaphysical assumptions, specifies limits to them. To deal with our situation requires that we think as well about what it *means* to think: how our mental life relates to our social existence and whether it is possible, or even desirable, for thought to play the age-old role laid out for it, that is, to prescribe standards for a truly human life.

To be a political philosopher in Lefort's sense requires that one be both attuned to the old questions and aware of the need to pose them anew. It requires that one be neither nostalgic nor prophetic. It involves the qualities found in the work of Hannah Arendt.

Hannah Arendt's unique and valuable contribution to the study of public life is her attempt to outline the nature of the political in our time, the ways in which people are bound together with each other and what this tells us about who we are and what we are capable of doing. While influenced by thinkers such as Aristotle, Kant, Marx, Nietzsche, Heidegger and Jaspers, Arendt is no disciple of any of them. But she does not simply maintain a critical distance from them. She also thinks through the dilemmas of their work in a way which puts this work in a new light not exclusively cast by either her perspective or theirs, but jointly, collectively. (In this sense the metaphor Arendt uses to describe the German social theorist, Walter Benjamin – that of a pearl diver who brings to the surface obscure and hidden gems not merely for the purposes of excavation but to bring forth the rich and the strange and so further our understanding of that from which they came – could as well be used to describe Arendt herself.) At its best, political thinking is itself a political act: it can only proceed dialogically.

In coming to grips with the demands of political philosophy and its historic foundations, Arendt seeks neither a literal restoration of that which has gone before nor an outright negation of what has become historically obsolete. It is not only impossible to restore the past, it is undesirable: the Western tradition of political thought was self-contradictory, its political values distorting as much as revealing the nature of public life. On the other hand, we are very much a product of this tradition and the social and historical forces which gave rise to it, and we cannot situate ourselves neutrally above or outside it.

Thus Arendt is neither a 'deconstructionist', intent upon demolishing conceptual thought, nor a political 'rationalist' with a system of notions within which experience must be tightly fitted. She emphasizes the importance of experience as it is actually lived by and, just as importantly, thought about by, (potentially) acting beings. What Arendt, I suggest, ultimately claims is that the mental activity needed by political beings is itself a political and collective one, even if the reflections at the heart of it are necessarily individual and solitary. And this political thinking can only take place within the framework of supportive institutions and practices: political thinking both makes possible and requires public life. Put another way, Arendt's distinctive concepts provide the basis for a powerful and challenging account of what it means to think, as well as act, politically, an account of what I would call citizen rationality, with roots both in public life and in the realm of the mind.

In this book, then, I attempt to trace out the connections in Arendt's work between public life and political thinking, and the ways in which each informs the other. In doing so I hope not only to explore the significance of Arendt's ideas but also to convey the 'spirit' of her work, something that seems to have proved elusive to many commentators. Few contemporary thinkers have been so difficult to pin down. She has been seen as a cultural conservative and pessimist on the one hand, a radical democrat on the other. While there is insight in virtually all of the accounts of her thought, what is most important about Arendt is less the development of a specific theoretical stance and more the attempt to capture the 'temper' of political life. This temper, which involves a certain sense of proportion in both political thinking and political acting, suggests a kind of openness to political experience, an openness denied, in Arendt's view, by both the rationalist metaphysics of classical philosophy and the historicist assumptions at the centre of so much modern thought and culture.[3] Such openness, which acknowledges that we act within contexts such that nothing is either inevitably fated or radically undetermined, entails a willingness to confront the prospect that even in the grimmest of times – 'dark times' as Arendt calls them – there are always possibilities for something better in the realm of human affairs.

This outlook in my view is most compatible with what might

broadly be called a left politics (although Arendt herself was no leftist or 'progressive'). Such a politics seeks to change the world and must thus be vitally concerned with the real possibilities of the present. But it must also acknowledge that the present is the milieu within which one must act and that no future state of affairs can be immanently deduced from it by a logic of inevitability, dialectical or otherwise. The other side of this coin is that political life is always, in a manner of speaking, in 'crisis' and only from a (falsely) transcendental perspective can any specific crisis be seen as the 'final' one, *the* definitive historical turning point. For Arendt, even the rise of Nazism and the Holocaust, the closest approximations yet to a clear-cut and decisive turning point in history, have not totally eliminated the possibilities for the expression of genuinely human capacities, although they have certainly threatened them. For those seeking a more genuine politics, and this is surely a major goal of any serious left, it is essential to shed the comforts of an apocalyptic pseudo-radical and revolutionary outlook which is the legacy of an incompletely transcended theological heritage. It is essential, in other words, to think without ideology, and without illusions, however comforting, about our situation – which is not to say without principles.

Thus for the political actor who is also a thinking being, Arendt lays out demanding requirements. But these requirements are accessible to all and not just a few. Those who see in Arendt's ideas the outlines of a radical and participatory democracy are not so far off base. Neither pessimist nor optimist (nor 'realist', at least as that term is normally understood), Arendt explores what it means to live both with a history which is inescapably ours but which does not fully determine us, and with our projections of new realities the pursuit of which gives meaning to our existence. She explores what it means to live, to use her own words, 'between past and future', between what has been and what is not yet.

My claim that Arendt outlines an account of political acting and thinking which are more in tune with fundamental human capacities than currently dominant forms of either implies another claim: that her work offers an ontology, a conception of what it means to be distinctively human. The issue of ontology is a controversial one in political theory. For Hannah Arendt, who specifically denied having an ontology, at least in the form of a systematic theory of human nature, this is especially so.[4] Yet in contrast to post-modernist or deconstructionist criticisms of ontological reasoning as inherently oppressive, I see ontological assumptions as not only indispensible for political theory but unavoidable: no account of who we are as humans can be coherent without claims about what makes us distinctive and, equally important, what makes human life worth living.[5] Ontological assumptions need not define a systematic human 'nature' or 'essence'. But they necessarily set out limits to what is acceptable if human existence is to be sustained.

It is important in light of Arendt's position to note what this entails: human beings are capable of acts which can deny and destroy who they are. I believe that Arendt's overt opposition to explicit and systematic ontology follows from her fear that it can blind people to what humans are capable of doing to themselves, not from a desire to disavow judgement about what is good or bad for them. Adolf Eichmann, the Nazi functionary tried and executed by the Israeli government following a widely publicized and controversial trial in 1961 for his role in the 'Final Solution', was for Arendt an important source of insight into the nature of a totalitarian state. She believed he could not be understood in terms of traditional rationalist canons. However, this did not mean that he could not or should not be understood and thus judged at all. If ontological assumptions orient us toward judgements about what is good or bad for human beings, then Arendt's thought is ontological, indeed powerfully so.

Moreover, Arendt's is a specifically *political* ontology. This is not only because she spells out the place of the political in a well-ordered human existence, but also because to be human for her is to live with others who are both distinct and like ourselves. Arendt calls this fundamental element of the human condition 'plurality'; her concerns with both the possibilities for it and the threats to it suffuse virtually all her writings. It is not too much to claim that the primary demand Arendt makes of us is that we attend more fully than we normally do in our individualistic culture to the reality that we live in a world with others, and that the hallmark of sound political institutions is that they are not only based upon plurality but that they also nurture it, make it a living and visible force in our everyday lives.

It is because Arendt brings ontological assumptions to her work, even if they are largely implicit, that she is able to develop a powerful critique of prevailing forms of thought and action; indeed it is because of the ontological character of her position that the bulk of her work is a critical account of the modern situation. I argue that this account turns on the relations among history, politics and citizenship, and that Arendt's treatment of these is informed primarily by the concepts of 'freedom', 'action' and 'public realm'. These concepts and experiences both illuminate the current and flawed relation of thought to action, and point toward a different and more satisfactory one faithful both to a truly public life and to the life of the mind.

From the vantage point which these concepts and experiences provide, Arendt argues provocatively that fundamental confusions plague our thinking and hence our practical commitments in the social world. Both thinking and acting must be reconsidered anew and with a fresh eye because each has come, in the name of a false understanding of itself, to encroach dangerously on the terrain of the other. Taking a cue from Aristotle, Arendt argues that there are, in other words, both authentic and perverted or distorted forms of thought and action. Such forms are embodied in what I call 'false' politics: institutions and practices that provide the form but not the substance of public life. These false modes of public life provide the targets for Arendt's reflections on the modern situation.

The presence of false forms of public life profoundly conditioned for Arendt the possibilities for the development of citizenship: the ways in which people relate to power, law and government and thus establish the terms under which they join together as co-participants in a common life. Although she does not work out a systematic account of citizenship in the manner of, say, Aristotle, Arendt nevertheless saw citizenship as a vital component of a genuinely public life. Indeed her most powerful writings, *The Origins of Totalitarianism* and *Eichmann in Jerusalem*, are at one level accounts of the disintegration of genuine citizenship and the emergence of varieties of 'anti'-citizenship, false forms of what Arendt calls 'organized living together'.

If the fate of citizenship in our time is so closely linked with distorted modes of thinking and acting, the rise of both was facilitated by, and in turn shaped, another critical phenomenon of the modern era: history. As both a theoretical concept and a politically and culturally influential understanding of human purpose, history, at least in its modern form, is, according to Arendt, a process which both compels and validates patterns of individual and collective activity held to conform to a 'logic' of historical development and the realization of an identifiable telos. This encourages passivity in the face of ineluctable 'forces' of which groups and individuals are merely agents. Conscious responsibility, moral sensibility and, in extreme cases, the very ability to think at all are for Arendt victims of an increasingly pervasive historical consciousness.

The complex relations among politics, history and citizenship provide the setting within which Arendt develops her own political philosophy. In this setting, she makes clear – and here she touches base with the Platonic foundations of Western political thought – that philosophy and politics are potentially antagonists. Yet they need each other, the one informing and checking the other. An improperly politicized philosophy or a 'thoughtless' politics destroys the necessarily delicate balance between them. In this light our situation raises difficult questions. Can there be a philosophy which seeks to inform politics without transforming it in its own image? Can there be a politics which is more than a blind clash of competing interests, yet does not seek to stifle plurality with the dubious claims of a false universalism? For Arendt, such questions are not of interest merely to philosophers or intellectuals. Rather, they can occur to all human beings in so far as they think and act. Thus they are questions that can be, and indeed must be, posed practically for political and social groups, and for the means and ends to which they profess commitment. It is this 'everyday' quality of the relation of thinking and acting, and with it the commitment to a freely discursive mode of presentation, that provides a specific and recognizable cast to Arendt's reflections.

Arendt thus strove to articulate the elements of a rationality adequate to the requirements of public life in the contemporay era. That this must be done with the very concepts which, in Arendt's view, have tended to obscure what is distinctively political, while at the same time carrying with them layers of politically relevant historical experience, indicates the always ambiguous, never completed, nature of political life *and* thought.

Because of her insistence that in the face of seemingly inexorable trends certain human activities – those she identifies with a genuine politics – are not only possible but necessary, Arendt has been criticized, if not dismissed, as a utopian.[6] Conversely, because of her frequent concern for the facts of lived experience, she has been criticized for celebrating a reified 'common sense'.[7] Such seemingly disparate characterizations follow from the unique character of her alleged 'utopianism'. If there is a utopianism to her thought, it is not a mystical yearning for distant shores. It is what I would call a *utopianism of the here-and-now*: an immanent utopianism rooted in the articulation of currently existing human capacities and competencies as they are manifested in actually existing societies, even if in a distorted form. There remains encased in the given order of things the basis for what Arendt, borrowing from Czech author Pavel Kohut, calls a 'new example', new forms of public life and private sphere. The possibilities for such forms will exist as long as people are recognizably human. The powerful words of the great contemporary German philosopher Hans-Georg Gadamer echo Arendt's own:

Don't we all then run the risk of a terrible intellectual hubris if we equate . . . the ideological confusion of the present with life as it is actually lived with its own forms of solidarity? . . . In other words, if it were the case that there were no single locus of solidarity remaining among human beings, whatever society or culture or class or race they might belong to, then common interests could be constituted only by social engineers or tyrants, that is, through anonymous or direct force. But have we reached this point? Will we ever? I believe that we would then be at the brink of unavoidable mutual destruction ... I am concerned with the fact that the displacement of human reality never goes so far that no forms of solidarity exist any longer. Plato saw this very well: there is no city so corrupted that it does not realize something of the true city; that is what, in my opinion, is the basis for the possibility of practical philosophy.[8]

In chapter 1, I examine Arendt's critique of history, a critique most fully elaborated in her essay 'The Concept of History', but also central to several other works. In her critique, Arendt is not so much concerned with history as a technical discipline or with the status of historical explanation, but rather the significance of historical consciousness for the quality of public life. In her view this consciousness shapes a way of thinking about the world that is dangerously inappropriate for truly public action. Yet the kind of thinking involved is widespread and not restricted to our conception of history alone – the domains of science and technology, so influential in modern societies, bear the hallmark of it. For obvious reasons, the work of Karl Marx stands at the centre of Arendt's treatment of history and her (much misunderstood) criticism of Marx provides an important contribution to a reconsideration of the meaning and value of Marx's work for advanced industrial societies.

Chapter 2 examines the core elements of what, for Arendt, is a genuine politics, a truly public life. In particular it examines the notions of 'freedom', 'action' and 'public realm', and the relation these bear to the conceptual framework Arendt develops in *The Human Condition*, her best-known work. I attempt to show that, while she gives her own unique twist to these ideas, they are neither incomprehensible nor so radically divorced from existing political reality that they function solely as literary or speculative devices. Her ideas for the most part work best in criticizing existing institutions. But without themselves sketching out new institutions, they do indicate what institutions, new or old, must provide if they are to be adequate to the demands of public life.

In this light the value of Arendt's work has been increasingly acknowledged by social theorists concerned with the nature of public things in contemporary society. I attempt to assess the relation of Arendt's position to this emerging body of theoretical work, and beyond this to pinpoint weaknesses and problems that accompany this position.

With the account of a genuine politics as a background, chapter 3 examines the elements of what I call a 'false' or 'pseudo' politics. It is here that the ontological character of Arendt's position comes through most clearly: if the possibilities for a genuine politics are checkmated, human action will find other outlets. Among the most important falsely political phenomena, at least in liberal democratic states, are mass culture, violence as a decisive arbiter of public affairs and, especially, organized political lying, the account of which provides one of Arendt's most brilliantly insightful contributions to our understanding of contemporary politics.

These forms of false politics vividly demonstrate the close connection between political thinking and political acting. Both formal philosophical reflection and everyday common sense are profoundly affected by, and in turn affect, such phenomena. The uncomfortable truth about false politics is the complicity of those ensnared within its grasp in reproducing it. Ideology and behaviour, the most powerful distorted forms of thought and action, make us irresponsibly responsible for our condition: we are encouraged both to see these forms as 'us', as ours (thus human beings are inherently aggressive and so violence is as 'American as cherry pie'; we have the right to redo reality if it makes us feel better; we should accept that culture is about either entertainment or self-improvement and can say nothing objective about 'real' life), and at the same time to see them as the product of fate over which we have no control and with which we should not trouble ourselves. It is these circumstances which make false politics so pernicious and difficult to confront.

The ultimate form of false politics, the fullest realization of its ominous properties, is totalitarianism. Chapter 4 is devoted to Arendt's magisterial study, *The Origins of Totalitarianism*, and her most controversial work, *Eichmann in Jerusalem*. Totalitarianism stands for Arendt at the intersection of the historical development of specific social and political institutions with the Western tradition of conceptual reasoning. There is a sense in which the total state represents a horrific 'realization' of certain universal values. It is this development which more than anything else shaped Arendt's ambivalence about the political role of traditional philosophy and brought forward the need to explore what it means to think politically.[9]

With the rise of totalitarianism, what is ultimately at stake for Arendt is the possibility of individual autonomy and judgement, a possibility she steadfastly maintains even in the face of totalitarian horror and the evident collapse of autonomy and judgement on all fronts. This is clear from *Eichmann in Jerusalem*, which completed her account of the totalitarian phenomenon. This work embroiled Arendt in a heated battle, the ramifications of which still echo in intellectual circles. Because the Eichmann study drew upon the analysis in *The Origins of Totalitarianism* in important ways still not generally recognized (and this lack of recognition mars the work of contemporary theorists of totalitarianism such as Claude Lefort, Cornelius Castoriadis and Agnes Heller, who consciously follow in Arendt's footsteps), the controversy surrounding it brought to the fore more than the question of Arendt's historical accuracy in dealing with the Holocaust, the primary target of the critical attack on Arendt's position. It also raised the issue of the experiential context and content of totalitarian rule, and thus the possibilities for forms of total control to be found in *all* states, including democratic ones. In short *Eichmann in Jerusalem* is a powerful contribution to political theory, a contribution not yet sufficiently recognized.

Chapter 5 analyses Arendt's account of revolution. Revolution represents for Arendt the most significant modern attempt to establish a truly public realm. It expresses the capacity of humans to begin anew, to insert themselves through word and deed into the world and so create a living public sphere. It opens up in a new way questions about the nature and worth of public affairs, and historically unprecedented possibilities for political participation. Revolution also exhibits what is for Arendt the positive side of tradition and its relation to the modern age: its provision of a home for those historical memories of attempts to create a public space. And 'attempts' is the critical word here. For Arendt, there is an important sense in which a genuine polis has *nowhere* appeared, not even in the classical world to which she is so often drawn for theoretical insight. The other side of the coin is that existing revolutionary theory fails to capture the unique character of revolution as the attempt to found a realm of freedom; indeed such theory works against the very goal it claims to seek.

Chapter 6 draws more systematically out of Arendt's account of politics and the political the elements of specifically political thinking, a distinctive citizen rationality. It makes clear the extent to which for Arendt, thinking and acting, the *vita contemplativa* and the *vita activa*, are not as radically separate as they might appear. Thinking as such has communal foundations; even in the solitude of the thinking activity, the world is, and must be, closely at hand. Thinking politically involves not merely or even primarily reflection upon recognizable political things, but rather a certain sort of relationship both to others and to oneself. Its chief hallmark is neither intelligence nor moral rectitude, but the capacity for judgement. It is in this light that

Arendt's turn to philosophy in *The Life of the Mind* and, especially, her efforts to draw out of Kant's work a distinctive political philosophy, must be understood.

In the conclusion, I review the main lines of the argument I have developed in the rest of the book and suggest that Arendt provides a unique way of rendering the political visible and relevant to people in an everyday setting. She does this by suggesting that there is a distinctively personal quality to collective life, but that this quality is by no means identical with modern notions and experiences of subjectivity or individuality. Here a theme that Arendt develops in her account of action, the importance of the 'web of relationships' within which individual humans are necessarily embedded, is especially significant. Nothing we do ever concerns only ourselves. Yet what we choose to do, or not to do, distinguishes us from others, in the end by showing to what extent we care for our collective milieu, for plurality. 'Who' we are as individuals depends upon how we are with others, and while our world is more than our intentions, it could not be what it is without them. In this respect, what Arendt has to say about her two primary mentors, Karl Jaspers and Martin Heidegger, personal profiles that are self-consciously political because of their very personal character, provides a clear demonstration of Arendt's way of thinking about these matters and a fitting conclusion to this study.

In dealing with the question of what it means to think politically, Arendt's writings bear witness to her *own* suspension 'between past and future', to her embeddedness within an historically circumscribed situation. This situation is fraught with both threats to a genuine politics and possibilities for its realization. Our era is like all other eras precisely because it is like no other one. Cautious hopefulness is the defining quality of Hannah Arendt's political thinking.

I have now been wrestling with the ideas of Hannah Arendt for the better part of twenty years. It has been a challenge worth the effort but, for me at least, a challenge nonetheless. Arendt wrote with a clarity and vigour not often found in academic philosophy and political theory. For some, this has condemned her efforts to pedestrian status, to a location on the margins of serious but ephemeral journalism. For others, it has meant that we need not devote much effort to an exegetical treatment of her work, but instead should push forward with the development of her ideas, extending them in new directions or building on them where they continue to speak to us, discarding them when they are no longer useful for contemporary concerns.

This work is both critical and exegetical. I have certainly tried to evaluate critically Arendt's key concepts and to show how these relate to ongoing themes and concerns of political theory and practice. But there is a great need to get clear about what her ideas are. Straightforward though Arendt's prose might be, her thought does make serious demands on us. Her ideas are not invulnerable to misinterpretation; they can and do generate vigorous differences of opinion about their intention and significance. In other words, Arendt is a powerful and important twentieth-century political thinker, and I have throughout the book sought to make the case that this is so. In my own mind I am clear about certain of her ideas, less clear about others. Those ideas with which I am still wrestling form puzzles which crop up at various points throughout this study. I fervently hope others will pick up on these and unravel them where I have been unable to do so.

Hannah Arendt liked few things better than a good conversation. This is my attempt to get one going with my readers.

1 History and the Decline of Politics

Towering over the work of Hannah Arendt is the figure of Karl Marx.[1] For Arendt, Marx's thought illuminates the tensions and contradictions of modern politics more fully and faithfully than does that of any other theorist. She sees him as the last great thinker in the Western tradition of political thought, a tradition which extended back to ancient Greece and until the nineteenth century provided the inescapable framework within which questions of human purpose were posed for people in the West. She takes seriously Marx's demand to 'realize' philosophy because this demand could arise only when philosophy itself, whose primary characteristic was precisely its un-realizability, was no longer capable of orienting people to their world and giving meaning to their existence. The 'end' of philosophy, the attempt to transform it into a practical guide for the revolutionary activity of the working class – according to Marx the sole legitimate heir to classical philosophy – pointed to new human possibilities which the old standards could no longer accommodate.

To be sure, the Western tradition was brought to an end not only in Marx's work but in that of Nietzsche and Kierkegaard as well.[2] Yet, given Arendt's distinctively political concerns, Marx's influence on Arendt was arguably the most profound. In the first place, Marx's impatience with contemplation and introspection, his desire to 'change the world' using the powerful forces of production created by capitalism, constituted a more definitive break with the main currents of the Western tradition than the equally challenging reflections of Nietzsche and Kierkegaard, who were in this respect more traditional philosophers. Secondly, while all three thinkers sought to break with the standards of Western thought, in the process remaining paradoxically wedded to them, Marx was ironically less ambivalent about their worth (which is why contemporary deconstructionists, intent upon overturning metaphysics, attack Marx in the name of Nietzsche). Arendt, too, was not so much opposed to the standards of Western thought as concerned about their distorted expression in social life. Finally, although the ideas of Nietzsche and Kierkegaard were not without political significance, Marx alone made politics itself the vehicle for the achievement of a more fully human existence. For him the world of action took precedence over the world of thought. Arendt was basically in sympathy with this position, at least in view of the alternative: a 'worldless' subjectivism which, as we shall see, was for her no small contributor to the problems of contemporary public life.

Arendt was certainly no Marxist and had little sympathy for Marxism in any of its forms, 'orthodox' or 'critical', 'Soviet' or 'Western'.[3] Yet her criticisms of Marx's ideas have little in common with traditional conservative ones. These criticisms generally take Marx to task for giving a false account of the human condition. Arendt's view is in fact quite the opposite. Particularly in his treatment of labour in modern society, Marx 'sounded a depth of experience reached by none of his predecessors . . . and none of his successors.' His thought is characterized by 'the faithfulness of his descriptions to phenomenal reality', and his 'loyalty and integrity in describing phenomena as they presented themselves to his view cannot be doubted . . .'[4] In her own way echoing Marx's materialist concerns, Arendt claims that if there is a problem with Marx's analysis, it lies not with Marx's ideas but with the historical conditions within which they emerged. Marx only gave a powerful voice to 'the authentic and very perplexing problems inherent in the modern world . . .'[5] His 'utopian ideal of a classless, stateless, and laborless society was born out of the marriage of two altogether non-utopian elements: the perception of certain trends in the present which could no longer be understood in the framework of tradition, and the traditional concepts and ideals by which Marx himself understood and integrated them.'[6]

There is something else as well. Arendt saw in Marx's work an evident concern for freedom and the desire to realize it more fully than ever before in history. Marx believed, and Arendt agreed, that the modern world held previously unheard-of material possibilities which could open up new opportunities for political action. For Marx, modernity made possible for the first time the (potential) realization of ancient dreams and hopes, particularly the liberation from needless toil, from compulsive labour.

Arendt shared at least some of these dreams and hopes. But she wondered whether Marx had grasped them properly and if modernity's achievements were as hospitable to them as he had thought. For Arendt, Marx was a powerfully contradictory thinker: his own ideas betrayed his deepest commitments. At the heart of Arendt's account of Marx is the claim that his defence of freedom and action ultimately served an iron necessity which denied freedom, and a passive and contemplative behaviour in the face of this necessity which was the antithesis of action. What might be said of an age in which its arguably most profound analyst could end up trapped in such contradictions?

For Hannah Arendt, the modern era is one of widespread and pervasive historical consciousness: the sense, deeply embedded in our culture, that we are the products of a temporal process which has 'made' us in a certain way, and that understanding the 'laws' by which this process has unfolded provides an indispensible guide to how we should organize our collective life. It is not the idea of history, *per se*, the idea that we are creatures who live in time, that is the problem. Rather, it is the fact that modern historical consciousness is 'process' consciousness – that we see ourselves as radically determined and thus unfree – that is the heart of the matter. In Arendt's eyes, this denies our reality as acting beings. And since the capacity to act is a fundamental human attribute, it never really disappears but goes underground, so to speak, where it affects the human condition in unacknowledged and therefore potentially destructive ways.

This chapter explores Arendt's account of history and its relation to public life. It examines the ways in which, according to Arendt, our sense of history has itself been historically transformed and how this transformation reflects changing conceptions of collective human purposes. These purposes involve above all the increasing recognition of the ability of humans to exercise greater command over the forces of nature, human and non-human, and what this means for traditional notions of both the individual and community. Here for Arendt lies Marx's ultimate importance. As a theorist and celebrant of labour, the human activity concerned with material reproduction and thus most closely tied to mastery over nature, Marx brilliantly spelled out the consequences of both the modern sense of history and the increasing organization of collective life around the demands of labour. The chapter analyzes Arendt's powerful and provocative critique of Marx's defence of labour and concludes with some suggestions of how Arendt begins to sketch out an alternative account of both individual responsibility and political community in the modern era.

I

In 'The Concept of History', Hannah Arendt identifies two distinct notions of history that have played a central role in Western culture: ancient and modern. The ancient notion of history was developed in the context of the Greek experience and was intimately associated with the polis. The modern notion dates from the beginnings of the modern scientific revolution, roughly the late Middle Ages, although its full impact was not felt until the seventeenth century. It is the modern notion which has been powerfully at the centre of the kind of historical consciousness which has for Arendt proved so baleful for a genuine politics, and it thus provides the primary focus of her account.

While Arendt is critical of modern historical consciousness, she has no doubt that human development has an essential historical component. Human capacities take shape in the flux of actually lived time, and only there. Indeed, because of its roots in remembrance, legitimate political experience requires a sense of the historical. For Arendt, history is a critical category; neither outright rejection nor blind celebration is adequate to the task of understanding our temporal situation. In the end neither the ancient nor the modern notions of history themselves can fully capture the demands of public life.

The motive for history is deeply rooted in human experience. It reflects the desire to bestow the immortality of nature on transient human deeds. History reclaims from the ravages of time those human acts, purposes and accomplishments which deserve to survive their perpetrators and live on in human experience.

It was the Greeks who first saw in history the worldly counterpart to a nature 'which comprehended all things that come into being by themselves without assistance from men or gods . . .'[7] For history the story is all. Its illuminating power, traceable to its capacity to weave apparently unrelated events into a narrative fabric that suggests a beginning and an end, and hence human meaning, 'reveals an unexpected landscape of human deeds, sufferings and new possibilities which together transcend the sum total of all willed intentions and the significance of all origins.'[8] In securing deeds from the futility of oblivion, history distinguishes the human from the non-human in nature.

That humans exist in nature is undeniable. In this respect Arendt agrees with Aristotle who 'explicitly assures us that man [*sic*] insofar as he is a natural being and belongs to the species of mankind, possesses immortality . . .'[9] But humans are part of nature in a specific way. They are capable of accounting for themselves, making themselves the protagonists of tales which illuminate human deeds. The human desire to create meaning animates the art of the storyteller who in this sense is the prototypical historian.

This is something the Greeks understood well. Arendt cites the example of Ulysses: 'The scene where Ulysses listens to the story of his own life is paradigmatic for both history and poetry; the "reconciliation with reality", the catharsis, which, according to Aristotle, was the essence of tragedy, and, according to Hegel, was the ultimate purpose of history, came through the tears of remembrance.'[10] This story is not a 'simple' narrative of events, but one shaped by the informing power of the storyteller's imaginative reconstruction of those events. More than curiosity about what happened or the desire for information is involved in the storyteller's art.

It is this imaginative dimension to history which links it with politics. History is about neither facts nor trends, inexorable patterns of temporal events, but about the experience of acting men and women. At the same time history as experience, unfolding in time and given meaning in a narrative account, is not the same as the account itself. The doer and the storyteller are not the same and what is allowed the historian – the ability to abstract from the flow of temporal events an underlying tendency or development that can be fitted into a pattern – is not available to the historical actor. On the other hand, the historian's categories are working hypotheses about the past, not the past itself.

Thus the historical actor and the historian need each other. And both in turn need a third party: the audience (which of course will include them both). The ancient historian and actor were helped out in this respect because they had an audience already at hand. This was the Greek polis itself, a form of institutionalized remembrance. History and politics are thus linked in a second sense: that of plurality, the presence of the many and not just the one. There is to any genuine historical account a necessary moment of reification or objectification. Its meaning can never be simply subjective. It must be given form in the thought objects of the historian's tale if it is to have worldly significance, the only significance that distinguishes genuinely human association from other forms of association. Ulysses, for one, knows the events and activities of his life. But he does not fully understand them because they form part of a lived experience defined by relations of plurality, of inter-subjectivity. The events of his life express human purposes and aspirations which cannot be grasped exclusively in terms of self-contained individual activities or states of mind. As the actor, Ulysses could not be his own chronicler.[11] His humanity was social and not simply atomic. The story which tells of the life of the person, or a group of people, takes on a life of its own and on these terms enters the world. The life taken on is given to it by the audience, by those for whom its events illuminate their strivings, needs and purposes.

Because the historical tale cannot be merely subjective, the question of historical objectivity looms large for Arendt. The hallmark of a genuinely historical account is precisely its objectivity. But the objectivity Arendt defends is not that of the modern natural sciences with their epistemological commitment to mathematical formulation and deductive and nomological laws. It is rather a sensuous objectivity which has the subjective as one of its elements. Ulysses could not be his own chronicler, his own historian. But neither were his intentions, desires or purposes irrelevant to the truth of the experience which the poet/historian sought to recount. This hermeneutic dimension of engagement with a life story articulated by another, or others, is for Arendt a critical component of history in both senses, as experience and as a narrative account of this experience. Arendt's claim is that history as understood by the ancients allowed for this in a way that modern history does not.

And because the story is the essence of history, the objectivity of history is necessarily associated with the objectivity of the historian. This objectivity, which Arendt equates with impartiality, owes its origins to Homer's decision to praise even-handedly the Trojans *and* the Achaeans, Hector *and* Achilles. Familiar with the experienceáof the Greek polis, in which the ebb and flow of argument and opinion determined the course of public life, the ancient historian could articulate without favour the opposing standpoints and actions of those engaged in historical events. He could write on the assumption that greatness shone forth for all to see and that great deeds in their universality transcend all considerations of partisanship.

But the objectivity of the historian had at its core a fundamental contradiction. This contradiction lay in the fact that while for the Greeks greatness was understood in terms of permanence, human greatness resided in the most perishable of human creations: words and deeds. The historian and the poet could attempt to resolve the contradiction by casting great deeds in story and song because they never doubted that the realm of human affairs was the forum for the emergence of human excellence. Plato and Aristotle, on the other hand, argued that nothing of enduring value could be had in the polis. Humans could link up with the truly immortal only in the contemplation of the unchanging essence of things as these presented themselves to thought. The opposition of philosophy to politics necessarily entailed its hostility o history. At issue, then, was not only the status of history but also the dignity of the political sphere itself.

Thus from Arendt's perspective, it was no surprise that the emergence of philosophy was historically linked closely to the decline of the polis (a development clearly vital for Aristotle's *Politics*.) The decline of the polis meant the collapse of that vehicle of remembrance which preserved great deeds for the ages. The legacy of the crumbling of shared understandings about the character and purposes of political life was the ambiguous relation of philosophy to politics. The capacity for politics and the possibility of history imply each other.

The classical or ancient understanding of history ultimately bequeathed to posterity two questions: (1) what is the basis of immortality? (2) who is capable of this immortality? To the first question, we already know the answer: great deeds which ought not to perish. However, in spite of its universalistic orientation, the Hellenic notion of history failed to answer the second question. Arendt cites Ulysses, the mythic hero. But in an essay on Bertolt Brecht, she also writes of the importance of the ballad form as a testimony to the exploits of those otherwise condemned through oppression to the oblivion of time.[12] This suggests that all people are capable of 'making' history, although the forms it assumes might differ. Like the political action with which it is so closely tied, it may be that history has an implicitly democratic dimension. The quest for worldly immortality need not be restricted to members of privileged groups or classes.

The modern experience and notion of history have both posed and answered these questions.

II

Given her generally laudatory assessment of the ancient notion of history, it is not surprising that Arendt views the modern understanding of history as seriously deficient. While she does not argue that we have witnessed a progressive decline in the character and conceptualization of our historical experience, she does believe that we have lost sight of the main qualities of a genuine history. To put it metaphorically: the capacity to tell stories, and the stories that can be told, have been transformed.

As Arendt sees it, of decisive importance here is the growth of modern science and, in turn, the emergence of the distinction between the 'natural' and the 'social' sciences, between the scientist and the humanist. At the heart of this development was a radically new relation of humans to nature. Where the ancient understanding of both history and science presupposed nature as the domain of immortality, the modern concepts of both assume a nature which is purely a complex of manipulable forces. In turn these understandings are embedded in the growth of large-scale processes of material production by which nature is transformed. These processes, which likewise presuppose nature as a sheer object of manipulation, deny by their very character the possibility of normative query. They are ethically mute, 'value-free'. The role of the scientist does not tell us whether the purposes for which science is used are good or just.[13] Human nature poses for science problems of social control, not possibilities of revelation. The stories a scientific culture tells have no 'morals'.

It is no accident that the assumptions, goals and limits of modern science should powerfully shape our concept and experience of history. The enormous capacity of the organized institutions of scientific work to alter the natural and social environment could not fail to impress itself upon a culture for which comfortable self-preservation had become the highest aim. In turn, the triumph of self-preservation conditioned another development with profound consequences for Western culture and its tradition of conceptual thought: the growth of scepticism about the truth-revealing capacity of the human physical senses.

Modern scepticism is nourished by the fear that because we cannot trust our senses, we will never be able to reach any truth or indeed be certain about anything. The experience that triggered the growth of this scepticism was the simple discovery that, immediate sense perception notwithstanding, the Earth revolved around the Sun and not the other way around. If immediate sense perception no longer fitted us to live in the world, if the objectivity of the world itself could no longer be guaranteed, we could turn not to objects of sensation, but to the fact of sensation itself, for confirmation of our existence as sentient beings.

The historical product of this radical transformation in the quality of experience and conceptual thought was, of course, the Cartesian ego. Descartes 'became the father of modern philosophy because he generalized the experience . . . [of doubt] . . . developed it into a new method of thinking, and thus became the first thinker thoroughly trained in that "school of suspicion" which, according to Nietzsche, constitutes modern philosophy.'[14] The productive union of science and industry, so characteristic of modern European and North American societies, was an almost inevitable outcome. If the senses could not be trusted, nothing revealed to them need be respected as bearers of objective truth and hence objects of contemplation as they had been for Aristotle's science. Given the unreliability of sense perception, the natural sciences became experimental and, in the process, began directly interfering with nature. According to Arendt, this interference knows no limit. Interference now lays the groundwork for more extensive initiatives later. Modern science is inherently 'progressive'.

To be sure, there is an 'indissoluble connection between our thinking and our sense perception', which makes it impossible to construct a model of science shorn completely of sense experience. At the same time, it is precisely the mistrust of such experience and its revelatory capacity which stands at the core of modern philosophy and science. Scientific reason, 'pure' reason in the Kantian sense, came to be the hallmark of science and truth itself. But, according to Arendt, this did not solve the problem: 'The trouble, in other words, is not that the physical universe cannot be visualized, for this is a matter of course under the assumption that nature does not reveal itself to the human senses; the uneasiness begins when nature turns out to be unconceivable, that is, unthinkable in terms of pure reasoning as well.'[15] As Arendt sees it, the peculiar fate of modern society is that its enormously developed capacity to transform nature is 'blind'. Social actors are incapable of identifying, let alone understanding, the consequences of their own activity.

Ironically, the mistrust of our senses was to have led to a more certain kind of knowledge than had ever existed before. If we are incapable of knowing the world given to us, we can at least know what we ourselves have made. As humans, we can act on the basis of patterns developed in the mind without apparent reference to the facts of experience, and can shape the world according to these patterns. If the external world holds no intrinsic purpose or meaning, then the problem of purpose can be avoided altogether by conceiving the world as a plethora of means to the realization of humanly determined ends – which, once they have been fulfilled, become themselves means to still further ends.

This transformation of thought and action has had an odd result. In spite of their ostensible materialism, the pragmatic and utilitarian attitudes and practices which began to emerge on a large scale have not led to the celebration of things created according to a fixed, preconceived plan (the classic image of what Arendt calls *homo faber*). They have led rather to the devaluation of things *as* things to the status of by-products of the realization of ends which transcended those things. In this development lies the origins of an idea with, in Arendt's eyes, profound implications for the modern concept and experience of history: the idea of nature as process. If things themselves lack meaning, they can be rendered meaningful by being swallowed up in the movement of something larger than any one of them.

Far from grounding us more firmly in our natural and social environments, however, modern scientific knowledge has generated even greater uncertainty and insecurity about our earthly existence. As Arendt sees it, this was inevitable, given the assumptions involved. What is missing from efforts to shape scientific knowledge according to the strict dictates of utilitarian rationality is precisely that which gives knowledge its significance: meaning. The positing of ends in the fulfilment of which humans transform nature is intended as a substitute for the objective meaning formerly held to be present to the contemplative gaze of the philosopher. But meaning cannot be created instrumentally, as an end 'product' for which it is possible to marshall the appropriate 'means'. Once meanings are degraded into ends, the distinction between means and ends itself can no longer be understood; hence all ends become degraded into means.

The ubiquitous utilitarianism of modern society has been so critical for history and humanity because of another powerful development: the massive expansion of technology. Although Arendt is not precise on this point, there are in fact two strains in the modern notion of nature and, correspondingly, in the theory and practice of science. Each strain has social roots in what Arendt identifies as two phases of modernity.

The first phase, the mechanized world of the Industrial Revolution, retained in society's relation with nature the traditional understanding of it as a source of useful objects. The human capacity involved was that of *homo faber*, the crafter of objects, who works up the material nature provides. Industrialization involved the mechanization of processes of work in order to produce objects more effectively and efficiently. It imitated nature's creative processes. While it no longer involved the contemplative grasp of the given, science was still restricted in its scope to the comprehension, initiation and utilization of natural forces for the purpose of material production.

The second phase witnessed a shift away from the substitution of humanly made for natural processes towards the actual initiation of such processes themselves. For Arendt, this represented a move away from fabrication towards action as the chief mode of appropriating external (and internal) nature. I will examine the human capacity to act, a central element of what Arendt calls the *vita activa*, in the next chapter. Here it is sufficient to note that a chief characteristic of human action is the unpredictability of its consequences, the inevitable rupture of intentions and outcomes. By acting into nature in a new way, we have introduced a certain kind of unpredictability into a realm – physical nature – that until the modern period had been relatively immune to it. The introduction of action into nature, which Arendt identifies most closely with the growth of nuclear physics, means that humans 'for the first time have taken nature into the human world as such and obliterated the defensive boundaries between natural elements and the human artifice by which all previous civilizations were hedged in.'[16] As Arendt sees it, we have reached the stage at which '[w]e can do in the natural-physical realm what . . . we could do only in the realm of history . . . [I]t has turned out that man is as capable of starting natural processes which would not have come about without human interference as he is of starting something new in the field of human affairs.'[17]

The mediating link between science and action is technology. Arendt suggests that while the practical or pragmatic application of scientific insights has rarely been the specific motive for scientific work, such application accords fully with the innermost intentions of the modern scientific enterprise, which arose when our attention shifted from the questions of 'what' to those of 'how'. As a social enterprise, science has explicitly political implications. Given the relation of history to nature, the growth of science and technology has inevitably altered our conception of history and hence our self-understanding as temporal beings. What modern history and nature (science) share in common – the concept of process – is the shorthand expression of a social development that has made it possible for humans to join their appropriation of nature with the management of their common affairs in an instrumental way. Arendt writes of the modern historical 'sciences' to demonstrate the pervasive impact of the new science on our political and social concepts, and she relates this to the growth of the contemporary social sciences. These sciences seek to 'prescribe conditions . . . to human behaviour, as modern physics prescribes conditions to natural processes . . . [and] . . . to treat man as an entirely natural being whose life process can be handled the same way as all other processes.'[18] Historical consciousness came to be viewed as an essential complement to natural science because it could bestow the meaning on human deeds and suffering which the natural sciences seemed unable to generate.

As the concept of nature underwent a two-fold transformation in modernity, so did the notion of history. And like the concept of nature, that of history was linked to the emerging demands of industrial society. Arendt's position here is complex and subtle. In her view, the early modern notion of history was contrasted more sharply with science than was later to be the case. This was not because thinkers and historians sought consciously to distinguish the realm of history as one immune to the lawlike behaviour of 'natural' entities, but rather because they saw history in the image of an earlier vision of nature. This vision had its roots in a more contemplative Aristotelian and medieval natural science which emphasized the collection and registration of facts. It was precisely this vision, and the metaphysical foundations it presupposed, which the modern age was to undermine.

In other words, according to Arendt, the historian's initial self-understanding, which to be humanly significant must correspond to society's own understanding of time, fell behind the objective course of events. In a world in which the scientist was rapidly becoming capable of making natural history, the historian was increasingly incapable of showing how this development shaped society and the very possibility of history itself. As history was being moulded in the image of an outmoded science, science itself was rapidly becoming historical.

The shift to a fully modern conception of history as (humanly made) process, and the consequence that history and natural science, whatever their apparent conflict, had common roots and a common purpose, followed in the wake of the increasing prevalence of Cartesian doubt and scepticism. As technology distinguished the later from the early modern concepts of science and nature, so it distinguished the later from the earlier versions of history. For Arendt, the important figure here is Giambattista Vico.

Vico is generally seen as the originator of the modern concept of history. To Arendt this is deeply ironic: in her view, Vico's work has a peculiarly ahistorical character. His emphasis on history did not arise from humanist considerations which saw in history the exclusive forum for the realization of genuinely human capacities. It came rather out of his belief that, given the unreliability of sense perception, humans are capable of knowing only what they have themselves made. Since Vico did not see the possibility of humans 'making' nature, it appeared that only in the realm of human affairs could we know genuine truth.

The presumption that human beings only make history but not nature was, of course, wrong. Since it was the process of making and not anything peculiar to history *per se* that concerned Vico, modern technology could conform fully to Vico's conception of knowledge. Technology not only distinguishes the later from the early modern conceptions of science and history, it provides the ground upon which the realms of history and nature have come together in the contemporary era.

The common roots of science, or nature, and history in the notion of process was masked by the nineteenth- and early twentieth-century debate over the alleged 'uniqueness' of the historical sciences. As Arendt points out, claims of incommensurability on both sides of the debate have given way in recent decades to the recognition that 'subjective' factors, plainly evident in history, are equally prominent in the natural sciences. Arendt sees a continuity between the natural and social sciences: the latter 'treat man as an entirely natural being whose life process can be handled the same way as all other processes.'

History as process represents for Arendt both the failure of meaning and the celebration of life itself (as opposed, for example, to the 'good life' of memorable deeds) as the highest human purpose. In our understanding of history, mere time sequence has come to assume a dignity it had never before possessed. Individual events, which for the ancients carried within themselves their essential meaning, now have yielded the capacity for revelation to an all-embracing mechanism, the sole bearer of significance.

Why these developments are so destructive of genuine human capacities is not immediately obvious. Arendt suggests that the concept of history has become a deterministic abstraction in the name of which large numbers of men and women have in this century been sacrificed. The idea of an inexorable law of history that leads inevitably to the realization of a fixed and final goal owes its lineage to such a concept. Arendt joins thinkers such as Leo Strauss in condemning the emergence of this 'historicism'.[19]

But Arendt's target is not simply modern historicism. She is not concerned simply to dismiss historical consciousness as destructive. To do so would be to succumb to the same error that plagues the blind celebration of the transparent logic of historical 'necessity'. The rise of historicism must itself be comprehended historically. The Greek notion of history and its relation to nature, for instance, were given form by and through the experience of the polis, the public realm. The character of political experience and a specific understanding of history imply each other. In thinking and acting *politically*, we cannot help thinking and acting *historically*.

This relation of history to politics is decisive for the argument Arendt makes in 'The Concept of History'. In fact, Arendt is not really concerned with history as a distinct form of social inquiry at all. She is interested in the fate of political action, and the relation of action to other modes of human experience, under radically changed social conditions. She raises these issues through a consideration of changing notions of history because the language of historical consciousness provides the categorical framework within which the demands of political association have been expressed. The modern computation of historical dates which takes the birth of Christ as a turning point was not just a technical convenience devised by scholars, but a feature of everyday life, because it corresponded to a new sense of the significance of time in society. One of the failings of contemporary historiography, and a defining characteristic of history itself, is that it has tended to lose sight of its social roots. History is seen as essentially 'spiritual', or at least as a reality that exists over and against individual historical events. While she does not single out Windelband, Dilthey and Rickert for specific criticism, Arendt has them clearly in mind when she writes that 'we have seen historians freely imposing upon the image of past facts almost any pattern they wish, with the result that the ruin of the factual and the particular through the seemingly higher validity of general "meanings" has even undermined the basic factual structure of all historical process, that is, chronology.'[20]

To see the political roots of Arendt's analysis of history is to clarify what might otherwise appear to be anomalies in her argument. Thus the early stages of modernity, during which modern historical consciousness began to form, were nevertheless characterized by a concern for politics unmatched since ancient times. For Arendt, the key figure in this development was Thomas Hobbes. Working on the assumption that political obligation could be put on a purely secular basis, Hobbes was among the first of the modern thinkers to address specifically the requirements and demands of the political realm. As C. B. Macpherson, Sheldon Wolin and others have pointed out, Hobbes believed that his mechanical construction, the Leviathan, could insure people a peaceful and commodious existence because it was fabricated according to the requirements of order accessible to human reason through mathematical calculation. Hobbes, too, was thoroughly convinced that humans could know only what they themselves had made and he was a theorist of politics because he believed that political institutions, although by no means immortal, could be the most stable and certain, and hence knowable, of human creations.

Yet it was this same dimension of Hobbes's thought which for Arendt illuminated the dilemmas of the modern experience. His 'error', which to be sure corresponded to the deepest commitments of the modern age, was in construing political *action* in terms of *fabrication*, doing in terms of making. I will examine the significance of this distinction for Arendt's political thought in the next chapter. The point here is that Hobbes's quest for a stable and permanent political structure reflected ironically his doubt about the permanence of the world itself, the domain of human institutions, practices and norms. He associated commitment to this world with the discredited metaphysics of the ancients. (This is why Hobbes's work is little concerned with political forms as such and the normative assessment of them that was so important for classical thought. This is most clearly evident in his well-known dismissal of 'tyranny' as a scientifically unreliable concept. Political forms had no autonomous 'objectivity'; they depended totally on the subjective purposes of the individuals who through contract created them. In short, Hobbes was the antithesis of the political philosopher in Claude Lefort's sense.) As political as Hobbes was, his thought provided in Arendt's view a harbinger of the decline of politics and the rise of history as process. She argues that the real meaning of the secularization of the realm of human affairs was that 'no matter what an individual might believe as a member of a church, as a citizen he acted and behaved on the assumption of human mortality.'[21] The new recognition of mortality, so at odds with the Christian belief in the immortality of individual life in a mortal world, spurred people on to rediscover antiquity, whose entire culture was predicated on precisely the opposite assumption. Yet people no longer had access to the authentic political experience that grew out of and generated this assumption. Both life *and* the world had come to be seen as mortal.

The Greek concept of fabrication, and its understanding of politics, were based on the assumption that the chief threats to worldly permanence were external: the elemental forces of physical nature and the barbarian hordes who behaved as nature-like objects. Hobbes's focus was different. His view that the chief threat to political stability was internal was not meant simply to point out the dangers of civil war, although he certainly considered this important. It was also meant to draw attention to both the need and the newly found ability to control the sources of human conflict in the individual him/herself. Hobbes believed that the new science, which had become increasingly capable of regulating external nature, could be even more successful in managing human nature.

Hobbes could proceed in this way because while he may have been dubious about the permanence of the world, he had no doubt about the permanence of human drives and aspirations, and in particular the quest for self-preservation. From Arendt's perspective, Hobbes's political philosophy was unworldly and subjectivist despite its hostility to classical metaphysics. It courted meaninglessness and hence encouraged the emergence of the idea of 'making' history, with a model or pattern guiding the maker. Historical narrative was a logical bearer of patterns and models.

The modern thinker who for Arendt most clearly recognized the consequences of history in this sense was Immanuel Kant. According to her, Kant saw that the 'melancholy haphazardness' of history could be redeemed by relating each historical occurrence to a hidden intention, 'the guiding thread of reason', that could shape worldly affairs. The meaninglessness of worldly events and hence politics, implicit in Hobbes's account of political obligation, could be overcome by incorporating the sense of history as the bearer of universal aims into the understanding of political action.

Yet Kant was ambivalent about history because he could not satisfactorily answer the question why earlier generations would labour only for the sake of later ones. Arendt sees this dilemma as inevitable. It is an indication of both the limits of historical explanation and consciousness, and the ultimately self-contradictory character of Hobbesian and post-Hobbesian political thought. The substitution of making for acting implies a purely external relation to both the context and outcomes of humanly initiated events or occurrences. It implies, in other words, the 'loss of hermeneutic power in the theoretical penetration of situations which were to be mastered practically. . . .'[22] That is, people lose a lived, conscious connection with the outcomes of their activities, which take on a life of their own. People fail to see their intentions and purposes reflected in their social life.

For Arendt, the collapse of this hermeneutic dimension is meaninglessness as such. Since history as process 'showed a peculiar and inspiring affinity with action', it could serve as a substitute for a genuine politics at the level of both conceptual thought and actual experience. But the modern use of history was not conceived as just a substitute for politics. It was seen as an actual replacement for a politics the unpredictability and unreliability of which had long been anathema to philosophers. Thus history 'has at least bestowed upon the record of past events that share of earthly immortality to which the modern age necessarily aspired, but which acting men no longer dared to claim from posterity.'[23] Modern history contains within itself both an affinity for action and an opposition to it. It is this dual character of history as process which gives it its truth and its falsehood, its capacity simultaneously to reveal and conceal the nature of human experience.

Modern history, then, somehow combines both action and fabrication, the 'thinking in terms of processes, on the one hand, and the conviction, on the other, that I know only what I myself have made. . .'[24] Hence the dilemmas of modern historical consciousness and experience; which reflect the ability of people at one and the same time to create norms, practices and institutions – what Arendt calls additions to the human artifice – while seeing them as gaining meaning from a nature-like process over which they exercise no control. In these circumstances, individual events and occurrences lose their unique character. But ironically they also fail to gain a comprehensive and compelling significance from the historical process of which they are seen to be part. The result is a meaninglessness which comes 'from the insight that I can choose to do whatever I want and some kind of "meaning" will always be the consequence.'[25] Such meaning is false because it lacks what genuine meaning must provide: illumination of the general through the particular.

Contemporary philosophers such as Richard Rorty, Jean-François Lyotard and Jacques Derrida see in this state of affairs no particular cause for concern. That humans can and do impose any meaning they like on their situation (subject to the constraints of the 'tradition' or 'language game' within which they think and act) testifies to the power of human creativity, the manifold ways people have of coping with their social and natural worlds. The 'crisis' of meaning identified by thinkers such as Arendt is in reality the crisis of a philosophy haunted by the failure of its misguided search for ultimate foundations, an absolutely certain knowledge.[26] Modern 'historicism' has made us aware of the unavoidable partiality of our beliefs and practices, their embeddedness in distinctive and incommensurable forms of life. Our everyday political dilemmas, and the monstrous political horrors of the twentieth century, are not the products of a crisis of (totalizing) reason. Rather, they have emerged precisely from attempts to impose one form of life as the true one on the irreducible plurality of human social possibilities. Whether they are partisans of scientific reason, or advocates of the dialectical critique of instrumental rationality, philosophers should jettison the arrogant assumption that they are the arbiters of the legitimacy of knowledge claims. People know, say and do more than philosophers allow; they should now facilitate the 'corporate conversation' (Oakeshott) through which people pursue their diverse wants, needs and purposes.[27]

These 'post-modern' or 'post-structuralist' currents of thought echo many of Arendt's own concerns.[28] Yet she does not repudiate the possibility or desirability of assessing 'forms of life' from the perspective of an adequate human existence. And Arendt not only acknowledges the existence of alternative ways of life which can be morally assessed. She also thinks that these can be judged *from within the confines of history itself*. In this respect she makes a critical point: even given that the unique and singular have become devoid of genuine meaning, meaning of a sort is generated within the historical process. In other words, there is a reason of a kind at work in history; as we will see, for Arendt a striking quality of totalitarianism is the 'reasonableness' of the institutions of the total state for people in desperate conditions.[29]

From the vantage point provided by Arendt's account, the post-modern critique of philosophy succumbs to an ironic error: notwith-standing its historicism, it is insufficiently historical. In spite of itself it presupposes the existence of a supposedly discredited comprehens-ive rationality which renders forms of life or ways of coping just that. To write or speak of 'life' or 'coping' already presupposes a certain sort of order. But post-modernist thought cannot get at its own presuppositions. It suffers from an a- or anti-politicism.[30]

This relation of Arendt's work to contemporary thought puts more clearly into focus her critique of history as process. The notion of process carries with it for Arendt the historicist assumption that everything that occurs has no independent standing, but is relative to some larger purposive, temporal movement. Yet her 'grand nar-rative', to use post-modernist language, does not draw its support from a position ostensibly outside history itself. Indeed she specific-ally dismisses critical accounts of modernity, based upon notions such as 'the disenchantment of the world' or 'the alienation of man', as empty abstractions which, among other things, entail an unwarranted romanticization of the past.[31] In other words, Arendt's position, when applied to the current situation, suggests that both philosophy and its post-modernist critique share more in common than what might divide them. What they share is an uncritical acceptance of process which, ironically, misses the root importance of both process-thinking and the experience which underlies it. The 'modern' tradition of social and political thinking devalues the particular by subordinating it to a universal the necessity of which only the philosopher (of history) can understand. The post-modernist alternative salvages the particu-lar, but renders it as a kind of universal endowed with an equal, and equally unquestionable, necessity. Neither poses the question of the impact of the modern situation on public life, and especially how the particulars become what they are and are interwoven together as the constitutive fabric of lived experience.

This suggests an important dimension to Arendt's analysis of process which, to be sure, Arendt herself does not explicitly develop. For it may be that what is at stake is not so much the desirability of process, but rather the relation of human beings to their own creations in a situation in which, with the rise of modern scepticism and science, it has become difficult to 'think what we are doing'. Process *per se* may in fact be an essential element of a genuine public life; although she does not appear explicitly to recognize its import-ance, Arendt understands action, the core element of a genuine politics, as above all the capacity to initiate *and* interrupt processes. Process-thinking raises the question of human creativity which, in different ways, is a non-question for both modern and post-modern thought. It is this concern which shapes Arendt's encounter with the work of Karl Marx.

III

Arendt's critique of history as process, then, is not simply dismissive, but attempts to get at its origins in the historically changing constellation of human capacities and purposes. The complex nature of her position points to perhaps the thorniest issue raised by her political thought. This involves the relation of her account to the dominant schemes of political values in modern Western societies. Where exactly does Arendt stand on the political spectrum? Is she on the right or the left? Is she a conservative or a radical?

Arendt herself eschewed such designations, believing them a poor substitute for thinking. Nevertheless, her work is highly relevant to such issues, if only because they suggest the limitations of ideologically based accounts of fundamental political values, that is, accounts based upon dogmatic and unquestioned assumptions about the world. Even more importantly, Arendt engaged the ideas of those who have played a central role in shaping the ideological divisions by which millions of people have understood their collective life. How she saw them through the prism of her own outlook can open up questions either long thought answered by the mere invocation of an ideological label, or never seriously treated at all.

This is particularly true of Arendt's analysis of Karl Marx. I have already suggested both that Arendt's political theory is most fully compatible with a broadly defined left position, and that Marx is for her the most significant modern political thinker. These propositions are of course connected. To speak about the left in Western-type societies (and increasingly in non-Western societies as well) is to come to terms with Marx's legacy. And while no Marxist, Arendt mounts a critique of Marx which accepts as descriptively accurate central elements of his account of modern capitalist society, while challenging the conclusions he draws from this account. Because for neither Arendt nor Marx could there be 'value-free' analyses of social phenomena, inasmuch as such phenomena are in large part constituted by the normative significance they have for human beings whose very identities have normative content, *descriptive* agreement involves at least some measure of *evaluative* agreement.

In my view, this area of agreement concerns the fate of human creativity in the modern era, the forms it has assumed and the ways in which people relate to their creations. Both Arendt and Marx are concerned that human creative powers have got out of control and threaten to overwhelm us. Put otherwise, both address the question of alienation: the estrangement of human beings from their capacities and the results of the exercise of these. However, from Arendt's vantage point, while Marx is concerned with the *self* alienation of people divorced from their productive capacities, the creation of things in response to biological need, the hallmark of the modern age is rather *world* alienation: estrangement from a domain of durable objects, including institutions and practices, which provide a permanent home for mortal human beings. To Arendt, Marx's emphasis on the need for humans to reclaim and reassert their species character, their species-being, complements the triumph of history as process, within which its components – in this case human beings themselves – are interchangeable and thus dispensable. Species-being stands opposed to plurality, the recognition that we are truly and humanly the same only in our differences. Plurality needs a world, not a sphere of socialized production, if it is to be actualized.

Thus for Arendt, Marx's solution to the problem of the modern age is itself part of the problem. From Arendt's perspective, both she and Marx are radical: each seeks to get at the roots of the modern situation. But Marx accepts fundamentally the way in which the modern situation has actually unfolded; Arendt is more dubious about the entire project while accepting it as the inescapable framework within which we must live, think and act.

Arendt's encounter with Marx is important not only because it shows his significance for her political thought. It also puts her own position more clearly into focus and helps clarify what in her view has been lost or absent in modern society as the result of the effects on human creativity of the rise of history as process.

In 'The Concept of History', Arendt argues that Marx 'is the last of those thinkers who stand at the borderline between the modern age's earlier interest in politics and its later preoccupation with history.'[32] Reflecting its historically ambiguous position, Marx's thought is a contradictory attempt to graft a theory of action onto an essentially contemplative philosophy of history. Arendt sees in this work the most explicit and consistently worked-out attempt to make the production of meaning the specific goal of human action in history. Unlike others who saw history as an object of fabrication, Marx was at least consistent enough to recognize that if history were actually 'made', there must be an end to the process of making, that is, an end to history. In her analysis of modern history, the development of which is so intimately tied to the fate of politics, Arendt finds Marx's work a crystallization and summation of the contradictions that history has bequeathed us.

At the heart of Arendt's analysis of Marx is a critique of labour and the role it has come to play in modern society. As a central element of the *vita activa*, labour is concerned with production in response to biological need, in Arendt's terms with the demands of life itself. Labour is an aspect of human life in every historical and social setting. But its character under modern conditions in particular illuminates the meaning of history as an everyday experience. It is no accident that the rise of modern historical consciousness coincides for Arendt with the emergence of what she calls 'labouring society', a society increasingly given over to the unlimited expansion of material production in the service of life. It is because he addressed both history and labour, and their existential significance, that Marx is for Arendt so critical to modern political thought.

Arendt's analysis of Marx forms the core of her account of labour in *The Human Condition*. Because of the provocative character of her argument, a clear exposition of it must respect two concerns. In the first place, as already pointed out, Arendt does not merely dismiss Marx's arguments. She believes he faithfully documented dominant trends in modern society and there is no question of his integrity or veracity. The labour theory of value, for example, was true to the character of modern social experience.

In the second place, Arendt no more rejects labour as an essential element of human existence than she repudiates history or historical consciousness as such. The issue in each case is a certain 'balance' among different dimensions of human social existence, and whether this balance has been put askew in modern societies. In other words, her argument is informed by an ontological perspective which asks us to assess the significance of certain developments in society for the achievement of certain purposes. This clearly links her analysis with Marx's own concerns, whatever might divide the two. At the same time, it makes clear that in criticizing the prominence of labour in the modern age, Arendt is not attacking those who labour. Her argument is not an elitist denunciation of the working classes in advanced capitalist or socialist societies. Indeed she has positive things to say about the political role played historically by these classes in modern Europe, as opposed to the role ascribed to them theoretically as bearers of a historical 'mission'.[33] Arendt's critique of labour and of Marx is more properly understood as at least potentially radical, not conservative.

Of the modern thinkers who put labour at the centre of their political thought, it was Marx who, according to Arendt, traced out most thoroughly the implications of organizing society around the simple reproduction of life itself. In Marx's distinction between 'productive' and 'unproductive' labour, she sees the clearest acknowledgement of the rise to dominance of a specific human 'type': *animal laborans*, the producing animal. The productivity of *animal laborans*, its ability to create an ever larger array of goods for immediate consumption, was the basis for the elevation of labour in modernity. And such productivity 'does not lie in any of labor's products but in the human "power" whose strength is not exhausted when it has produced the means of its own subsistence and survival but is capable of producing a "surplus", that is, more than is necessary for its own "reproduction".'[34]

With Marx, Arendt accepts that the elevation of labour carries significant social and political implications. In particular she accepts Marx's claim that surplus labour power is the key factor in social reproduction. She agrees that this surplus provides the means of life for those not actively engaged in its immediate production, and that its use requires a mechanism of expropriation – in the modern era, capitalist private property.

What Arendt does not accept is the conclusion Marx draws from these assumptions. Marx viewed capitalism as a necessary stage in the historical realization of a free society. He saw in capitalism the basis of a future abundance and thus applauded the process of accumulation central to a capitalist economy. It is precisely on this point that Arendt parts company with him. She argues that in defending capitalist accumulation, Marx was in fact promoting not the conditions of future freedom, but rather the destruction of any possibility of it. This is because, for Arendt, labour is grounded ultimately in bodily necessity and its claims. And unlike the spurious necessity of history, that of labour is real, pressing and enduring. Yet like its counterpart in history, the necessity of labour demands subordination to its claims, which must be met before it is possible to engage in 'free' activities.

For Arendt, as for Marx, the issue here is how to manage the demands of necessity, of labour, in order to reduce its scope in human affairs. Arendt insists that Marx's vision of a 'socialized mankind' extends rather than reduces the grip of necessity on human social life. In a manner recalling Max Weber, Arendt argues that far from challenging the fetishism of labour characteristic of capitalist society, and the unfreedom that comes with it, socialism completes it. Both capitalism and socialism are in her eyes regimes of expropriation:

they both deny people a stable place in the world from which to act. They both reduce, if not eliminate altogether, the prospect for freedom, since our freedom is always won in our never wholly successful attempts to liberate ourselves from necessity.[35]

While never a conscious enemy of liberty, Marx succumbed to the lure of necessity because he made a critical error: he obscured the distinction between work and labour. For Arendt, work is 'worldly'. That is, it creates additions to the human artifice, to culture, broadly defined, as our 'home' on earth. By contrast, labour 'actually is the most natural and least worldly of men's activities.'[36] Marx, however, believed that labour was the ultimate world-building activity. He thus found himself in the grip of a fundamental contradiction, one which led him to argue that the task of socialist revolution was not the emancipation of the labouring classes, but rather emancipation from labour altogether, since 'the realm of freedom begins only where labor determined through want and external utility ceases . . .'[37]

Yet in Marx's own terms, emancipation from labour meant emancipation from necessity. The enormous productivity of *animal laborans*, of life itself, would be impossible. And the recognition and celebration of this productivity is, according to Arendt, at the heart of his vision. To dismiss it would be to forfeit the ability, unmatched by other modern thinkers, to grasp modern reality at its roots.

As Arendt sees it, Marx throughout his work had defined the human being as *animal laborans* and held labour to be the most human of our activities. At the same time, he claimed that the classless society would render unnecessary altogether the power to labour. He thus ended up with 'the rather distressing alternative between productive slavery and unproductive freedom'.[38] In the final analysis, Marx's celebration of abundance, of necessity, triumphed over his concern for freedom.

In other words, Marx failed to recognize that the elimination of necessity would mean the elimination of the human metabolism with nature, our 'emancipation' not only from production but consumption as well – the condition of human life itself. With the growth and spread of automation, Arendt sees this utopian dream of a life without labour, if not consumption, as potentially achievable. For her, the problem would be how to ensure sufficient opportunities for the exercise of our bodily energies so that the capacity for consumption could be sustained.

It is here that, according to Arendt, Marx made his most serious error. He embraced 'the illusion of a mechanistic philosophy which assumes that labor power, like any other energy, can never be lost, so that if it is not spent in the drudgery of life it will automatically nourish other, "higher" activities.'[39] Since we can never be free from necessity, it would reimpose itself as the inexorable and unlimited expansion of our consumptive appetites, to the point at which the life process would swallow up all that represented the 'unnatural' demands of the world. The futility of the life process, which leaves nothing durable in its wake, cannot be overcome, but only hidden by the dazzling abundance of a consumer society.

The ultimate irony of the triumph of *animal laborans* is that while consumptive activities are in a labouring society highly visible, they have their basis in the 'strict and even cruel privacy [of] the experience of bodily processes which life manifests itself . . .'[40] The world of labour and consumption is a private world. Lacking a common world, a labouring society cannot sustain a genuine politics. As the objects of what is increasingly a waste economy barely survive the moment of their production, so the activities of *animal laborans* leave few remembered traces that can be preserved in narrative form. A labouring society is thus capable of neither politics nor history. Everyone lives in a kind of eternal present, governed by the cyclical rhythms of the human metabolism with nature, in which everything is always the same and nothing new ever happens.

Since Marx certainly believed his theory to be both political and historical, Arendt in effect argues that he was forced by the logic of his position to contradict his deepest commitments – to the point at which, she claims, he predicted the 'withering away' of the public realm 'with an unjustified glee'.[41] Nonetheless, Marx's weaknesses are his greatest strengths. His decidedly non-utopian ideal of a socialized humanity reveals clearly the hidden claim of modern industrial society. This claim is nothing but 'the age-old dream of the poor and destitute, which can have a charm of its own so long as it is a dream, but turns into a fool's paradise as soon as it is realized.'[42]

Arendt's interpretation of Marx is controversial, even idiosyncratic. Her account is beset by a number of problems. For one, Marx intended the labour theory of value to apply strictly to capitalist society; for another, his distinction between 'productive' and 'unproductive' labour (which Arendt sees as rooted in his supposed celebration of the labour process) related exclusively to the issue of whether or not such labour contributed to the generation of surplus exchange value. Finally, there is evidence from Marx's own writings that what Arendt calls labour he identified with alienated labour, a specific historical form of the social organization of production which he thought would be historically transcended. In summary, Arendt fails to take adequately into account Marx's concern with an alienation not of the self, a concept which he seems in any case to have repudiated as an element of bourgeois ideology, but rather of the world as the forum for the exercise of human powers. In other words, she fails to recognize Marx's desire to promote the very possibilities for free action that so much concern her. In this respect Arendt shares an ironic bond with 'orthodox' or 'scientific' Marxists. For her, as for them, Marx is a deterministic defender of 'laws' of historical necessity.

At the same time, recent critical analyses of Marx's thought have pursued themes strikingly similar to those of Arendt. Where undertaken from a broadly socialist perspective, these criticisms take Marx to task for his insensitivity to questions of human agency and choice, for his 'productivist' bias and even for the latent positivism of his supposedly revolutionary science.[43] Where still committed to the need for radical political and social change, but sceptical about the contemporary value of Marx's project, they renew Arendt's doubts about the quality of existence in, and even the institutional conditions for, a labouring ('full employment') society, and point to patterns of social stratification and political conflict which cannot adequately be understood in Marxian class terms.[44] Whatever the vantage point, these analyses exhibit a concern for questions of normative political theory similar to Arendt's own.

Given the contemporary political and intellectual climate, it might be wondered if an account of Arendt's critique of Marx has any currency. Certainly in the neo-conservative milieu which has emerged recently almost everywhere, but particularly in Britain and North America, radical projects of any sort, much less Marx's vision of social transformation, appear to lack substantial social roots in the behaviour and outlook of large numbers of people. Marxism itself is precisely the sort of 'grand narrative', or totalizing perspective, so badly out of fashion in dominant intellectual circles.

Nevertheless, as a means of exploring its contemporary significance, there is still value in situating Arendt's work in relation to Marx's legacy. Aside from the great influence Marx exerted on Arendt herself, this is true for a number of reasons. One is in fact the advent of neo-conservative economic and social policies in Western capitalist democracies. These could presage a return of 'old-fashioned' economic class conflicts as the living standards of the employed and marginal sectors of society are threatened. Another involves recent and current developments in Eastern Europe. These could have the ironic effect of publicizing within these societies structures of domination and inequality, exposure of which is central to the very Marxist heritage that has played such a large role in them. Finally, what might be called the hermeneutics of political discourse requires an ongoing engagement with Marx's ideas, as both the 'right' and the 'left' continue to define themselves in terms shaped by his legacy (e.g. 'anti-socialism'; 'non-working non-class'). While the apocalyptic and falsely utopian claims of traditional Marxism may have been undermined by historical developments, the body of Marxian ideas may still be thought a fertile source of prospective insights into the contemporary political situation.

In this light I would like to focus on one specific issue which is germane both to the common ground Arendt and Marx might share and to the concerns raised by movements of political opposition both in contemporary industrial democracies and in Soviet-type societies: the question of human needs.

Whatever her criticisms of Marx's thought, Arendt is strongly influenced by his critique of modern society. Her most specific account of the increasingly central role played in political and historical thought by the concept of process makes this clear. This account attributes this role largely to the concern of post-seventeenth-century theorists to explain the rapidly growing accumulation of wealth in market-oriented societies. It was natural for thinkers to understand the generation of wealth in the image of the life process, for of all human activities, 'only labor, and neither action nor work is unending, progressing automatically in accordance with life itself and outside the range of wilful decisions or humanly meaningful purposes.'[45] Perhaps unwittingly, Arendt here reveals the common element shared by the life process and the capitalist labor process: the seeming inability of people to subject either to conscious human direction and control.

Marx himself, and the best who followed in his wake – Lukács and the Frankfurt circle most notably – were vitally concerned with the problem of the rational regulation by men and women of the process of social reproduction. They saw that the increasingly sophisticated rationalization of the labour process took place at the mercy of irrational drives and goals shaped and animated by social conflict and domination. Arendt does not find such a conceptual framework congenial. But she seems aware of the problem of rationality. Indeed her distinction between labour and work appears to rest finally on the view that fabrication, rooted as it is in the creative imagination of the maker who can subject his or her efforts to transform the stuff of nature to the requirements of a preconceived model, imparts a conscious human stamp to a natural process of which he or she yet remains a part. In her admission that the distinction between labour and work has not normally been rendered in either political thought or everyday life, Arendt acknowledges that the line between conscious and unconscious transformation is a historically shifting one that may be difficult to draw under specific circumstances.[46] Nevertheless, she steadfastly insists upon drawing it and sees in it the source of an unbridgeable chasm between Marx and her, regardless of whatever they might share in common.

Arendt's claim that Marx is the supreme theorist of the labour process hinges on what she sees as his brilliantly accurate depiction of this process and his fundamental acceptance of it. In itself the labour process is not 'bad'. Because there seems to be misunderstanding about this, it is worth making the point clearly: labour is essential because the human condition of labour is life. Arendt does not wish to do away with labour as an activity unworthy of human beings. In fact she attributes just such an inhuman goal to Marx himself. We may be more than *animal laborans*, but we *are* also *animal laborans*. We remain bound to necessity and must be aware of this if we are consciously to transcend it through the construction of a worldly artifice. In a manner that echoes her concern about the effects of historicism upon our ability to recognize our genuinely historical character, Arendt fears that human beings will 'forget' the demands of necessity, and so the futility of a life devoted to it; this underscores her unease about the pursuit of abundance in industrial society. Humans need to labour. But they lose the sense of what labour means when all they do is labour, or when all their activities serve the life process.

For this reason, Arendt is a much more unstintingly harsh critic of capitalism than is Marx. Unlike Marx, there is for her no 'civilizing moment' in the process of capital expansion, and socialism as the redemption of human experience is doomed to fail because there is little in capitalism to redeem.[47]

It is now evident why history as process is so destructive of actual experience. It carries over into the one realm in which the capacity to tell stories is crucial the anonymity of labour. And there is no story buried beneath layers of exchange value that can be brought to light by a revolutionary transformation of the relations of production, no story that reveals in their glory genuine human capacities. Arendt cannot hold out hope for what Marx calls the end of human pre-history. The silence and futility of labour breed only further and deeper silences, until the voice of that necessity which drives the labour process is itself muted. Arendt's strongest objection to history as process is that it can have no purpose other than the process itself.

Arendt's analysis here is pregnant with ontological implications. Something disappears from the range of human possibilities when the labour process triumphs. In light of the ubiquity of labour, one might wonder how it is possible for there to be evidence of alternative human pursuits at all, including the capacity to reflect on the limits of the labour process itself. In fact, Arendt leaves open the possibility not only that both action and work retain deep, if precarious, roots in contemporary society, but also that the distinction between labour, on the one hand, and both work and action, on the other, may not be as absolute as it might seem.

Here lies perhaps the most serious difficulty with Arendt's interpretation of Marx: her unwillingness to concede, in a manner consistent with her own argument, that labour can express the conscious intent or pluralist character of work. Arendt notes that Marx distinguished human from animal productive activity in terms of the imaginative vision that guides the labourer. But she claims that Marx here 'no longer speaks of labor, but of work – with which he is not concerned; and the best proof of this is that the apparently all-important element of the "imagination" plays no roles whatsoever in his labor theory.'[48] This is not an obvious conclusion. It becomes even less so in light of Marx's criticisms of the dehumanizing effects of capitalist production and private property, particularly their penchant for transforming potentially human activity into merely animal functions and for systematically dulling human intellectual faculties.[49] These arguments have clearly influenced Arendt. Why would she ascribe to Marx conclusions she herself, arguing from similar premisses, would never reach? Putting it another way, why would she attribute to Marx views against which he himself seems to argue? The answer turns precisely on the problem of human needs.

Although somewhat overshadowed of late by political and intellectual developments (the crisis of socialism, the rise of neo-conservatism, the growth of post-modernist thought), there have recently appeared several important studies of the question of needs in the writings of Marx.[50] A full discussion of this work is beyond the scope of this book. In their essentials, however, these studies claim that the genuinely radical core of Marxian thought, and the basis for whatever contemporary political relevance it might have, lie less in Marx's detailed analysis of the mechanics of capitalism than in his highly original attempt to show how our sensuous nature, our needs, are shaped and transformed through our appropriation of external nature; how capitalist society, in unleashing enormous productive forces, is the first society in which the intimate relation of human production and human nature is obvious; and hence how it is now, or will be soon, possible for men and women consciously to formulate their goals and purposes in freedom and autonomy once the fetters on the free development of needs erected by capitalist market relations are removed. That capitalism expands the range of possible needs, while simultaneously thwarting their realization, is the contradiction at the centre of its dynamism and instability, and the basis for its ultimate supersession by socialism.

Marx's treatment of needs makes clear that capitalism reproduces itself not just economically but socially, politically and culturally as well. It cannot be radically altered simply through a change in economic class relations. A critical theory of needs demonstrates both how difficult radical social and political change actually is and also why it is difficult: because of the dualistic character of need articulation and satisfaction entailed by the expansion of capitalist production.

Of course Marx did not provide the final word on the issue. He paid insufficient attention to the symbolic as opposed to the material correlates of needs and their satisfaction (and perhaps only in this sense is Arendt's analysis of him as a labour theorist in her terms fully sound) and so drew too absolute a distinction between use value and exchange value as a keynote of his theory.[51] In a related manner he had too sanguine a view of the naturalness and beneficial character of science and the manner in which it mediated the human encounter with outer nature as a source of need satisfaction.[52] And he failed to recognize that his understanding of human needs as a basis for radical change could stand at odds with an emphasis on class interests as the foundation for political action against capitalism; here the problem is that the notion of interest is too fully imbued with the egoistic logic of capitalist society to be an adequate ground for a radical politics.[53] Nevertheless he pointed out a dimension of the modern labour process that Arendt misses, and in so doing suggests why this process could serve as a vehicle of universality in the face of the eclipse of a meaningful history and a genuine politics.

Arendt does not put the question of needs at the centre of her political thought; indeed there is evidence that she sees the fulfilment of needs and the exercise of freedom as fundamentally at odds.[54] At the same time, she cannot avoid the issue of needs and what might be called the experiential basis of need formation when she specifies the concrete qualities of labour. For while labour may be 'mute', rooted in the demands of life, 'conditioned' by life, it is not equivalent to life itself – something both Arendt's supporters and critics often appear to miss.[55] As part of her effort to spell out the differences between work and labour, Arendt distinguishes between specialization of work, the pooling of identifiable individual skills for the purpose of creating a finished product, and division of labour, the organization of the quantifiable productive energies of individuals who in principle and in practice are indistinguishable and interchangeable. Although the purposes underlying each mode of collective organization are radically different, Arendt acknowledges that there is a tendency to see the two as identical. She attributes this to the fact that each mode of activity 'owes its origin to the strictly political sphere of life, to the fact of man's capacity to act and to act together and in concert. Only within the framework of political organization, where men not merely live, but act, together, can specialization of work and division of labor take place.'[56]

Arendt does not follow up this brief remark. But it has important implications for her theory of action. It appears that the labour process, the most unworldly and apolitical of human pursuits, is not possible under modern conditions of production without some measure of politics. Since politics is concerned with purpose beyond self-interest, labour must in Arendt's terms bear at least the possibility, admittedly suppressed and distorted, of such purpose. It must, in other words, contain the prospect for plurality, in this case manifested in the existence of a community of separate though related individuals whose efforts to organize the reproduction of their social life are subordinated to the pursuit of consciously determined and distinctively human ends. This is what Marx hoped, and what Arendt's theory can reasonably accommodate.

As things stand, the relation of labour to society remains in an important sense obscure. The point may be put this way: given the incapacity of *animal laborans* for distinction and thus speech or action, how is it possible for it to have a sense of history at all – even history as process? *Animal laborans* must in the end be capable of some kind of self-understanding. In spite of Arendt's observations about the attempt to construe action in the image of fabrication, it is no less true that action and labour share something in common: process. Both action and labour involve the initiation of processes. And labour, not simply action, is under the conditions of modern production capable of such initiatives – given the close association of science and productivity, Arendt's account of modern science implies that this is the case. Only because action and labour share process in common is it possible to have a concept and experience of history, however limited, in contemporary society.

The notion of radical needs suggests a way out of this dilemma in Arendt's position. For it implies the conscious articulation of the purposes to which human energies are to be put and the social institutions required for the successful realization of these purposes. Radical needs may be considered 'thought' needs, a non-automatic basis for the twin processes of production and consumption. Social

movements which have called into question quasi-naturalistic defini-
tions of necessity sustained by concrete economic and political interests, and enforced by authoritarian bureaucratic structures which seek
to immunize themselves from popular accountability, may be understood in these terms. The iron grip of necessity (efficiency, productivity, competitiveness and the like) is seen to have human fingers.
Even traditional 'economistic' trade union organizations have
begun to question the demands of economic 'necessity' by increasingly emphasizing health and occupational questions, and incorporating ecological concerns into their political and collective bargaining
claims.[57]

Yet if these recent forms of political mobilization are characterized
most commonly by the quest for free social spaces protected from
the reach of both capital and the state, the purposes for which
autonomy is sought can and do vary. To take one example, some
neighbourhood movements have protested against the location of
nuclear waste disposal sites in their communities. But others have
vigorously opposed the location of public housing developments, or
court-enforced, racially open housing plans and school integration
programmes.[58] Whatever the merits of particular political agendas in
local cases, the direction of political activity exhibited by some social
movements would seem troublesome to many.

My argument, then, that the differences between Arendt and Marx
can be reconciled around the notion of radical needs appears here to
founder. Without the idea of class interest and the notion of correct
class consciousness to serve as 'objective' criteria by means of which
political and social action might be judged, it seems there is no basis
for assessing the 'progressive' or 'reactionary' character of a social
movement. (This is in fact the main objection levelled by orthodox
Marxists against the alleged substitution of social movements for the
proletariat as the agent of radical change.) And given the evident
rootedness of social movements in the everyday conditions of social
reproduction, it seems that political conflicts and struggles that take
shape around these conditions might not create a public sphere open
to all, but rather domains of exclusion according to the principles of
race, class or gender. The committed 'Arendtian', on the one side,
and Marxist, on the other, might well reaffirm the unbridgeability of
the gap between them.

It is precisely this kind of dilemma which provides an opportunity
to think both *with* and *against* Arendt, and in this way develop the
critical possibilities in her position, even where she does not explicitly
spell them out. While it may be true that Arendt does not allow that
labour could harbour the seeds of plurality, even though her position

could enable her to do so without violating her fundamental commitments, at the same time her critique of labour as process makes a point of fundamental importance to a critical assessment of contemporary political options. Because of its intrinsic connection to individual and social reproduction, need, even of an avowedly radical kind, contains a moment of 'self-ness', a 'blind' drive for fulfilment which, because it contains an element of lack and dread, excludes or repels. Pain and desire have their reasons but are not themselves reason.

To be sure, they are not as a result immoral or 'evil', nor would Arendt contend they were.[59] And their existence provides no inherent justification for an unchanging and a historical apparatus of repression in the service of a 'morality' which, as Max Horkheimer points out, whips up the very passions it so sombrely condemns. The great Marxian insight, that artificially contrived scarcity distorts human drives, and a society in which this scarcity was sharply reduced, if not eliminated altogether, would strip these drives of their 'demonic power' (Horkheimer) because life and death would no longer be so immediately at stake, remains vitally important for critical thought. This is especially true in an era such as the current one, in which new forms of social Darwinist ideology, such as the drive for 'competitiveness', have emerged almost everywhere.

Nevertheless, Arendt's argument forces us to (re)consider the relation between abundance and freedom, and the nature of human drives in any conceivable human society. For Arendt, advances in material productivity have failed to lay the foundation for new forms of political action. They have only meant that *animal laborans* has become 'greedier and more craving' in its appetites.[60] They have not promoted greater freedom; indeed quite the opposite. This is clearly a contentious claim, even given that Arendt does not equate *animal laborans* with the working classes in industrial societies. But the questions remain. Do aspirations grounded in the material life process invariably contain an element of moral ambiguity, which means that even were it possible to consider what a radically transformed society would look like, one would still be faced with the prospect of social claims to satisfaction which would exclude or deny – in other words, with the problem of injustice? And given that we remain bound to our present societies, with their evident domination, injustice and misery, do not needs, even radical needs, necessarily reflect this sorry state of affairs? If this is the case, are contemporary movements for social change which speak the language of needs an instance of pouring old wine into new bottles, of pursuing the old in the guise of the new?[61]

These are difficult questions for left politics. But Arendt's work not only provokes these questions. It gives us clues about how to answer them. In the final section of this chapter, I want to indicate how Arendt's analysis of history and her encounter with Marx suggest conceptions of both collective life and individual action which attempt to meet the challenge of process-thinking and its social and political implications.

IV

I noted earlier how important the emergence of a complex division of labour was for Arendt in the development of the labour process in modernity. She claims that while division of labour and specialization of work share a common political origin, the former is ultimately anti-political. I suggested that this was not an obvious or necessary conclusion. Yet there is a quality of the labour process as it is actually organized in industrial societies which Arendt carefully notes, and which is crucial to the issue here. She argues that division of labour is based on the fact that when two people put their labour power together, they can behave toward one another as if they were one person. They behave, in other words, as if each were identical, the same and exchangeable. Division of labour is thus the very opposite of the human political capacity to work together co-operatively, although on the surface it resembles it.

If individuals are the same and exchangeable, then all are equally superfluous or dispensable when their labour 'power' is used up. Indeed, the only measure of their worth is their contribution to what Arendt, ironically borrowing again from Marx, calls the 'collective labor force', the only subject of the labor process in the context of the division of labour. As we will see, the prevalence of exchange-ability and implied superfluity of the labourer links division of labour in a subtle but ominous way with the structure of the totalitarian mass movement.

For Arendt, there is a certain existential quality to the 'labourer': an anonymity inherent in the very reduction of individual skill to abstract labour power. As she sees it, politics is about appearing before one's peers in a public space where one can see and be seen, and is not invisible or mute. People denied the opportunity to 'appear' lose something valuably human. What they lose is the opportunity, in Arendt's terms, to reveal 'who' they are. This notion of a 'who' which stands at the centre of political action is a difficult and demanding one in Arendt's thought. It clearly involves individual identity, but not of the kind associated with particular gifts or talents, or the typical characterizations much favoured by social sciences such as psychology. Indeed Arendt claims that personal qualities of this sort involve not the 'who' but rather the 'what' someone is. Knowing 'what' someone is allows for an external account of the individual which can be useful in locating this individual in relation to the everyday processes of social life. By contrast, when individuals show who they are (and 'show' is the only way to do it), they 'reveal actively their unique personal identities and thus make their appearance in the human world, while their physical identities appear without any activity of their own in the unique shape of the body and sound of the voice.'[62]

Two important implications follow from this. In the first place, disclosing one's 'who' is radically different from outlining one's characteristics. As Arendt sees it, this disclosure can never be achieved intentionally, as if this identity were 'owned' and thus disposable as its owner saw fit. 'On the contrary, it is more than likely that the "who", which appears so clearly and unmistakably to others, remains hidden from the person . . .'[63] This suggests a second implication: that the presence of others is vital for disclosure. And this presence must be of a specific character. Those to whom one reveals oneself must be open to this revelation. As I see it, this means that 'who' someone is cannot 'matter' to them in the same way that the qualities which comprise 'what' someone is can. Someone's personal identity, her 'who', must impinge upon others in a way that is different from the effects of objectively describable characteristics. In the everyday sense of the term, people must be 'disinterested'. Disclosure for its own sake should be all that counts. For while the person so disclosed cannot own her identity, *neither can the others in whose eyes this disclosure takes place.* In a very powerful way, to disclose oneself is in Arendt's view to *be*: the specifically political quality of her ontology is clearly evident here. Openness to others and to oneself is the key, and this means that in the course of disclosure, anything can happen. It is because political action can disclose in this sense that for Arendt it is 'free'.

Arendt calls this distinctive form of collective life 'sheer human togetherness'. It involves a situation 'where people are *with* others and neither for nor against them . . .'[64] Only where people come together in this way can the revelatory quality of speech and action come to the fore. In this respect, Arendt's analysis of the 'who' suggests again the powerful influence of Immanuel Kant. In large measure she reformulates Kant's notion of an intelligible or noumenal ego, while giving it a special communal twist. Kant sought to establish the possibility of the rational subject acting according to a universal law it freely gives to itself outside the bounds of empirical causality, and in so doing expressing its nature as a morally autonomous agent. (Kant's influence on Marx is considerable here and is especially evident in Marx's notion of a realm of freedom beyond necessity.) Arendt reworks Kant's claim in a non-transcendental fashion, for the 'who' possesses an existential or experiential content; it does not exist outside its concrete emergence in a public space. Thus it does not entail the opposition, to which Kant's position points, between a moral world and an empirical one. But Arendt does share his view that human beings cannot be fully understood, or indeed fully human, without the possibility of universality and ultimately the political institutions which could express and guarantee it. For Kant, this involved the kingdom of ends. For Arendt, it involves a world in which people can be with others, and neither for nor against them – a world of solidarity which overcomes the isolation of each from all inherent in Kant's prescriptions, rooted as they are in his assumption of the 'unsocial sociability' of human nature.[65] Without this solidarity, this 'human togetherness', there can be no disclosure of 'the unique and distinct identity of the agent'. There can only be instrumental relations between people which ultimately rob them of their human dignity.[66] There would, in short, be alienation.

Thus, for prospective political actors, Arendt's position poses some demanding requirements. These might be summarized by a Kantian-flavoured question: 'What kind of world would I be creating by my actions, and would I want to live in it were someone else creating it?'[67] This question does not exclude any particular basis for action. It does not in principle exclude political action around, for example, the organization of the productive apparatus; thus it can accommodate what I have called radical needs. But it does require a certain 'stepping out' of one's situation, a conscious act of imaginative identification with others as potentially unique agents who are capable of personal revelation, of showing 'who' they are. It involves entertaining the possibility of something new and surprising from the interaction of potential agents, the disruption of established and anticipated patterns in social life. In other words, it involves the possibility of what Arendt understands to be genuine history.[68]

We are thus back where we began in this chapter. There I argued that for Arendt, history and politics inhere in each other. Her critique of the concept of history, ancient and modern, and of Karl Marx as a theorist of the labour process, seeks to demonstrate that our capacity to live genuinely historical lives, and thus political lives, has come under siege. Too little are we 'with' others. Too often are we 'for' them, as under the division of labour and its institutional variants, including certain kinds of social movements, or 'against' them, as in warfare.

For all of his powerful insights into the divisive, anti-solidaristic consequences of capitalist development, from Arendt's perspective Marx failed to transcend the framework within which he was forced to think. He did not outline satisfactorily the elements of a new human community, forms of sheer human togetherness. But how can we know whether people are with each other, and not merely for or against them? With his notion of a universal interest, embodied in the proletariat, Marx at least had a standard of judgement about appropriate or inappropriate forms of human association. Obviously this standard is not available to Arendt. And unlike Marx at his most optimistic, Arendt never accepted that there could be clear-cut guarantees about a 'proper' drawing of the boundaries between genuine and false forms of association. Just as history expresses both great deeds deserving of glory and infamous ones meriting condemnation, politics as the provision of spaces in which people appear and reveal themselves can hold unpleasant surprises. Politics is difficult and has risks (although it is not itself 'risk'). Arendt tells us that genuine political action, free action, is inspired by principles such as 'honor or glory, love of equality . . . distinction or excellence . . . but also fear or distrust or hatred.'[69] What are the hallmarks of human solidarity, of the identity in difference that is human plurality? In chapter 2, I suggest that the concepts of 'freedom', 'action' and 'public realm' provide Arendt with the standards of assessment of political life. What is unique about these notions is that they capture the openness and indeterminacy of the demonstration of human capacities in a condition of sheer togetherness without falling prey to relativism or nihilism – without in other words parting company with Arendt's ontological concerns.

2 Freedom, Action and Public Realm: Hannah Arendt's Polis and the Foundations of a Genuine Politics

As a model for the organization of public life, and as a paradigm of the meaning and significance of politics as a human pursuit, the Greek polis has long held a profound allure for political theorists and actors alike. The experience of the one hundred and fifty or so 'city-states' most closely identified with the Hellenic world around the Mediterranean Sea, and in particular with the Athens of the fifth century BC, has proved decisive for Western thought and practice, not least because of its influence upon subsequent forms of political association – most notably those of the Romans whom Hannah Arendt considered the most political of people.[1] The ideal of a comprehensive citizenship which engages people not just as isolated individuals but as members of a social body, and which holds out the possibility that the laws which govern society can be the direct products of citizen participation, has recurred again and again down to our own century. It seems to address a pressing human need or aspiration which has persisted over time.

Arendt acknowledges the significance of the dream of an integral citizenship. It is the core of the quest for political freedom that has emerged at various historical junctures, most recently and dramatically in the revolutionary upheavals of the modern age.[2] It is also the phenomenon most directly threatened by the advent of modern 'anti' or 'false' politics, the growth of bureaucracy as the dominant political institution in the contemporary world, the triumph of *animal laborans* and the 'social' in modernity. It is in the context of a reconsideration of the polis that Arendt develops her account of 'freedom', 'action' and 'public realm', the critical standards by which she seeks both to grasp the decline of a genuine politics in the modern age and to suggest what a form of political association built upon plurality, sheer human togetherness, might look like.

Because of the way it functions in her thought, the polis is for Arendt both a historical and a normative phenomenon. Both dimensions of the polis must be understood in their interrelation if we are fully to appreciate the magnitude of the issues confronting us as potentially political beings. While the polis is a historical phenomenon, it is also in an important sense itself the source of Western history, at least in political terms. As Arendt argues in 'The Concept of History', the remembrance of great deeds which deserve immortality already presupposes the polis as a form of institutionalized remembrance. Thus when in Arendt we read the polis as history, we must also read history through the mediating power of the polis.

In presenting the polis as a paradigm or model of public life, Arendt treads a well-worn path. What is unique or significant about her reference to this time-honoured standard? In the first place Hannah Arendt's polis is a metaphor. She fully understands that the conditions which gave rise to it – the existence of small, largely homogenous populations organized through a relatively simple division of labour (which included slavery) and bound together by a religiously based social consensus – cannot be duplicated in the modern world. She wants us, rather, to reflect upon certain conceptual and practical distinctions which she believes were fundamental to the polis, and can only be retrieved if we look afresh at its meaning and the purposes it fulfilled. Her use of the polis, then, is not intended to provide empirically testable hypotheses about actual and possible political institutions, forms of organized social life. Nor is it a heuristic device to stimulate the scientific imagination through the provision of analogies which are themselves 'unscientific'. It is designed rather to allow us to make sense of the historical judgements of political communities about the boundaries of collective life and the relation of citizenship and law to other domains of human existence. In particular, it permits us to see why for the Greeks the human capacity for political organization, the *bios politikos*, was built upon and in turn conditioned the distinctively human properties of praxis and lexis, action and speech, properties which required a public realm if they were to be given full majesty.[3]

In the second place, Arendt is aware that the polis was the origin not only of Western political history but also political philosophy. Our very understanding of the historical polis owes much to those like Plato and Aristotle whose judgements about it were profoundly shaped by philosophical considerations. But our reliance upon Plato and Aristotle in this respect has not been an unmixed blessing, for both harboured strong reservations about the ultimate meaning and worth of political life.[4] Whether thinking philosophically about politics distorts both philosophy and politics, whether each is antagonistic to the other and whether the prime victim of such a conflict might be not philosophy, as is commonly assumed, but politics – these questions are all crucial to Arendt's evocation of the polis as the paradigm of a genuine politics. They are crucial, in other words, to Arendt's attempt to work out new forms of genuine political thinking and to identify new possibilities for political action.

Finally, Arendt sees the polis as radically distinct from the modern state. Clearly this involves some obvious and oft-noted characteristics of the modern state which distinguish it from the polis: the fact that it is large, bureaucratically organized and impersonal; that it engages its citizens/subjects in an external way best understood by the logic of interests; and that its fundamental task is to maintain peace and order among potentially conflicting individuals. But the distinction between state and polis includes for Arendt something more. As suggested above, the polis as a form of life represented the quest for a certain kind of excellence, a shining forth in word and deed of distinctively human capacities which could be preserved in story and remembered over time. In the polis acting individuals showed their 'stuff', their virtuosity, their capacity to move and persuade those around them with just the 'right' combination of words and actions. Such demonstrations of human verve and skill stood, so to speak, on their own; they were their own justification and needed no 'external' ends to validate their worth. In other words, they were meaningful and not (primarily) useful.

In this respect the revelation of human capacities in the polis manifested a distinction which, according to Arendt, has been forgotten in modern experience: that between 'for the sake of' and 'in order to'. To undertake something for the sake of something else is to make it meaningful in relation to some standard of worth established independently of both what is undertaken and its consequences. The connection to the notion of a 'who' revealed in action before others is clear. In revealing 'who' one is, an actor proceeds deliberately, but the end result cannot be consciously willed and is itself ultimately defined by others according to an evaluative standard. These others are bound together in a set of relations among equals, a form of 'sheer human togetherness' for which the polis provides a model.

To reveal one's 'who' is to act for the sake of both oneself and others whose sense of reality depends upon the recognition of a distinctively human presence that can only be rendered in this way. By contrast, to undertake something in order to realize something else is the basic utilitarian formula according to which the only relevant relations are those between means and ends. This involves a domain within which everything is in principle and without limit capable of being transformed into means to something else. It involves, in other words, an instrumental world. The sense entailed by 'in order to' clearly relates to questions of 'what' someone is in terms of describable and manipulable capacities and qualities, with the implication that all relations between individuals are purely external, technical and non-revelatory.

From Arendt's perspective, the modern state provides a powerful testament to the suppression of 'for the sake of' by 'in order to', the reduction of meaning to utility. As a complex bureaucratic order with its hierarchically organized mobilization of resources, which themselves serve as means to the fulfilment of further aims and goals, the state implements 'policies' which are shaped by 'interests' and fulfil 'needs'. But it cannot provide a home for the initiation of free action for its own sake. The modern state both discourages action and undermines the conditions of its very possibility – by binding people together in a purely instrumental way.

Such complex concerns provide the background for Arendt's concepts of 'freedom', 'action' and 'public realm'. Like the notion of the polis with which they are associated, these concepts have both descriptive and normative dimensions. That is, they draw upon historically recognizable forms of these phenomena, but break with the purely descriptive and historical by recalling suppressed dimensions and possibilities which can be associated with freedom, action and the public realm, and which point to more satisfactory forms of all three. The combination of the mundane and the strange in Arendt's account makes it both arresting and difficult, as well as open to radically conflicting interpretations. It also provides additional grounds for what I have argued is Arendt's attempt to encourage a rethinking of both political institutions and practices, and our ways of thinking about how we think. In short, it is central to her political philosophy, in Claude Lefort's sense of the term.

In this chapter, then, I examine the key elements of Arendt's account of public life, a genuine politics. I then seek to demonstrate the suppleness of this account by suggesting various issues and practices in modern social life which are germane to Arendt's work and upon which it casts light. Finally, I assess two significant critical analyses of her ideas which relate these ideas to important alternative conceptions of public life: liberalism and feminism. I argue that, while frequently penetrating, these analyses exhibit significant limitations which ironically demonstrate the often submerged critical potential of Arendt's position.

I

'The raison d'etre of politics is freedom and its field of experience is action . . . Men *are* free – as distinguished from their possessing the gift of freedom – as long as they act, neither before nor after; for to be free and to act are the same.'[5] In a nutshell, this is the central proposition of Arendt's entire political theory. The fullest expression of freedom is found in action. But for action to be possible, relations among individuals must be free relations. The complex interconnection of freedom and action gives Arendt's account of a genuine public life its distinctive character.

As I noted before, Arendt's analyses of important political ideas generally start from a critique of existing accounts of the political phenomena in question. Her treatment of freedom and action is a model of this approach. According to her, currently dominant notions of freedom are inherently contradictory in a way that has profoundly shaped our conception of ourselves as political beings. The mark of process-thinking is clearly visible here for the contradiction lies in the fact that while we tell ourselves that we are free and responsible, we orient ourselves according to the principle of causality. In other words, we have confounded the distinction between freedom and necessity, in the process remoulding our concept and practice of freedom in the image of necessity.

Here Arendt's reservations about the historical effects of philosophy upon politics are profound. In cultural terms the meaning of freedom has been transformed from a distinctively political into a philosophical question, from a matter involving our relations with others into a purely 'inner' question, a feature of the dialogue between me and myself which is the hallmark of philosophical thinking. The clearest expression of this change is the widespread identification of freedom with the inner domain of the will. To be free is to will into being a particular state of affairs against the barriers which inevitably resist the will's thrust.

While the origins of the change in the status of freedom can be traced back to Plato's and Aristotle's opposition to the polis and its citizenship, it was with St Augustine that freedom became fully a philosophical issue. The context within which this occurred was decisive. As Arendt sees it, the problem of freedom appeared in the work of Augustine as part of the effort to divorce freedom from politics and to arrive at a formulation such that one could simultaneously be a slave in the world and still be free. The collapse of the ancient world and its political forms was obviously critical here and made the questions of freedom and slavery particularly pressing. But the full significance of the transformation of freedom did not become clear until the seventeenth and eighteenth centuries. In the writings of Hobbes and Spinoza, even perhaps Kant, freedom was understood as outside the realm of politics altogether; indeed the less politics, the more freedom. Politics became compatible with freedom only to the extent that it was possible to be free *from* politics.

The idea that freedom exists in the power of the will to realize its aims has characterized most modern thinking about freedom. Particularly as it has emerged in the writings of Christian thinkers from Augustine onward, the will has come to be seen as an organ of self-liberation, a means by which it is in fact possible to be a slave in the world and free at the same time. The will, which commands execution of the aim cognition sets for it, allows people to transcend the limits of an alien and hostile world, even as they remain unfortunately bound to it.

Of course the idea of liberation is an essential element of any meaningful notion of freedom. But according to Arendt, the modern understanding of freedom is anti-worldly: self-liberation has come to mean liberation *from* the self as the locus of worldly desires and intentions. And since the power of the will is its ability to command, this power is a matter of strength, not freedom. To link freedom with the will is to leave the sphere of politics and enter the realm of necessity. Arendt argues that strength is a mutely natural, singular quality of the individual. Thus the will can bear no communal properties. At best, individual wills can come together through contract. At worst, they remain forever isolated and inevitably in conflict.

However, as an instrument of self-liberation, will-power is doomed to fail. This failure is inherent in the very capacity of willing itself, for '[i]t is as though the I-will immediately paralyzed the I-can, as though the moment men *willed* freedom they lost capacity to *be* free. In the deadly conflict with worldly desires and intentions from which will-power was supposed to liberate the self, the most willing seemed able to achieve was oppression. Because of the will's omnipotence . . . the will-to-power turned at once into a will-to-oppression.[6] In being set against our own desires, we have become antagonists with the world – and with ourselves.

Again it is Augustine who provides for Arendt the clearest formulation of the dilemma inherent in willing. In developing the notions of will and will-power, Augustine was struck not by the power of the will but its impotence in the war of me and myself. Thus he believed one to be at odds with oneself, 'as though there were two wills present in the same man, fighting with each other for power over his mind.'[7] The I-will, in conflict with the I-will-not, illuminates the experience of the I-will-but-*cannot*; it remains forever bound to an intractable self. For Arendt, all this is inherently anti-political. The perception of bondage to the self leads to the desire for liberation from the self – and from other selves – that can come, paradoxically, only when the individual retreats fully into the realm of the self, that is, in the activity of thought. Arendt's ambivalence about political philosophy follows from her uneasy sense that the triumph of traditional philosophy over politics was a pyrrhic victory.

The major consequence of the transformation of freedom from a political into a philosophical experience was the increasingly close association of freedom with sovereignty, the ideal of a free will independent from other wills and ultimately prevailing against them. For Arendt, the identification of freedom and sovereignty has been a pernicious development, for 'it leads either to a denial of human freedom – namely, if it is realized that whatever men may be, they are never sovereign – or to the insight that the freedom of one man, or group, or a body politic can be purchased only at the price of freedom i.e. sovereignty of others.'[8] Like the idea of a free will, the idea of sovereignty is anti-political. In the final analysis only the one can be fully sovereign. The ultimate political expression of sovereignty is tyranny. Hence, '[t]he famous sovereignty of political bodies has always been an illusion, which, moreover, can be maintained only by the instruments of violence, that is, with essentially non-political means.'[9] The modern 'sovereign' state, ostensibly the most political of social institutions, is both founded upon and reinforces anti-political relations and practices. Arendt puts the matter bluntly: 'If men wish to be free, it is precisely sovereignty they must renounce.'[10]

The transformation of freedom into an 'inner' experience of the will, and thus an equivalent of sovereignty, radically individualizes it. Such 'freedom', which exists as a kind of compulsion, perfectly suits a society in which individuals are set against each other as self-interested competitors, and enjoy little solidarity. This is why Arendt sees modern liberalism, with its strong commitment to individualism against community, as frequently hostile to liberty, even as it ostensibly defends it.[11] In liberal cultures, particularly those of

Britain and North America, the lethal combination of sovereignty and the will has undermined real possibilities for free action, paving the way for, among other things, the triumph of process-thinking that I discussed in the previous chapter.

By contrast with the inherently individualist understanding of freedom that has accompanied its conversion into a philosophical question, Arendt argues that genuine freedom is inextricable from community and the historical possibilities for establishing communal arrangements. In a manner that suggests Benjamin Constant (whom Arendt indeed quotes in *The Human Condition* in the introduction to her critique of Marx, a critique she patterns after Constant's critical assessment of Rousseau), the liberty Arendt defends is that of the political community, not that of the individual against the community. It is for this reason that freedom and action are necessarily interwined: freedom is a political or communitarian phenomenon while action is at the heart of a genuine politics.

It is at this point that the complexities and tensions of Arendt's account of freedom, and thus action, come into focus. In arguing on behalf of freedom *as* politics, as opposed to freedom *from* politics, Arendt does more than simply draw out the conflict between what Isaiah Berlin has called negative and positive freedom, between freedom as the absence of restrictions by others on what I choose to do, and freedom as self-mastery and its concomitant claim that to be free is to participate actively in making the decisions that govern one's life. Arendt's arguments are clearly germane to this debate; they certainly suggest at one level an affinity with those which support positive freedom. But the real thrust of her position involves something more. To see this we must recall two themes which broadly characterize Arendt's view of the history of the Western political tradition and the nature of the modern age. First, Arendt finds in traditional political philosophy from Plato onwards a hostility to the unpredictability and uncertainty of action, which make action ill-suited to the philosophic task of comprehending the permanent and unchanging metaphysical standards which define reality. Secondly, although the anti-political consequences of this position were visible enough in the ancient world, their full effects were, oddly, not felt until the modern era. As we have seen, modern political theory from Hobbes onwards increasingly defined freedom as freedom from politics. The philosophical grounds for this claim were worked out in the thought of Descartes and his successors, notably Kant, and emphasized the purely inner, spiritual quality of freedom. Since in the modern age knowledge has come to be identified with what we ourselves have made, and since to be knowable and thus 'real' freedom must conform to this ideal of knowledge, it can only be an 'inner' experience. All we can know with any certainty about ourselves as beings capable of freedom are our own sensations, be they of pain, as in the utilitarian account, or of our basic moral urgings, as in Kant's work.

So the transformation of freedom into an inner matter of the will was a response to a real and pressing set of circumstances. And it undoubtedly has had certain benefits, as befitting the Enlightenment context within which it came to fruition. These benefits involve potential limits on what free human beings can do: for Hobbes, to take one example, by drawing upon our self-knowledge we see the absolute necessity of peace; for Kant, to take another example, our self-knowledge gives access to the moral laws which allow us to live together by treating others as ends and not means.

What I suggest Arendt provocatively and powerfully argues in her account of freedom and action, is that for humans to be genuinely free, they must not only renounce sovereignty but the pursuit of sovereign 'knowing' itself, that is, the control and certainty which the understanding of freedom as purely inner freedom has made possible. It is the close association of freedom with inner certainty and moral control that has made her account of freedom and action difficult for many to accept: it seems that she wilfully gives up the possibility and even the desirability of moral limits to political action.[12] But Arendt does not see it in this way. Rather, freedom as it has come to be understood and embodied in our institutions and practices has functioned as a surrogate necessity – we are free to do what we must – and this has permitted precisely the transformation of people into means or instruments, elements in a complex social division of labour. Put another way, the moral limits to action supposedly inherent in the 'philosophical' definition of freedom have not prevented political outrages, even in the name of freedom and reason themselves. (In this respect Arendt's position parallels Max Horkheimer's and T. W. Adorno's account of the 'dialectic of enlightenment'.)

To be sure, as I noted in the previous chapter, freedom and action, if understood as essentially worldly and not spiritual phenomena, do indeed carry certain risks. That genuinely free action is an 'external' matter is another way of affirming that politics requires an audience. That the audience may be hostile, or unreceptive or inattentive to the real implications of what unfolds before it, does not change the relation of audience to actor, although it may alter its moral character. After all, distrust and hatred can be principles of action. However, it is wrong to assume that Arendt fails to provide a moral context within which freedom is exercised. Solidarity as sheer human togetherness entails a basic acceptance of others in their distinctiveness, a commitment to plurality. This acceptance is itself a limit on what people can reasonably do to each other: in a sense Arendt attempts to provide a more compelling phenomenological basis for the exercise of Kant's categorical imperative, a basis Kant himself was unable to provide. And the argument that existing political communities fail to embody solidarity is no more an argument against Arendt's position than the equally defensible claim that because Kantian moral integrity and responsibility find little place in the everyday world of political life in modern societies, these are irrelevant to serious political analysis.

Risks, however, there are and the very language Arendt uses to describe action indicates how important what might be called an element of hope is in her account. In contrast to the compulsive strivings of the will, which remain tied to the never-ending struggle against desire, one's own and that of others, free action expresses a moment of transcendence. The achievements of action are, literally, miraculous: they always interrupt some natural or social process in totally unexpected ways. For Arendt, miracles are primarily political and worldly, not religious and other-worldly. It follows that 'a capacity for performing miracles must . . . be within the range of human faculties'[13], for the capacity to generate the unexpected, to begin something new, is literally the capacity to act. Arendt uses the term 'miracle' because she wants to shock us into recognizing anew what was once thought obvious about the realm of human affairs but is now in danger of slipping from view: that ours is a world of potentially creative individuals 'who because they have received the two-fold gift of freedom and action can establish a reality of their own.'[14]

For action to be 'genuine', faithful to its capabilities, it must express certain distinctive qualities. In the first place action suggests virtuosity, a kind of performing excellence valuable in itself and not in terms of some product which outlasts the action and takes on an independent existence. It is because there is to action, and thus freedom, a strong element of performance that Arendt ascribes so much importance to appearing before an audience as a critical component of a genuine politics. This appearance requires its own unique 'space' where virtuosity can take shape, not as an inner matter, but as 'a worldly reality, tangible in words which can be heard, in deeds which can be seen, and in events which are talked about, remembered, and turned into stories . . .'[15]

In the second place, if action is to have these qualities, it 'must be free from motive on the one side, from its intended goal as a predictable effect on the other . . .'[16] It must be free from both 'the judgment of the intellect' and 'the command of the will'.[17] This is not to claim that motives and aims are unimportant in stimulating action. It *is* to say that to be free an action must transcend them. It must be subject neither to the guidance of the intellect, which formulates aims, nor the will, which carries out the judgements of the intellect. What a free act does express is a principle. In contrast to an aim or a motive, a principle inspires an action from without. It is given its fullest manifestation in the completed action and loses none of its strength or validity once the act has been completed, although it requires action to come into the world at all. As we have seen, these principles are varied: 'honor or glory, love of equality . . . or distinction or excellence . . . but also fear or distrust or hatred'.[18] If the political actor is a kind of performer, the standard of critical judgement for the performance is the principle that inspired it.

But why should political action and thus freedom be understood in this way? Why should it not be about, for example, the struggle for power or the clash of interests, themes that most of us would identify with politics? In fact, as the various principles which inspire free action suggest, there is nothing in Arendt's position which precludes a struggle for power or a clash of interests from providing the context for genuine political action. In principle most recognizable social phenomena can serve as bases for performative achievement, for revelation. Arendt never intended that her account of freedom and action should be unrecognizable from the perspective of actual lived experience.

Nevertheless Arendt's account of free action is difficult, one of those puzzles to which I referred in the Introduction. Understandably it has been controversial, its meaning and implications a source of debate. Certainly the criticisms of the American political theorist George Kateb, which I will examine later in this chapter, turn substantially on the problem of action. I am not certain that either Arendt's critics or I are fully clear about her position. But it might be helpful at least to attempt to establish more fully than is normally done the context within which Arendt formulated her position and so get a sharper picture of its content and limits.

If Arendt's overall account of freedom was framed by certain assumptions about the Western tradition of political thought and the modern age, her understanding of action itself was conditioned by specific developments that have taken root as the demands of the modern world confronted the claims of traditional thought. In my view, in developing her notion of 'action', Arendt was reacting against two distinct but related currents of twentieth-century political thought and practice. Both have had, and continue to have, profound implications for our understanding of politics.

The first development is the 'scientization' of politics, an important theme in many critical accounts of the modern situation, including Arendt's. As Arendt's account of history makes clear, this involves the assumption that the methodological canons of the natural sciences provide the only grounds for legitimate knowledge. The effect upon politics is to transform political practices, and human beings themselves, into objects capable of being understood as matter in motion, and thus governed by laws similar to those which determine the behaviour of non-human natural phenomena. Arendt finds evidence of the scientization of politics in a wide array of contemporary institutions and practices. Prominent in this respect are theories of behaviourism, most economic analyses and what Arendt calls in her account of the role of the United States in the Vietnam war in the 1960s and 1970s the 'scenerios' of national security managers.[19] Where politics is conducted as a species of science, the possibilities for action are seriously diminished, if not eliminated altogether.

The second development is perhaps less obvious but no less important. This involves forms of what might be called political romanticism. The critical assessment of romanticism is less visible in Arendt's work than is the critique of science. But it is evident enough, for example, in her criticisms of 'grandiose aims' in politics, as well as, arguably, in her expressed fear that the conditions under which the state of Israel were created, laudable as this creation was, could well create the basis for future and continuing injustice and conflict.[20] In another context it involves less a specific political theory or practice than a mode through which political understanding develops. In this sense it is evident in various attempts to link traditional conceptions of morality to political life; as such it figures, as we will see, in Arendt's depiction of Adolf Eichmann and the critical attacks on this.

The uniqueness and significance of Arendt's treatment of action is that it seeks to transcend these positions while at the same time accepting that they express important dimensions of modern social and individual life. Individuals seeking to think *or* act must take them into account. In the very suggestion that the principles which inspire and are manifested by action are and must be distinct from both 'the judgment of the intellect' and 'the command of the will', Arendt suggests a historical and dynamic character to the notion of action which is not usually associated with it, perhaps not even explicitly by Arendt herself. Intellect and will denote distinctively modern characteristics of the individual. And they are also, not coincidentally, associated with those currents of thought Arendt finds threatening to a genuine politics: scienticism (intellect) and romanticism (will).

In this light something surprising emerges: it is not a greater affinity between action and conventional morality that would limit the potentially dangerous and destructive characteristics of politics. It is precisely their *distance* that in Arendt's view makes action more, not less, sensitive to these threats. Arendt is certainly aware of these threats. To repeat: not just the desire for freedom but 'hatred and jealousy' can be principles of action.

Indeed, where properly undertaken, action could provide the only bulwark – an admittedly tenuous one given modern circumstances, to be sure – *against* the politically unconscionable. The point is that in so far as it expresses both scientific rationality and romanticism (and they are surprisingly united in their hostility to worldliness), modern politics *has* produced unconscionable states of affairs. It is not action run wild but the absence and forcible suppression of any possibilities of it that are the hallmarks of political horrors such as totalitarianism.

To suggest that action can provide a uniquely strong bulwark against the politically unconscionable is also to claim that it possesses its own moral standards, means by which its effects can be registered and weighed. If action is marked above all by its unpredictability and irreversibility of outcome, then the standards peculiar to it must deal with and limit these. For Arendt these limits inhere in action itself and involve two powerful if difficult human faculties: the power to make and keep promises and the power to forgive.

In defending the power to make and keep promises as the primary antidote to the unpredictability of action and the always changing qualities of the human beings who undertake it, Arendt ironically links up with the modern tradition of the social contract which, from Hobbes onwards, has been such a powerful current in political thought. Yet for Arendt, committing ourselves to abide tomorrow by what we have agreed to today is a moral act only imperfectly reflected in existing contracts guaranteed under private law, or even the constitutional provisions of the liberal state. For these practices presuppose what Arendt explicitly rejects: the identification of freedom with sovereignty. For Arendt, the making and keeping of promises can only work if people acknowledge their *lack* of sovereignty, in other words the basic human condition of plurality. That humans must do so is evident from Arendt's account of what exactly this faculty rectifies. It must deal with what Arendt calls a 'two-fold darkness of human affairs': the basic unreliability of human beings who can never guarantee that they will be the same people tomorrow as they are today; and the impossibility of forecasting adequately the consequences of what one does in a community of equals where all have the capacity to act.[21] This two-fold 'darkness' and the uncertainty with which it is associated is the 'price' we pay for a freedom which by its nature is non-sovereign, and for a plurality which reflects the joy of sheer living together among beings whose fundamental sense of reality requires the presence of others. The ability to keep one's word, an island of certainty in a sea of unpredictability, is 'the only alternative to a mastery which relies on domination of one's self and rule over others . . .'[22]

If the faculty to make and keep promises is the only antidote for the unpredictability of action, the fact that we cannot foresee the consequences of what we do, the power to forgive is the only way to counter the irreversibility of action, the fact that we cannot undo what we have done. While the power to forgive suggests an extraordinary response to acts of evil or wrongdoing, Arendt sees it as a much more mundane matter, although no less exceptional for that. Even where we had not intended it, our inability both to predict and control the consequences of our actions means that unpleasant and unpalatable outcomes can always ensue. Only by being forgiven, by being released from the consequences of what we have done, can a process which would otherwise proceed in an uninterrupted way be brought to an end in the only humanly appropriate manner: by the acknowledgement of a plurality of equals which includes the one who forgives and the one who is forgiven. Without being forgiven in what is incipiently a communal and thus political act, 'our capacity to act would, as it were, be confined to one single deed from which we could never recover; we would remain the victims of its consequences forever, not unlike the sorcerer's apprentice who lacked the magic formula to break the spell.'[23] The power to forgive is the only response to the irreversibility of action consistent with the fundamental qualities of action itself. Like action, the exercise of this power can never be fated or predetermined.

For Arendt, what is unique about these capacities is that, unlike more conventional moral standards which have their origin in the relation of me to myself, that is, in thought or philosophy, the power to make and keep promises and the capacity to forgive necessarily have a distinctively political origin. They are based upon experiences which are possible only in the presence of others, never in the inner experience of ruling and being ruled which since Plato has provided the basis of our more conventional political morality. Arendt's claim is radical: only these capacities can provide the foundations of a genuinely political morality because only these have their roots in the fact of human plurality. The moral judgements which follow from their exercise must return us to a world of equals; they can never simply be means of self-control as if we were by ourselves in the world. In short, only these capacities reflect and reinforce non-sovereignty. We can never forgive or make promises with ourselves, or, if we think we can do so, this is only because we have had the experience of making promises to, or being forgiven by, others.

Here Arendt's notion of a 'who' revealed in action is once again vital. Just as who one is can never be the predetermined product of an actor's conscious choice, so the person who is forgiven, must also be the one who reveals him- or herself to others – and only they can so judge. Ultimately this is why no one can forgive herself. For here, 'as in action and speech generally, we are dependent upon others, to whom we appear in a distinctness which we ourselves are unable to perceive. Closed within ourselves, we would never be able to forgive ourselves any failing or transgression because we would lack the experience of the person for the sake of whom one can forgive.'[24]

The capacity to make and keep promises and the power to forgive are at one and the same time both strongly embedded in everyday experience and immensely frail. All hinges upon the possibility of a political community which incorporates plurality and, what is now clear, its attendant qualities, notably a kind of reciprocity, a mutuality of acknowledgement and respect, a solidarity. The mode of being together which sustains these is anchored ultimately by what Arendt calls the public realm. If Arendt's primary concern is the 'recovery' of the public world,[25] this is because only where there is such a world can freedom as non-sovereignty and action as its necessary expression find a place in society. In other words, only if there is a public realm can there be a politics which is not simply the domination of one by another.

The public realm is for Arendt the scene of an existential drama that has as its stage the 'inter-est', a 'worldly space' that unites individuals while simultaneously separating them. It is thus the basic condition of plurality and provides the forum within which the 'living essence' of a person can show itself in the flux of speech and action.[26] It stands in contrast to the private realm, the 'proper' home of the labour process, where the requirements of biological existence, the reproduction of the material basis of life, are met, and the sphere in which relations of intimacy which cannot withstand the glare of publicity find their true place.

As the vehicle for self-revelation, the public realm incorporates what Arendt calls a 'space of appearance'. The existence of this public space allows us literally to be seen and heard by others who can thus assure us of the reality of the world and, equally important, of ourselves. While the concept of 'space of appearance' has important institutional implications[27] – by suggesting the necessity of political culture in the broadest sense – its main significance is in pointing to those human capacities which can only be realized in the presence of others, as opposed to those which require a 'private realm', a domain of intimacy, of the personal in our everyday sense. To deprive humans of the possibility of acting and speaking together in a common world is to imprison them 'in the subjectivity of their singular experience, which does not cease to be singular if the same experience is multiplied innumerable times.'[28] It is the nature and end of the activity, and not merely its spatial or temporal characteristics, that determine its status. Wherever people come together to establish a common ground, and seek to take the initiative and inject themselves by word and deed into the events going on around them, they have created a public realm, a forum for action that is itself the outcome of action.

The essential condition for the existence of a public realm is of course plurality, the fact that individuals live with others and not simply by themselves. But the actualization of plurality in all its manifestations as a living reality, and not just as a possibility, requires the achievement of another state of affairs: 'worldliness'.

As noted in chapter 1, in contrast to the production of things required for biological regeneration, the 'world' as Arendt defines it is the creation not of labour but of work, of *homo faber* rather than *animal laborans*. Obviously both labour and work 'produce' in the sense of transforming nature through the systematic deployment of human energies whether directly or indirectly (that is, through means of production or 'instruments', and technology). But while the criteria governing production for *animal laborans* is consumption, or destruction, for *homo faber* it is utility, or durability. *Homo faber* works up nature according to a mental image or model of the end product to be brought into the world. This standard in terms of which physical materials are formed into durable objects points to the need for the creations of *homo faber* to appear as 'objective' realities in a way that articles of consumption, which are bound by their nature literally to dis-appear, cannot. In this respect, while it is the middle term between 'labour' and 'action' in the *vita activa*, work shares more in common with action: both can assume a public character.[29]

In building the world as a human artifice, a 'reified' domain of use objects and those peculiarly 'useless' objects we call works of art, *homo faber* provides for human beings, who are by nature unstable and mortal, a stable and stolid habitation, a genuine world. And this must be a 'common world' which simultaneously unites people while at the same time separating them.[30] Such 'worldliness' sustains institutionally the existence of human plurality and thus renders possible that disclosure of each distinct individual for which the space of appearance exists. Where a domain of stable and familiar objects is absent, the world loses its power to gather people together, to relate and separate them. It no longer has room for 'interests'. This situation 'resembles a spiritualistic seance where a number of people gathered around a table might suddenly, through some magic trick, see the table vanish from their midst, so that two persons sitting opposite each other were no longer separated but also would be entirely unrelated to each other by anything tangible.'[31] The result is a deep uncertainty 'not only of all political matters, but of all affairs that go on between men directly, without the intermediary, stabilizing, and solidifying influence of things.'[32]

For Arendt, this state of affairs points to the difference between what she calls 'organized living' under the sway of the labour process, on the one hand, and a genuine political sphere, on the other. To live without a world, to live under the conditions of what Arendt calls 'world alienation', does not of course mean that there are no physical objects, or that they do not enter into relations among people. It means, rather, that our existential attitude towards them does not permit us to appear and exhibit those qualities which can only be realized through action in a common world.[33] Perhaps the clearest examples today of 'unworldly' objects in Arendt's sense (and she was quite aware of this) are nuclear weapons, which have no real 'use' but which paralyse action, and most certainly affect the relations people have with one another.

In the modern age, *homo faber* has done its part to bring about the loss of the world it helps create. The distinguishing hallmark of *homo faber* is its utilitarianism: the process of making things is determined by the categories of means and ends. This utilitarian perspective is vital if the world is to come into existence at all. It cannot, however, govern the world once it has been created. Yet this is precisely what has happened in modernity. The constant devaluation of ends into means for the realization of further ends, which themselves become means, and so on in unending procession, is at the core of the modern crisis of meaning, the collapse of the distinction between 'for the sake of' and 'in order to'.

It is in the nature of *homo faber* that it strives to render all relations between humans and objects, and thus humans and their creative capacities, in utilitarian terms. In Arendt's view, however, this tendency has been exacerbated in the modern era by the labour process,

which has absorbed work and increasingly subordinated its performance to the rhythms of labouring. The end of the economic significance of the craftworker who produced for an exchange market in
products, and the rise of large-scale, increasingly mechanized labour
processes and the organization of human energies as saleable labour
power – a process which for Arendt roughly parallels the transformation of commercial or merchant capitalism into industrial capitalism[34]
– resulted in the 'degradation' of work, its subordination to the
requirements of making a living. It is for this reason that, according
to Arendt, there is contemporary confusion between 'specialization
of work' and 'division of labour'.[35]

The fusion of work and labour in modern 'labouring society has
thus, in a manner of speaking, radicalized the utilitarian thrust in the
culture. Where human energies are given over to the rhythmic metabolism with nature which can know no real distinctions, even the
distinction between means and ends loses its significance.[36] At the same
time, the problem inherent in all utilitarianism – that, as Lessing put
it, there can be no 'use' for use, no end in itself – led to the quest for
an ultimate ground which could give sense to an otherwise meaningless
procession of means and ends. In a society in which production was
for the sake of consumption, and vice versa, the solution to the
problem was to establish 'man' as the end in itself, the 'measure' of
all things. For Arendt this 'humanism' is inherently subjectivist and
hence contributes decisively to the loss of an objective world required
for a genuine history and politics. At the same time, as an object 'man'
loses his subjectivity so that in the end both subject and object are
lost to a process of always becoming, the labour process itself.

The fusion of work and labour, the breakdown of a proper balance
among the components of the *vita activa* and the consequent undermining of the conditions needed for both a genuinely public and a
truly private realm, is what Arendt understands as the rise of the social
realm in the modern age. The triumph of 'society', the elevation of
the essentially private domain of material reproduction to the status
of a public matter, has seriously undermined the prospects for a fully
public life. This triumph has weakened the ability both of the capacity
to make and keep promises and of the power to forgive to check the
potentially destabilizing effects of action. Deprived of a proper public
forum, action finds other, more ominous outlets. The effects of the
loss of a 'common world' are visible in a number of ways; perhaps
the most notable here involves what Arendt sees as the virtual abolition of property and its transformation into wealth. Property is the
final element in Arendt's picture of a genuinely public world.

Like freedom itself, the modern institution of property and our accompanying understanding of it have from Arendt's viewpoint parted company with the historical experience in the polis which gave rise to them. Just as modern politics and the modern state claim to defend freedom while actually undermining it, so they also celebrate property while in reality abetting its destruction.

The property Arendt sees as vital to a common world and a public realm is necessarily 'private'. It connects the genuinely private and truly public spheres, the realms of necessity and freedom, each of which must be given its proper place in a truly human society. But the private property Arendt defends is very different from the private property which characterizes modern civil society. In Arendt's view, as the chief condition for admission to political life, private property had a very specific objective content: it signified one's location in a particular part of the world, a tangible place of one's own, as head of one of the families which comprised the political realm. At the same time it provided a refuge from common affairs, required because a 'life spent entirely in public, in the presence of others becomes, as we would say, shallow . . . [It] loses the quality of rising into sight from some darker ground which must remain hidden if it is not to lose its depth in a very real, nonsubjective sense.'[37]

What is now commonly called private property, however, is in reality wealth – and the two are not identical although we often see them as such. Indeed for Arendt they are antithetical; hence our potentially wealthy societies are ironically becoming increasingly propertyless. This is inherent in the very nature of wealth itself. Wealth involves those objects of use and consumption required for biological existence. To possess wealth means to master the necessities of life and thus to be free to enter the common world. Because of the freedom it makes possible, wealth, too, can sustain a genuine politics. As private property provides the institutionalized boundaries which mark off the private from the public spheres and thus preserves the integrity of both, so private wealth organizes the realm of necessity within the walls of the household such that one can leave it and enter political life.

But wealth lacks the durability and stability of property. It is in the nature of wealth that it is capable of expansion, that it can, in other words, be accumulated. Thus while the ancients considered property sacred, they never viewed wealth in the same way. One who chose to expand his holdings without limit literally became a slave to them, a servant of necessity. Only in modern society has wealth become 'sacred'.

Because it is ephemeral, the existence of wealth can never be guaranteed as fully as can one's private share of a common world, an objective world of useful objects. Only the process of wealth generation itself – in other words accumulation – can bear at least some of the marks of the permanence of property. And this permanence can itself be secured only if everything is in principle capable of being appropriated and thus absorbed by the process of wealth generation. With C. B. Macpherson, Arendt agrees that infinite accumulation and infinite appropriation entail each other. As she sees it, this has grave consequences for the stability of the common world. Continuous appropriation, or accumulation, destroys property in the older sense. Arendt understands this as the literal destruction of tangible use objects as they are dissolved in the process of production and consumption that gives the accumulative drive its phenomenal form. But she also sees the basis of accumulation in the political, historical and institutional process of expropriation, first of the Catholic Church after the Reformation, then of the peasant classes in Europe. In the end private property is sacrificed to the demands of accumulation when the two come into conflict. What modern states defend is not 'property as such but the unhampered pursuit of more property . . .'[38]

Thus while Arendt is a staunch defender of private property, she is an equally staunch critic of capitalism, as we saw in her encounter with Marx. It is now clear why. As the regime of accumulation par excellence, capitalism destroys property and thus a vital foundation of a genuine politics. In analysing wealth and property, Arendt in effect distinguishes between property as a stable base for free activity and property as capital, the substitution of exchange for use value as the governing criterion for production. With the blurring of the distinction between property and wealth, 'every tangible 'fungible' thing has become an object of consumption; it lost its private use value which was determined by its location and acquired an exclusively social value determined through its ever changing exchangeability whose fluctuation could itself be fixed only temporarily by relating it to the common denominator of money.'[39] In the end the impermanence and exchangeability of modern private property in terms of the abstract commodity, money, undermines a life of both common pursuits and genuine privacy.

So for Arendt, freedom, action and the public realm are the anchors of a genuine politics. They both require and reproduce a common world, the only mode of collective existence within which human plurality and solidarity can be secured. They illuminate those conditions which would make possible the realization of Winston Smith's utopian hope in *Nineteen Eighty-Four*: that there could be a world in which people would be different from one another, and yet not live alone.[40] But as her account of property makes clear, modern political institutions tend to preserve the form but not necessarily the substance of important public phenomena. What might it mean to restore this substance to contemporary political life? What would such an attempt mean for existing institutions and practices? What new ones would be required? In short what is the fate of plurality and solidarity as Arendt understands these?

II

A critical account of politics such as that of Hannah Arendt always poses the problem of institutionalization: how the critical perspective in question can be embodied in concrete norms and practices, made a realizable and accepted component of the everyday outlook of the people who in the end would have to make it viable. As I noted in the Introduction, Arendt has frequently been criticized as a utopian with an unrealistic and unsatisfactory theory of politics. This criticism can take two forms: either the demands she makes of political actors are unreasonable, given human nature, or existing institutions, particularly in liberal democratic states, are more acceptably 'political' than she allows. Whatever the specific criticisms, at stake is the relevance of Arendt's key concepts for an enhanced understanding of contemporary political dilemmas.

If I am correct in seeing Arendt's work as devoted less to an examination of politics in the narrow institutional sense and more to an exploration of the political as Claude Lefort defines it, it follows that one need not expect or demand of her a full-scale account of alternative institutions and practices. To 'think what we are doing', as Arendt defines her task in *The Human Condition*, does not in itself generate specific institutional prescriptions.

In any case, Arendt is not indifferent to institutional questions as these are normally conceived. While references to specific institutions dot her work at various points, two particular sets of concrete proposals for institutional reform stand out. The first involves her well-known emphasis on the importance of the council form of government, organs of popular participation and decision-making during modern revolutionary upheavals, and her consequent proposal for the creation of such participatory forms, 'elementary republics', in existing bureaucratic states, East and West.[41]

As Ferenc Feher and Agnes Heller have pointed out, this links Arendt to an important Central European republican tradition which is currently experiencing a revival there with the collapse of the power of the Soviet Union, and which could well be adapted to other states as well.[42] The emphasis, found, for example, in some of the writings and pronouncements of Czech playwright and political leader, Vaclav Havel, on a citizen virtue not immediately subject either to the pressure of economic interest or the temptations and demands of traditional power politics accords well with many of Arendt's own themes.

The second set of proposals is, perhaps surprisingly, less well known. These involve Arendt's arguments in *Eichmann in Jerusalem* for the establishment of a new international legal code, with the real possibility of enforcement, which would deal with the crime of genocide. I will say more about this in chapter 4 and my discussion of the Eichmann book. Here it is worth noting that Arendt's proposals are tied to a powerful attempt to deal with perhaps the central issue in all political theory: justice. That 'speculative' theory and concrete institutional analysis need not be mutually exclusive but may indeed be mutually reinforcing is a matter worth pondering further when one attempts to make sense of a complex thinker such as Hannah Arendt.

While acknowledging Arendt's own concern with institutions, in my view her key concepts are most valuable in outlining a picture of public life which challenges what she sees as disturbingly dominant anti-political values and practices in modern society, phenomena which undermine community and solidarity. In this respect what is most important in dealing with her work is to get clear about what I would call her political topography: the range of matters which can reasonably be included in the public sphere as Arendt understands it. Put another way, her position requires us to ask: what is the *res publica?* What are public 'things'?

At the heart of Arendt's account of the political is the concept of public space, a space of appearance which is the heart of a genuine public realm. Although its key elements are presented rather abstractly, this concept is fundamental to her treatment of the various manifestations of the human capacity to act in the modern world, even in circumstances hostile to action. From the actions of those 'men' in 'dark times' whom Arendt profiles in a book of that name, to the periodic upsurges of revolutionary activity from the eighteenth century down to our own time – in other words as both individual and collective phenomena – the modern era has witnessed examples of civic virtue, of solidarity, of the quest for immortality that ruptures everyday routines. In Arendt's terms, these historical examples, all the more striking because they fly in the face of modern trends, are not only about public space. They *are* public space itself, testimonies to the ability of humans to foster the conditions of plurality by creating additions to the human artifice.

Public space implies both a type of activity and a context within which it takes place. As it turns out, this means that even where they seem at their most speculative, Arendt's concepts in fact do have institutional significance. And because these relate to worldliness, the entirety of the 'unnatural' habitat which houses mortal humans, institutional questions have a more comprehensive meaning than that normally associated with state or government bodies. They relate, for example, to the built environment within which everyday life takes place, a life shaped by the structures of what the French social theorist Henri Lefebvre calls 'the bureaucratic society of controlled consumption'.

When seen in this way, Arendt's treatment of public space links up with contemporary debates about the nature of urban life under contemporary conditions, the capacity of urban forms to provide public access to common sites within which people could assemble as equals enjoying each other's company as competent actors – in short, as a plurality of citizens joined in solidarity by a common world. Reflecting 'the substitution of productive or processual norms, for the more traditional criteria of worldliness and use', the contemporary urban environment has come to be viewed, by urban social theorists and political activists, as inimical to community and democratic participation.[43] Its rhythms express and reproduce the patterns of production, distribution and consumption integral to modern capitalism, processes which require disciplined subordination to mechanistic, organizational purposes – what Arendt calls 'behavior'.

The meaning of these processes, for Arendt literally their 'value', appears to inhere in the objects of production and consumption independently of those who supposedly make 'use' of them. This problem of meaninglessness seems to be at the centre of critical/radical urban political action, from modest efforts to preserve from destruction 'heritage' properties which can contribute to the development or preservation of a popular sense of historical identity, to 'reformist' attempts to restrain the power of local real estate and development interests, to full-scale challenges, which have included novel forms of civil disobedience and 'expressive' politics, against efforts to reconstruct neighbourhoods according to the logic of 'efficiency' or the 'market'.

Urban-based political activity has simultaneously pointed towards both the relevance of Arendt's analysis for understanding the contemporary urban milieux and the limitations of most prevalent radical conceptions of social change. Simply put, these conceptions are based largely on temporality, not spatiality. The most notable is, of course, orthodox Marxism, with its emphasis on phenomena such as the falling *rate* of profit. Such an analysis fails to comprehend a capitalism that reproduces itself through the production of commodified space in the form of lived social environments.[44]

And the nature of urban experience establishes grounds for Arendt's critique of modern notions of property. Neither one's temporal nor spatial location in the world can be understood or secured by a property institution tied to the requirements of accumulation. Thus the vaunted move in Eastern Europe and the Soviet Union itself toward a 'market' economy, which would supposedly put private property in the hands of the people and foster both economic efficiency and political freedom, is more properly understood from Arendt's perspective as the establishment of new mechanisms for the generation of wealth – and the continuing denial of a worldly space for free action. On the other hand, traditional socialism with its emphasis on the 'socialization of the means of production' seems equally incapable of guaranteeing a stable, worldly location within which individual and collective identities can be established. Recent thinking by some socialist theorists about property suggests that a form of 'private' property may play an essential role in a radically democratic, egalitarian society.[45]

The establishment of spaces of appearance and their 'worldly' foundations are clearly important issues in any assessment of Arendt's position. But they are not the only issues, nor necessarily the most significant ones. If the public sphere and the action which it makes possible reveal 'who' one is, that is, certain distinctively human qualities not apparent in other human activities, then the issue of *how* people go about revealing themselves, what purposes move and inspire them, likewise becomes crucial. While Arendt's analysis of freedom is obviously critical here, there is a more general concern involved. This has to do with the formation of prospective actors, the foundation and nature of their self-understandings as beings capable of worldly pursuits. In this context the question of meaning, 'for the sake of', takes a central place. Arendt implies that where the physical objects that people encounter, including those reifications of human purposes we call culture, fail to establish the possibility of human insertion into the world, and do not allow for the initiation of something new which breaks the routine of everyday existence, they lose the capacity to establish a sense of place for people.

This loss has a profound effect upon the purposes that people can develop. Objects which fail to unite while separating people in a common world can be negotiated by individuals seeking to make their way in the relationships within which they find themselves. In what they do, people can display a certain kind of rationality, a consistency of behaviour. But this is precisely the instrumental attitude in terms of which individuals are 'for' or 'against', but seldom 'with', each other. To the extent that they express themselves in this setting, it is as 'personalities', that is, 'what' as opposed to 'who' they are. Unlike the essence revealed in a genuine space of appearance, a personality can be 'manufactured'. For Arendt, this administered generation of effects is evident in a wide range of important and pervasive modern social and political phenomena: the role of the image-makers in the American national security apparatus responsible for the conduct of the Vietnam War;[46] the 'fame' which comes with 'the one-week notoriety of the cover story . . .'[47]; and even the ultimate 'self-made man', Adolf Eichmann, who created for himself a historical fable within which he was the chief protagonist, the 'star'.

These phenomena involve modes of social and self-identification which pose fundamental questions of how political actors are formed. In the past, according to Arendt, one's sense of self, history and the world was shaped by tradition and education. But both are now in crisis. Traditional standards have been turned upside down and no longer illuminate enduring questions for us, while modern education by and large prepares the young for 'life' and not the 'world', thereby delivering them over to the iron grip of necessity.[48] As potentially acting beings, we are, ironically thrown back upon our resources as thinking beings who must, as Arendt puts it, pave anew the gap we occupy between past and future.[49]

Precisely because what Arendt calls the 'banister' of tradition can no longer help us, and because other institutions which ought to take up the slack seem to have been absorbed by the demands of the life process, questions of self and collective identity must, from Arendt's perspective, become politically critical. Who appropriates history and its associated reifications, and why, become vitally important because these matters define what citizenship can mean in contemporary states. What is at stake are the sources and supplies of political legitimacy.

Two related examples illustrate this feature of Hannah Arendt's political topography. The first, which will be discussed further in chapter 4, is the debate over her 1963 account of the Eichmann trial, and in particular the politically and ideologically charged responses to some of her specific observations and judgements. As Arendt herself explained it, the Eichmann 'controversy' made her aware in a way that she had not been before of the politics of historical interpretation which can develop when 'a highly topical subject . . . is drawn into that gap between past and future which is perhaps the proper habitat of all reflections.'[50] She became aware, in other words, that scholarly debate can have public consequences – and conversely that political imperatives affected, and had to affect, the form and content of scholarship when such scholarship touched upon matters of historical identity.

The second example is more recent. It involves the so-called *Historikerstreit* which burst forth in the Federal Republic of Germany in 1986. This controversy, which first involved professional historians and, in part because of the intercession of Jürgen Habermas, was broadened to become a public matter, involves the meaning of Germany's past, and in particular the Nazi era and the Holocaust, for the current and future understanding of the German nation and its political role in Europe and the West. As all participants have recognized, even those who have sought to defend their positions from criticism on the grounds of superior technical expertise, the questions raised by the controversy have important implications: whether the horrors of the Nazi regime are unique or 'merely' part of a century of terror; whether the Nazi era was an aberration or an expression of the forces at work throughout German history; and whether the time has come to put the past in a new light in order to get on with the business of constructing a history which 'promise[s] direction signs to identity, anchorages in the cataracts of progress'.[51] Such questions loom as especially pressing in light of both the unification of the two Germanies and the impending economic integration of Western Europe.

The perception that the controversy over German identity is clearly lodged in the gap 'between past and future' indicates the continuing relevance of Arendt's reflections. The issue of identity and what could count as public questions, and how these could be registered – in short the content and character of the public realm – are at the very heart of the dispute.[52] Moreover, the issue of identity is closely linked with the possibilities for solidarity, especially with the victims of Nazi terror. Would a German 'identity' be predicated upon an 'us' versus 'them' mentality, with 'them' being identified with some external 'threat' as well as with those who ostensibly serve this 'threat' by fixating excessively upon a guilt-ridden conception of the German past? The attempt by Habermas to promote in the context of the dispute a 'post-conventional' as opposed to a 'conventional' identity, a universalist versus a particularistic outlook on the world, reflects a clear concern with this issue.[53]

Thus Arendt's conception of public life can trigger creative consideration of the range of social phenomena which impinge upon the possibilities for solidarity and self-revelation. The conceptual distinctions at the core of her analysis provide, if not the banister of tradition, at least historically drenched clues about what we should seek in coming to grips with our common affairs. Seen in this way Arendt's account of public life can range very widely indeed, perhaps more widely than even Arendt herself would have thought possible.[54]

III

Because of the unusual, not to say idiosyncratic, character of her key concepts, Hannah Arendt's political thought has proved sorely vexing to many interpreters and political thinkers. Christopher Lasch, the American social theorist, writes for others when he notes the 'richness and suggestiveness of Hannah Arendt's thought' and the 'boldness of her thinking, which cannot be fitted into one of those imprisoning categories that so many right-thinking people depend on for infallible standards of political rectitude'. He argues that her work is *sui generis* and has been unjustly criticized or dismissed by those who have sought, without success, to assimilate it to a particular intellectual tradition. Nevertheless, he finds that while her analysis is suggestive, it is also at the same time misleading. She has 'raised some of the most important questions that can be raised about modern history'. But there appears to be in her work 'a good deal of confusion . . . judgements that seem arbitrary and perverse . . . misreadings of the historical record'.[55]

Such disparate views suggest the difficulty both of situating and evaluating Arendt's contribution to political and social theory, and of critically assessing the critics and criticisms themselves. What sorts of criticisms are likely to penetrate to the core of Arendt's arguments?

Aristotle's political thought, which exerted an immense influence on Arendt's own, pursues two distinct but related concerns, both of which define the texture of the polis. On the one side is the great question of the *Politics*: what is a citizen? On the other is the issue of exactly who can qualify for citizenship. Both concerns in turn pose issues of institutional arrangements and individual and collective identity.

If my account of Arendt's polis is correct, then both these matters and related issues ought to be near the centre of the more penetrating criticisms of Arendt. I think this is indeed the case. Two critical assessments stand out here: George Kateb's account of Arendt's position on representative democracy; and Mary O'Brien's wide-ranging critique of Arendt's ideas as expressions of 'male-stream' thought. These writings not only put into focus central elements of what for Arendt is a genuine politics. They also point toward critically important features of what I have called 'false' politics, those arrangements which deny plurality and action, worldliness and solidarity.

In a number of published works, George Kateb undertakes an immanent critique of Arendt's political thought.[56] That is, he accepts the validity of her concerns and is sympathetic to her standards of political judgement and conduct. Nevertheless, he finds many elements of her work deficient in terms of her own claims, especially as these involve her assessment of American political and social institutions. He attempts to show that American political experience, and liberal democratic political experience in general, is more hospitable to political commitments than she was generally prepared to allow. In particular, he urges a reassessment from Arendt's own perspective of the merits of representative democracy.

Kateb argues that Arendt ought to have taken a closer look than she did at the institutions of representative democracy as potential and actual forums for political action. He interprets Arendt's position as hostile to representative, electoral institutions on the grounds that they are prone to the dominance of economic questions and interests, and hence, from the point of veiw of action and worldliness, corruptible. Because voting gives power to people in their private capacity, it puts a premium on private satisfaction as opposed to what she calls 'public happiness': the quest for the maintenance of a common world and a space of appearance. 'The misfortune is that representative democracy, in its unyielding actuality, is very little more than the consecration of selfishness and self-regardingness.'[57]

The corruption of the state by economic interests includes more than the deployment of state power on behalf of economically powerful groups at the expense of the less powerful. It also extends to attempts to 'ameliorate the conditions of the disadvantaged' when such attempts become questions of political debate rather than matters of successful administration for which there are clear-cut, purely technical choices. (For Arendt the field of administration is very wide indeed and includes, for example, the provision of decent housing for everyone as a matter of course.) As Kateb sees it, the 'politics' of the welfare state is for Arendt a contradiction in terms: 'Her conception of political action at its best simply does not accommodate the dailiness of reformist and welfarist politics, and such politics is, in turn, a principal part of the politics of representative democracy.'[58]

By contrast Kateb argues that the politics of economics shows evidence of real political action. The 'agonistic' quality which Arendt so closely identifies with political action may be found in the 'connections between firms and entrepreneurs and pressure groups (on the one side) and elected and unelected officials (on the other side) . . .'[59]

More importantly, however, the conjunction of Arendt's polis and representative democracy is not simply empirical. It is also moral: 'representative democracy is a genuinely distinctive political system with special moral claims, and a system that should lead someone of Arendt's outlook to praise it, if only as "second best".'[60] Kateb argues that representative democracy fosters a wide variety of laudable political and moral phenomena, particularly the willingness to resist atrocity. For a thinker like Arendt, who in the 1960s came out strongly in favour of civil disobedience as a constitutionally legitimate corrective to the enactment of unjust laws and the pursuit by political authorities of unconscionable policies, the ability to foster resistance ought to be given pride of place in her political outlook.

And the connection between representative, democratic government and political morality is not accidental. According to Kateb, it inheres in the nature of representative institutions themselves. This is because the much-maligned electoral system, which stands at the heart of representative democracy, makes possible a continuous and active reassertion of popular consent and hence control over political authorities. Political power is subject to constant religitimation and thus can never be reified as an object standing above or outside society. Hence the 'regular workings of the electoral procedure comprise a *chastening* of political authority. By its dependence on the will and choice of the people, political authority loses all majesty . . . The result is a heightened readiness to resist authority, to resist government, when office-holders forget who they are, when they forget that they are servants of the people.'[61] Kateb attributes to Arendt the claim that representative democracy enforces passivity on the part of citizens. He argues, to the contrary, that the consent required to make representative institutions work is anything but passive. A system of government which has resistance to authority built into it must encourage a citizen activism that, while frequently mundane in its direction, sets limits to the pursuit of the unlawful and unconscionable.

For Kateb, Arendt's indifference/hostility to representative democracy because of its alleged inferiority to direct citizen participation in government results in more than a failure to see elements of a genuine politics in actually existing democratic states. It also results in a subtle corrosion of the sense of obligation required for a representative democracy to work, and the undermining of the cultural prerequisites which make resistance possible. By giving short shrift to the electoral process as a genuine basis for legitimate authority and the laws based on it, indeed by arguing that electoral consent is 'entirely fictitious', Arendt unwittingly appears to side with those for whom representative democracy is simply a facade for oligarchy, or a pale imitation of a genuinely democratic polity. If the spirit of resistance to atrocity is to be preserved and encouraged, we must keep representative democracy alive. We must treat its institutions as legitimate, its policies and laws as authoritative.

To be sure, Kateb does not restrict the significance of this categorical imperative to the legislative arena alone. If it is to provide a substantial basis for political obligation, it must go together with a process of democratization in all areas of social life, particularly the workplace. At the same time, obligation to the laws enacted by democratically elected legislatures is necessarily imperfect: there is only an approximate fit between legislative decisions and the will of the people understood as a constitutionally empowered, electoral majority. Nevertheless the electoral system, combined with constitutionalism, are at the centre of a representative democratic culture and, even if only 'second best', warrant our and Arendt's support on more than instrumental grounds. And there is evidence that they may be more than 'second best'.

Kateb makes a good case for what might be called a politics of liberal decency. He draws attention to facts of political life in existing liberal democratic societies which are worth noting, even for those sharply critical of the inequalities and injustices which continue to haunt these societies, their official democratic ideologies notwithstanding. He is also surely correct in pointing to the need for further democratization in such societies and in criticizing Arendt for being, in spite of the tenor of her analysis, 'largely averse to a democratization of authority relations outside the public sphere'.[62]

Nevertheless, Kateb's critique is insufficiently attuned to the depth dimensions of Arendt's account of public life. While he sees politics virtually everywhere in contemporary liberal democratic states like the United States, he appears ironically to have a narrow view of things political. His public sphere seems restricted to the electoral arena, and although he emphasizes the need to promote a representative democratic culture, and identifies its primary qualities, he gives little indication of how a depth connection between democratic values and electoral participation actually develops. The formative processes which I have suggested are central to Arendt's concerns are left obscure. Kateb seems to require a solidarity which, because of its serializing character, the exercise of the franchise itself is not likely to promote, but which is needed if the electoral process is successfully to foster resistance to atrocity. Kateb might argue that extending democratic practices to all areas of social life would have the educative effect needed to ground representative institutions. But we need to know more about what such democratization might involve, in terms of Arendt's argument and indeed whether contemporary efforts to achieve it are in fact succeeding.[63]

It is doubtful, too, that, in light of the experience of Weimar Germany, Arendt could so readily accept that representative democracy serves as a barrier to atrocity. She seems to have been influenced by the frequently incisive critiques of representative bodies which began to emerge in the Weimar period and which pointed to the eclipse of the role of parliament, and hence the electoral process, in actively determining state policy.[64] These criticisms take on added lustre given the current state of Kateb's model, American representative democracy: decreasing levels of general voter participation with the active electorate increasingly dominated by while, affluent male voters; the evidence over the last two decades of the exercise of increasingly uncontrollable executive power; and the continuing, and disturbing, salience of race in electoral competition at national, state and local levels of government.[65]

It is doubtful, then, that representative institutions can themselves carry the load that Kateb assigns to them. This is not of course to suggest that they are unimportant or insignificant for a democratic society. Kateb may well be right in arguing that Arendt should recognize representative democracy as a viable 'second best' political option. But he does not deal sufficiently with the question of why, from Arendt's point of view, it might be seen as limited. He does not, in other words, explore why the kind of participation in public life Arendt defends cannot be secured by means of representative institutions, or at least by them alone. He does not examine fully enough the nature of solidarity and citizenship.

To be sure, as Kateb properly makes clear, there is no sure-fire guarantee against the politically unconscionable; it is always a threat in human collectivities. Nevertheless, there is more in Arendt's conception of public life that is sensitive to this potential than Kateb seems to allow – and perhaps an even greater sensitivity to the frailty of political life than his defence of representative democracy can accommodate.[66]

If George Kateb writes from a perspective basically in sympathy with Arendt's own, Mary O'Brien self-consciously and resolutely stands outside the Western tradition of political thought and its committed practitioners, including Hannah Arendt. A radical feminist, O'Brien attempts in *The Politics of Reproduction* to explore and explain the core elements of 'male-stream' thought: the dominant conventions, notions and ideas which throughout Western history have rationalized and legitimized male dominance. Since thought is indelibly linked to practice, male-stream thought at its most self-conscious draws from male experience, all the while distorting or dismissing, where not actually suppressing, the experience of women. In male-stream thought, women have been consigned to the margins of his-story, rendered invisible as social actors. This is especially true with respect to the long-established split between public and private realms: the world of male citizens conducting political affairs which are celebrated as the highest expression of what it means to be human, over against the private sphere of labour and domesticity, the world of women and their work. And within the generally despised private domain, no activity has been more discredited and/or overlooked than reproductive labour – without which, however, there can be no other human activities at all. In singling out the private – public split as crucial to the subordination of women, O'Brien powerfully articulates a central concern of contemporary feminist thought, one which has contributed to the vital role feminism has played in illuminating the working structures of patriarchal domination.

Given the significance of the distinction between private and public realms in Arendt's thought, the relation of her work to feminism obviously becomes an important question. For O'Brien's part, Hannah Arendt is a female proponent of male-stream thinking. She 'accepts the normality and even the necessity of male supremacy, and . . . believes that the functions and structures proper to the private realm have expanded historically in a way which has well-nigh destroyed the public realm.' Arendt's understanding of the human condition 'is in fact a view of man in the literal as well as the generalized sense, and . . . the lack of analysis of the human condition of women is ultimately a failure to analyze adequately the vita active itself.'[67]

In setting out the distinction between private and public realms, Arendt upholds a central tenet of male-stream thought: that there is an ontological need for 'man' to escape the reproductive sphere of first nature and create a higher, more fully human domain of second nature, a truer, political life which is the only genuine home of morality, culture, community. For O'Brien, this ontological dualism became necessary for men because they were excluded, or alienated, from the process of reproductive labour, the ground of the genetic continuity of the species; the expression of this exclusion which most haunted male consciousness was the uncertainty of paternity. Men thus had to create a reified political continuity and its accompanying historical myths which would compensate for man's alienation from reproduction, and in fact displace genetic continuity as the real locus of human identity.

If the uncertainty of paternity was the 'problem', the 'solution' which came to be embodied in this political 'superstructure' was the male potency principle. This involved not only the power and privilege of the male seed, but more generally the creative capacity of men to produce a humanly worthwhile social existence. But given the realities of reproduction, and the consequent tension in male reproductive consciousness which reflected the ambiguous role of any individual in the continuation of the species, male potency could only express itself as the forcible overcoming of alienation. Potency entailed conquest – of woman; of man himself; ultimately, of all nature.

The implications of O'Brien's analysis are thoroughly radical. The citizen in the public realm and the owner of private property – the two-dimensional existence of 'man' in the ideal polis – are products of the quest for male supremacy. The 'universal' notions of citizenship and ownership articulate the interests of the brotherhood of men, who, because they are ironically 'free' from the requirements of reproduction, must band together as appropriators of the identities of women and children through the institutions of marriage, paternity and property. As O'Brien notes, paternity is not a 'natural' relation to a child, but a 'right' – and a right is inherently social and political. A system of rights undergirds relations of forced co-operation among men, the ultimate achievement of which is the transformation of uncertain paternity into universal patriarchy.

Wrapped up with the dynamics of mastery, the male potency principle and its supportive ideological buttresses, including all we think we know about politics and citizenship, now threaten massive social and environmental destruction from which men themselves will be unable to escape. It must be supplanted by the 'feminist principle': 'the principle which upholds the value of individual lives against collective death, of integration of the natural world against the "masterful" destruction of that world, of the abolition of the phoney wall between public and private, first nature and second nature, continuity and discontinuity'.[68]

In pursuit of this task, the political thought of Hannah Arendt is no aid, but a barrier. In fact, as O'Brien sees it, Arendt's ideas are deficient on grounds not specifically 'feminist' alone. Because she works with a materialist and dialectical analysis derived, in spite of their immersion in male-stream thought, from Hegel and Marx, O'Brien chides Arendt for giving an idealist account of political life in ancient Greece: 'the category of action in Arendt's analysis remains predictably abstract and unsatisfactory; it is never quite clear, for example, what . . . fathers of families who are to spend their "whole life" in the public sphere are actually doing there.'[69] To counter what she sees as Arendt's pristine conception of a politics untainted by the quest for private advantage, O'Brien turns to the arguments of Pericles himself, who was quite aware, even if Arendt is not, that practical considerations of life and property, and indeed the requirements of patriarchal control itself, played a critical role in the polis.[70]

But the bulk of O'Brien's critique strives to show that Arendt's thought stands opposed to the feminist principle. The separation of public and private, and the professed superiority of the former to the latter, provide of course the clearest evidence, and a number of male supremacist consequences follow accordingly. Chief among them is a rather cavalier and ahistorical view of violence which, according to O'Brien, Arendt accepts as an essential element of mastering necessity and hence a core feature of the private realm. In O'Brien's eyes, Arendt's treatment of violence is flawed in two crucial respects. First, she fails to see that, in the Greek polis, violence was by no means restricted to the private realm, but was also evident in the class struggles and imperialist ventures which decisively shaped public life. At the same time, the violence characteristic of the private sphere necessarily possessed a political component. Arendt 'does not appear to understand that this private violence is possible only where it is legitimated by public action, and that in this sense it is always political violence.'[71]

Secondly, Arendt's claim that violence is required to master necessity – in effect a claim that it has ontological status – demonstrates that, in spite of her expressed reservations about modern science and the rise of the labour process, she is a proponent of the domination of nature. Oblivious to the possibility, central to feminism, of a more integrative relation of society to nature, Arendt accepts the 'male-stream' opposition of 'man' to nature and the need forcibly to subordinate nature to our purposes. The only distinguishing hallmark of Arendt's position is that such domination must be a private, not a public, matter.

In the end, Arendt's indifference to the real dynamics of both public and private realms, particularly the 'social relations of reproduction', and the close and necessary interrelation of the two, mark her as a female proponent of male supremacy. The artificial nature of her categories reflects her attempt to ground the separation of public and private in an arbitrary stratification of human activities . . . undertaken from an exclusively male perspective, a fact which itself is a tribute to the strength of the tradition of male-stream thought'.[72]

Because of its radical character, O'Brien's account gets more thoroughly at the deepest qualities of Arendt's thought than do other treatments. Unlike George Kateb, for example, O'Brien would have no difficulty with Arendt's alleged reservations about representative democracy because she would see its institutions as based upon forms of domination and control which Kateb's 'male-stream' blinkers would prevent him from seeing. She is thus sensitive to the ontological focus of Arendt's writings. She identifies this with a phenomenological orientation, 'where the intention of the analyst is unified with the object to be examined', in this case 'the totality of the activities of labour, work and action'.[73] According to O'Brien, Arendt's phenomenological ontology of activity precludes certain kinds of abstract categorization and metaphysical speculation which can stand in the way of concrete thinking. Hence Arendt writes not of abstract nature in general, but of human nature in particular and, unlike Aristotle, does not identify an abstract reason as the defining quality of humanity – this because such reason has the tendency to engage in metaphysical flights of fantasy. If for O'Brien Arendt's categories are ultimately 'thoughtless', they are peculiarly suggestive nonetheless.

By criticizing Arendt in the way she does, O'Brien can demonstrate unacknowledged commitments and unexamined assumptions in Arendt's arguments. This is especially true of Arendt's treatment of necessity and her tendency to view labour, productive and reproductive, as narrowly biological and timeless.

Yet O'Brien's own conception of public and private, and thus necessity, seem themselves peculiarly static and ahistorical. The shift from a household-based economy to a 'public' one dynamically shaped and altered the meaning and content of the public – private distinction. Whatever its limitations, Arendt's analysis presupposes and attempts to explain this historical development; indeed her concept of the 'social' cannot otherwise be understood. O'Brien does not seem to take this into account.[74]

This problem in turn reflects a more general one: a failure to follow up more fully on the immanent critical elements of Arendt's ideas, although O'Brien's own approach would allow her to do so. In part this involves some misunderstanding of Arendt's intentions. Thus Arendt's notion of violence as a constituent element of the private realm does not mean that she sees it only there, but rather that viewing it in the way she does allows her to distinguish freedom from necessity. This distinction is as central to O'Brien's own work as it is to Arendt's. And there is no indication Arendt believes that certain people, women and slaves for example, ought by nature to be subject to violence, even though in the Greek polis they obviously were.

O'Brien contrasts Arendt unfavourably with Aristotle, but oddly misses a crucial difference between them: that Arendt has no concept of natural inequality. Again, while historico-ontological in its focus, Arendt's analysis of public and private is designed to illuminate a complex of attitudes and practices, not fixed spheres eternally occupied by certain social categories of individuals.

On the relation of violence to the domination of nature, O'Brien has a stronger argument. But even here she goes too far by arguing that Arendt supports the domination of nature. Arendt's criticisms of modern science and world alienation, as well as her critique of sovereignty, are more fundamental than O'Brien allows. And given the relation of the domination of human to non-human nature, a relationship which is important to O'Brien, Arendt's refusal to ontologize specific social relations of hierarchy undercuts a fundamental ideological and institutional prop for the project of domination.[75]

And O'Brien seriously misinterprets Arendt by claiming that in Arendt's view, 'interpretation of social life from the standpoint of history rather than that of ontology is an intellectual and social disaster.' As I have argued, Arendt criticizes not history *per se*, but rather history as process, a concept of history which expresses the destruction of a genuinely historical existence. The difference is not simply terminological. It, too, involves the dynamic quality of her categories and the possibilities for self-revelation and solidarity.

But beyond questionable interpretation, there is the matter of political topography, the possible range of concerns which Arendt's thinking can explore. Here I would like to borrow from another feminist thinker, Carole Pateman, and suggest a different interpretation of Arendt, one which acknowledges O'Brien's insights about the relation of Arendt's ideas to patriarchal ideology, but which points to greater critical possibilities in her work than O'Brien might countenance.

Carole Pateman shares Mary O'Brien's view that Hannah Arendt articulates a male supremacist position. Nevertheless, she develops an account of public and private which in my view shares common ground with Arendt's and can put into relief its dynamic character and critical potential.[76] Pateman argues that in classical liberalism, where the modern distinction between public and private has its major roots, there have in fact been two conceptions, rarely distinguished from each other, of the split between public and private realms. For the most part, the split has been understood as occurring either between civil society and the state, or within civil society itself. Either way, the private realm is the sphere of economic life, the governing principle of which is freedom. The public sphere, or the state or government, is the domain of coercion. The political task in liberal society is to limit the encroachment of the inherently despotic state on the domain of freedom, protecting men in the pursuit of their various 'trades and callings', as Hobbes put it.

What is notable about this conception of public and private is that both terms are already, in a manner of speaking, 'public'. The split between them reflects a kind of in-house quarrel between two notions of, and institutional expressions of, (largely male) social identity: citizen versus bourgeois.

But according to Pateman, there is another, 'hidden' public–private duality, one of obvious significance for feminism. This is the split between the domestic sphere of largely female productive and reproductive labour, and a largely male public realm, whether it is conceived of as 'civil society' or the 'state'; or whether there is seen to be a public–private split *within* civil society itself. This separation of public and private, which undergirds and makes possible the 'public' separation between the two realms, seems to be hidden in two senses. In the first place, there is the obvious historical fact that those consigned to the domestic sphere have been silenced, denied a voice with which to speak into history. In the second place, theoretical and practical efforts to 'publicize' this sphere by incorporating the domestic domain into the dominant public–private division have frequently failed to take into account the qualitative difference between the two senses of public and private. The relation of the domestic sphere to the public realm is not simply one of an overlooked or suppressed moment of the private realm of freedom, either within or as civil society, to the state. The theoretical and institutional recognition of the hidden public–private split fundamentally challenges the very logic of the more visible, well-known and public one. This challenge resides in the suggestion of a more integral, less contentious relation of human beings to their capacities than that which sustains the dominant public–private separation. Even if the domestic sphere is made an object of political analysis and struggle, the 'hidden' split remains hidden if the challenge goes unacknowledged or unanswered.

Put otherwise, relations of domination which the public–private split incorporates cannot fully be challenged simply by opening up the ongoing 'public' relations of public to private to the participation of those formerly entrapped in the hidden domestic sphere. The 'visible' public–private split always and already is structured by and as a relation of domination. Put more bluntly still, oppression – of women, of nature, indeed of men themselves – cannot be ended just by 'elevating' women to the status of citizens and property-owners within the dominant public–private relationship. And it is here that the historical importance of feminism comes into play. Because of its particular sensitivity to the hidden public–private split, feminism can point beyond prevailing conceptions and practices of citizenship to new forms of solidarity and community, which are 'grounded in the interrelationship of the individual to collective life, or personal to political life, instead of their separation and opposition'.[77]

Pateman's account allows for a revealing treatment of the strengths and limitations of Arendt's analysis. From the vantage point of Pateman's two-sided conception of the public–private split, it seems that Arendt, like most liberal theorists, collapses the two. For her, the elevation of the private to public status in modernity, that is, the rise of the social, entails the 'publicization' of domestic life now transformed into the large household called the economy. But although she might on this point share common ground with them, Arendt is no economic liberal or defender of capitalism. This is because she quite properly attributes the violence and unfreedom of domestic life to the private (i.e. economic) sphere which liberalism had defined as the realm of freedom.

In so collapsing the two conceptions, Arendt falls into the patriarchal trap of obscuring the nature of the domestic sphere. But she eludes the equally essential patriarchal claim of the free character of the private understood as the social or the economic. Thus her demand for the restoration of public space, of power as the pursuit of a common purpose, stands, in opposition to domination in both the domestic and private domains. As with Pateman, so with Arendt: the very logic of prevailing notions, and the range of social practices which these notions are intended to illuminate, reveal inconsistencies and contradictions which undermine claims of their worth and permanence.

In the final analysis, one can ask of feminism the following 'Arendtian' question: is it concerned with the status of public life and of citizenship from the vantage point of a fuller and more adequate realization of both? I would say the answer is 'yes', and that Arendt's account of public life provides an important critical resource.[78] Ironically, Mary O'Brien seems to agree. She concludes her discussion of Arendt, public and private with references to largely neglected historical examples of women in periods of great political and social upheaval, such as the English Civil War, when women were 'bursting into the public realm' in pursuit of distinctively political aims.[79] But far from refuting Arendt's argument, such examples confirm it. They are precisely what Arendt has in mind when she writes of genuinely free action, of people injecting themselves by word and deed into affairs going on around them.

The criticisms of George Kateb and Mary O'Brien promote a careful assessment of the meaning of Arendt's 'polis'. They help illuminate the concrete content of a genuine politics in Arendt's sense. They do more, however, than provide targets at which Arendt's arguments might be directed. Because of their concern with the complex socio-historical practices within which public life has been conducted, they also, to use Hegelian language, make clear the mediations through which Arendt's concept of the public realm must pass if it is to designate more than an abstract utopia, be it democratic (Kateb) or elitist (O'Brien).

In other words, if Arendt not only shares the concerns of Kateb and O'Brien but in certain respects can address them more adequately than they can, then one must show that her reflections have a basis in the actual properties of identifiable social and political practices and institutions. At the same time, these reflections must comprehend those practices and institutions in a way which demonstrates that, as working realities, they fail to live up to their claims to foster a free, reasonable existence. In my view Arendt's analyses of what I call 'false' politics do exactly this.

3 The Public Realm under Siege: False Politics and the Modern Age

By 'false politics', I mean those forms of social life which deny solidarity and citizenship as Hannah Arendt understands these. In my view, forms of false politics comprise the bulk of those social and historical phenenomena which engage Arendt's attention throughout her work. In a number of contexts she goes to bat on behalf of her understanding of a genuine politics against widespread, if not always widely accepted, institutions and practices which for her cast light upon the nature of modern experience.

Yet the very idea of a false politics suggests that the relation of human purposes to the prevailing institutional structure is complex and ambiguous. While these institutions at one level deny the expression of genuinely political impulses, at another they 'realize' these impulses, or at least derive their binding character, their 'spirit', from them. In other words, if the instruments of false politics are distorted expressions of genuinely political purposes and drives, then they must also have a certain 'rational' content: they may be said to incorporate the reasonableness of unreasonable circumstances. As Aristotle understood, there can be many workable regimes, some very far removed indeed from a life of reason and happiness.

Thus forms of false politics can be understood as distorted manifestations of a genuine politics which emerge where conditions for a genuine politics are absent. Their existence supports Arendt's account of the problem of modern history: that at one and the same time people create additions to the human artifice, while seeing them as gaining meaning from a nature-like process over which they exercise no control. They suggest the extent to which Arendt's account of public life is at heart ontological: that there are distinctively human wants, needs and purposes which can only be realized through political action, and that it is therefore possible to distinguish between genuine and spurious expressions of these.

The most significant manifestation of false politics is totalitarianism. It is of such obvious importance for Arendt's thought as a whole, and is such a distinctive form of false politics, that it will be treated separately in the next chapter. Here I focus on phenomena which are characteristically, if not exclusively, found in liberal democratic states. Their presence, and Arendt's treatment of them, suggest that although it is in a sense the crystallization of the forces which make for a false politics, totalitarianism is not the end of the story. Threats to public life, denials of something fundamentally human, abound in our own societies and may be all the more ominous both because they are more subtle and because they may even be gratifying.

What exactly, then, are forms of false politics? Arendt's accounts of freedom and public space, and what I have argued are implied by these accounts, suggest that the extent of false politics can be very wide indeed. Particular phenomena such as state and bureaucracy, violence and ideology are likely to come quickly to mind as obvious candidates for inclusion here. And indeed, from Arendt's perspective, they are included, and I treat them in this chapter. Yet because the range of concerns potentially covered by Arendt's notion of the public realm is broad, the domain of false politics, an inverted public world, is not exhausted by specifically institutional or ideological matters. In what follows I argue that two crucial modern developments not often fully recognized for their significance for Arendt's position – the crisis in culture and political lying – intertwine with and at the same time distil the essence of other, more visible, expressions of false politics. Both of these developments profoundly affect the identities people establish and the ways of being together they might share. Their deep roots in contemporary societies illuminate their capacity to anchor a 'working' social order, an unnaturally 'natural' political universe which can be very difficult to challenge in the name of what can only appear to everyday consciousness as a highly speculative, and thus false, alternative.

At stake in Arendt's critical assault on false politics is the character of her challenge to the political *status quo*, an issue that I first raised in chapter 1 in relation to her account of Marx. What is the nature of Arendt's radicalism as a critic of existing society and its values and institutions? In the name of precisely what alternative does she pose her critical challenge? As futile efforts to subsume her ideas under this or that ideological label attest, this is by no means a simple or straightforward matter.[1] In my view this is because her dissection of what I call 'false' politics is the other side of her positive account of a genuine politics grounded in freedom and action in a public realm. As I argued in chapter 2, these notions are difficult and, in some ways, potentially troubling. So, too, are her criticisms of existing political and social forms which, like her accounts of labour, freedom and action, take as their starting point existing institutions and practices, while ultimately breaking with them. If a genuine politics has risks (although such politics is perhaps less risky than what now passes for politics, at least where the capacities for making and keeping promises and for forgiveness play a role), then the challenge to existing institutions and norms also has risks. Arendt's powerful indictments of modern mass culture and political lying may be said to exhibit this quality. They are insightful and provocative; they are also ambiguous with respect to certain important norms and values. In the end I defend Arendt's position while recognizing (I hope) aspects of it with which people might reasonably disagree. But then, Arendt herself would probably not have wanted it otherwise. To put it another way: Arendt's critique of false politics involves, for me at least, more of those puzzles I noted in the Introduction.

In this chapter, then, I first examine the crisis in culture and political lying. I move on to discuss more overtly political forms of false politics, notably the state and ideology, that in our century have been critical for the development of our sense of political location and political identity. Finally, I examine political violence, a complex phenomenon which puts into bold relief the main elements of false politics and which provides a link between the everyday realities of constitutional liberal democracies and the extreme case of totalitarianism. All the way through, I attempt to maintain in the forefront of my discussion the need Arendt identifies for new modes both of political action and of political thinking as a response to our situation.

I

Hannah Arendt's critique of modern culture owes its origins to a theme not only in her work, but also in that of other important twentieth-century critics of culture, such as Walter Benjamin and T. W. Adorno: the decline of community, of human solidarity, of plurality. In Arendt's case, this theme is developed through her analysis of the collapse of worldliness and the accompanying erosion of individual and collective memory. Hence the concerns central to an understanding of a genuine public life – the nature of the world and one's orientation to it – are at the heart of Arendt's account of cultural crisis. In particular she introduces here two concepts central to her political thought: 'mass society' and 'judging'.

The crisis in culture has its roots for Arendt in two historical developments. The first involves the rise of 'society' and the consequent admission to political and social power of the propertied middle classes in the nineteenth century. The second is the increasing predominance of 'mass entertainment' in the twentieth. The paramount expression of this crisis, particularly in the nineteenth century, was the increasing subordination of artistic creation to utilitarian norms. This development became particularly evident in the tendency on the part of audiences to appreciate art not for its formal properties of beauty and proportion, but for its ability to promote personal self-enrichment and self-improvement.

At the centre of this transformation was a new 'subject' of aesthetic reception: the 'philistine' who subjects all experience, artistic and otherwise, to the utilitarian calculus. Particularly in the context of an argument that is in part a criticism of mass society, Arendt's reference to the philistine is clearly provocative. It conjures up images of an elitist, aesthetic hostility to sober bourgeois values and institutions, a contempt for the concerns of people in their everyday lives. As Henry Pachter reminds us, the attack on the philistine was a staple of reactionary thought in the first decades of the twentieth century, an important element of the 'politics of cultural despair' which helped lay the basis for the rise of Fascism and Nazism.[2]

Against this possible interpretation, I want to argue that Arendt's account of the philistine, and, *inter alia*, mass society, points in another direction: toward a community of equals in solidarity, that is, toward a genuine 'polis'. In this sense Arendt's critique of culture shares more in common with contemporary analyses of the anti-democratic, inegalitarian tendencies of consumer capitalism than with the reactionary assault on liberalism and democracy. The key here is once again the need for a proper balance between the elements of the *vita activa*. However, there indeed are difficulties in Arendt's account, interpretative puzzles which any honest treatment of her ideas here must admit and confront.

The question of balance in the *vita activa* is brought forward in a distinction crucial to Arendt's analysis: that between art and culture, between the requirements necessary for bringing things of beauty into existence and the proper mode of intercourse with them once they have come into the world. More starkly, the distinction calls to mind the tension between the demands of fabrication, on the one hand,

and the nature of action, on the other. The term 'culture' itself is suggestive. Its root is the same as that of the verb 'to cultivate', and the noun 'agriculture'. All express the view, peculiar to the Romans, that care and concern for our habitation on earth, and for the monuments of our past, are at the core of civilized human association. The 'cultivated' individual is one at home in the world, able freely to move gracefully among those products of human artifice that establish the claims of the human species to immortality. Hers is what Cicero called the *cultura animi*, 'a mind so trained and cultivated that it can be trusted to tend and take care of a world of appearances whose criterion is beauty'.[3]

Arendt's reference here to a 'world of appearances' is suggestive. Appearance is, after all, the chief characteristic of a truly public realm. It may be that politics and culture have in common certain fundamental existential qualities. Perhaps action and beauty, the hallmarks of politics and art respectively, stand together against labour and fabrication. Perhaps beauty is not merely an 'ideal', does not inhabit a subjective, immaterial, spiritual realm divorced from lived experience. Hence the split between what Georg Simmel called 'subjective' and 'objective' culture – between personal commitments and worldly reifications – violates the true nature of cultural life.

It is with these considerations as a backdrop that Arendt confronts the crisis in culture. In fact this turns out to be a crisis of a specific kind of culture: mass culture. As Arendt sees it, mass culture is intimately tied to 'the not much older' phenomenon of mass society, and both have come to enjoy a measure of intellectual respectability long denied them by 'serious' opinion. How this has come about, and why it has proven baleful for both culture and society, are among Arendt's concerns here. However, her more important purpose is to understand the precise relation of mass culture to mass society, and how this relationship differs from the relation of culture to society in other historical periods. It is essential to grasp this, for Arendt wants to understand not merely what is 'false' about the relation of mass culture to mass society, but, more subtly, what is necessary about it: what needs of human association this relationship serves under current historical conditions. It is part of Arendt's attempt to understand the current contours of the political in Lefort's sense of the term.

For Arendt, mass society came into being when the majorities of the populations of Europe and North America were admitted into what were formerly the exclusive preserves of the wealthy and leisured. While this suggests a purely quantitative dimension to the notion of 'mass' – namely, the problem is one of too many people doing what only a few were able to do before – Arendt gives to her account a qualitative character. For her, mass society in a numerical sense is not the exclusive domain of those qualities commonly attributed to 'mass man': loneliness, excitability, lack of standards, absence of judgement, enormous capacity for consumption, egocentricity, world alienation. Such qualities 'first appeared in good society, where there was no question of masses numerically speaking.'[4] There is thus inherent in Arendt's use of the term 'mass' an element of irony, a dialectical twist; this suffuses her entire analysis of culture. At stake, then, in Arendt's critique of culture is not simply the mere fact of a mass presence in the cultural realm, but the specific character of what Arendt calls the intercourse of people with cultural things.

Arendt's analysis of mass society forms one aspect of her account of the rise of the social, and thus the labour process, in the modern world. This analysis therefore shares many of the same, largely negative assumptions of the more comprehensive argument. Thus as Arendt sees it, the distinguishing hallmark of mass society is its unworldliness, its voracious appetite for the consumption of all things – not the least the things of culture. This growth of the 'consumers' society' has fundamentally altered the nature of our intercourse with cultural things. These things no longer serve as vehicles for the development and expression of *cultura animi*. Rather, they have become fodder for a qualitatively new kind of socio-economic institution: the entertainment industry.[5] Entertainment is the 'culture' of a society in which the possibilities for culture as a concern for the stability and permanence of an objective world have been vitiated. It is, in other words, the culture of a social world that has lost its sense of tradition.

For Arendt, the emergence of the consumer society and its quest for entertainment have not been wholly negative developments. With the collapse of tradition has come the opportunity to re-examine the basis and character of our cultural and political experience. For this task 'mass society is much less in our way than good and educated society . . .'[6] Entertainment has organic links with the requirements of the life process and we all need diversion and amusement. Moreover, the challenge to worldliness that entertainment provides at least is obvious. The threat to genuine culture posed by 'good and educated society' is more subtle. This is because such a society is supposedly geared to the preservation of culture, in this case 'high' culture, culture as the sphere of superior values untainted by the demands of everyday life. But for Arendt this very separation of culture from experience is part of the general crisis of culture itself. This so-called 'high' culture is no different from the 'low' culture or entertainment, to which it is misleadingly contrasted – with the exception that 'high' culture can be more readily deployed as a vehicle for self-improvement, the basis for an abstract elevation of the spiritual side of our nature.

It is for this reason that the philistine is so significant for Arendt's analysis. At one level, the philistine is the object of the modern artistic critique of society, the contemporary focus of the artist's more or less permanent antagonism to the social world. But Arendt's use of the term has broader, more explicitly political implications. The philistine has not been a historically invariant actor on the social stage. The notion of philistinism, and what it expressed, underwent a subtle but powerful transformation. Whereas in the earlier nineteenth-century stage of the modern artistic rebellion against society, the philistine was one who was simply 'uncultured', commonplace in his judgements about the world, in the later stages of modern social life, the dominant interests in society itself began to adopt an all-encompassing interest in cultural matters. Culture became a weapon in the hands of the newly powerful bourgeoisie in its struggle for status and power, while at the same time serving as an ostensible escape from the reality of this struggle.

Arendt sees in this two-sided development the seeds of the modern entertainment industry and the subordination of art to life: of the objective, tangible world of things that provides for humans a habitat on earth, to the irresistible demands of consumption in the service of the life process. At the heart of this development is a fundamental contradiction. If the philistine seeks at one and the same time both to deploy art as a means of self-improvement and to abandon reality itself, this means that he is of two minds with respect to artistic objects. Even as he seeks 'sweetness and light' in art, he denounces it for its 'uselessness'.

In the final analysis, the philistine destroys culture in the very pursuit of it. This is because whether he seeks escape or self-improvement, the philistine relates to artistic objects in a purely utilitarian way, and this militates against the preservation of an objective world that incorporates beauty as an objective property. A work of art, a thing of the world, 'comprehends and gives testimony to the entire recorded past of countries, nations and ultimately mankind . . . [A]s soon as the immortal works of the past became objects of social and individual refinement and the status accorded to it, they lost their most important and elemental quality which is to grasp and move the reader or the spectator over the centuries.'[7] In these circumstances culture became just another 'value', that is, 'a social commodity which could be circulated and cashed in in exchange for all kinds of other values, social and individual'.[8]

The conversion of culture into a value which can enter the market-place like any other value not only destroys the worldliness of cultural artifacts, but also, if more subtly, the capacity for memory and hence a genuine sense of history, a sense of where we have been and thus where we might be going. It was under these conditions – characterized by the assault on worldliness, memory, transcendence itself – that the populations of market societies entered the ranks of the leisured. And it was under these same conditions that the entertainment industry, the voice and guarantor of an eternal present, the producer of worldless and timeless objects, first came into its own. As Arendt sees it, the threat posed by the entertainment industry is not that it provides relief from toil, for we all need that, but rather that in its insatiable demand for sources of consumer goods, it ransacks culture and tradition for artifacts that can readily be altered, that is, denatured and cheapened for easy consumption. Once leisure serves not as an alternative to but as an aspect of necessity – once, to recall the German tradition of political thought, the realm of freedom is organized as an extension of the realm of necessity – culture becomes subordinate to the production cycle and so loses its worldly character.

What occurs here is a kind of process of de-objectification. Genuine objects, worldly creations, are not simply contingent agglomerations of sensuous qualities. Rather, they possess determinate shapes and forms; they are matter that has been mediated by and through the form-giving power of the imagination.[9] Aesthetic qualities, and especially beauty – for Arendt the basic aesthetic dimension – become contentless, subjective preferences, 'ideal', when objects become pseudo-objects formed by the imperatives of the labour process. De-objectification in the sense meant here involves not the elimination of form as such, but the institution of a specific form – the commodity form – which is destroyed, only to be re-created, in the course of the life cycle of production and consumption. The forms of art objects, which were created to appear and express permanence and stability, now literally dis-appear. They serve to orient people in an instrument-ally rational way to the demands of the labour process. The very basis of art itself is undermined. Arendt notes: '[t]here are many great authors of the past who have survived centuries of oblivion and neglect, but it is still an open question whether they will be able to survive an entertaining version of what they have to say.'[10]

In criticizing mass culture in the terms outlined here, Arendt shares common ground with other analysts of mass society. Her account bears obvious similarity to the arguments of T. W. Adorno and Max Horkheimer in *Dialectic of Enlightenment* about the culture industry as a powerful force in contemporary capitalist societies. Such a comparison is by no means trivial politically: in my view Arendt, like Horkheimer and Adorno, is more interested in what mass culture does to the people whose concerns it supposedly reflects than with its mass character as such. To put it another way: there is no inherent reason to suppose that Arendt views the triumph of mass culture as either the product of, or the necessary complement to, some presumed inability of ordinary people to enjoy a genuine, transcendental artistic experience. But to see this requires a more systematic examination of the specific connection between culture and politics in Arendt's argument. For what I ultimately intend to argue is that Arendt's unique understanding of the political both provides a ground for, and is given one of its sharpest and most compelling expressions in, her account of the crisis in culture.

The very character of culture as the intercourse of people with objects of art is moulded by the same elements which shape genuine political experience. In a fundamental way the capacity for political experience and the ability to be moved and enlightened by works of art require the same individual qualities. This is so because for a genuine politics to exist there must be a truly human world, a domain of humanly-made things which provides a home for people on earth. For Arendt, the most worldly of all objects, subject neither to the functionalism of things produced for consumption nor the utility of objects produced for mere use alone, are works of art. They have a permanence, a sheer durability, unmatched by any other human product. She writes: 'It is as though worldly stability had become transparent in the permanence of art, so that a premonition of immortality, not the immortality of the soul or of life but of something immortal achieved by mortal hands, has become tangibly present, to shine and to be seen, to sound and to be heard, to speak and to be read.'[11]

Arendt's account of art as worldly creation *par excellence* carries within it an important political implication. When she claims that the 'premonition of immortality' which art exhibits is neither that of the soul nor of life, in effect she challenges both ancient, or classical, and modern conceptions of political purpose. The ancient polis, the world of Plato and Aristotle, was a fusion of the ethical and the political, the domain of soul-craft. The modern state, whose most provocative defender is Hobbes, exists above all to foster self-preservation, life. Neither genuine art, part of a world within which a genuine public realm can be housed, nor politics is about soul-craft or self-preservation.

And neither the capacity to make and keep promises nor the ability to forgive, Arendt's bulwarks against the unpredictability and uncertainty of action, is soul-enhancing or life-preserving. These lack the didactic qualities associated with the proper instruction of the soul, as well as the useful benefits associated with the successful calculation of self-interest. Rather, they make possible the equal and reciprocal acknowledgement by each and all of a shared situation, a life of solidarity. In this respect they have a powerful quality in common with artistic reception (and, strikingly, receptivity, or non-sovereignty, is essential for Arendt both to political freedom and artistic experience): art is after all about neither self-improvement, the modern secularized variant of soul-craft, nor mere diversion.

How we 'receive' others who act in a situation of sheer human togetherness and how we receive works of art are related in another way: they both involve appearance in a public space. It is with respect to this connection that Arendt examines the idea of beauty. She notes that what is inherent in any thing as a thing is that it has a shape, and 'whatever has a shape at all and is seen cannot help being either beautiful, ugly, or something in-between. Everything that is, must appear, and nothing can appear without a shape of its own; hence there is in fact no thing that does not in some way transcend its functional use, and its transcendence, its beauty or ugliness, is identical with appearing publicly and being seen.'[12]

Arendt does not imply that we can or should assess people and their worth in the public realm by whether they are 'beautiful' or 'ugly', although understanding 'who' someone is has the quality of an artistic experience – it involves something more and other than simply weighing the strengths and weaknesses of a person's qualities from an instrumental point of view, that is, from the vantage point of 'what' the person is. To be sure, for action to survive the moment of its undertaking and to live on in memory, it must be reified into a story that can be told, and in this respect will necessarily partake of the qualities of beauty or ugliness. But action and the acting human being, and the story that can be told of these, are not identical. (Arendt challenges Marx's claim that humans create themselves, not on the grounds that such a claim is blasphemous, but rather because it attempts to make people their own chroniclers, that is, it collapses action and fabrication or work.) To put it another way, politics is not art. Arendt's account of false politics is not an expression of disgust on the part of the aesthete at the everyday realities of political struggle and compromise in a pluralistic society. (Some interpretation of this sort seems at the core of George Kateb's criticisms of Arendt's views on representative democracy.)

However, there is some sense in which the ability to distinguish the beautiful from the ugly – what is normally called taste – is connected to the ability to act and to respond to action in the public realm. This connection arises from what Arendt, perhaps surprisingly, claims is the human source of a work of art: the capacity for thought. Comparing the capacity for thought to the capacities for exchange and use, Arendt argues that

[t]hought is related to feeling and transforms its mute and inarticulate despondency, as exchange transforms the naked greed of desire and usage transforms the desperate longing of needs – until they all are fit to enter the world and be transformed into things, to become reified. In each instance, a human capacity which by its nature is world-open and communicative transcends and releases into a world a passionate intensity from its imprisonment within the self.[13]

Art makes thought real, fabricates thought things, transfigures our feelings and emotions in a way that manifests the creative but essentially inner world of thinking itself.

Arendt further distinguishes thought from, on the one hand, cognition, the acquisition of knowledge in pursuit of practical aims, and, on the other hand, logical reasoning, the ability to make deductions from self-evident premises or to subsume particular examples under general rules. I believe she does this not merely in order to catalogue the distinctive qualities of the human mind, but rather for another reason: to indicate that unlike cognition, which is intimately bound up with modern science and the transformation of our natural environment into a human 'world', or logical reasoning, which is rooted in the structure of the human brain and reflects a 'brain power' very much like our power to labour, there is nothing necessary or inevitable about the appearance of thought in the world. In other words, thought is tied more closely to human freedom than is either cognition or logical reasoning.

In this respect art and action are strikingly similar. They both involve human capacities which need not be actualized. Moreover, the milieux within which they appear, if at all, are likewise linked. The milieu for action is of course the space of appearance, the (political) public realm. That of art is culture itself. In a sense culture constitutes the artistic space of appearance. Whether art is exhibited in museums or churches literally determines the character of culture as the mode of human intercourse with art. In its broadest sense the public realm provides more than a space for action. It also allows for the display generally of things whose essence is to appear and thus to be (potentially) beautiful. Thus art and politics are mutually dependent: 'The fleeting greatness of word and deed can endure in the world to the extent that beauty can be bestowed upon it . . . The common element connecting art and politics is that they are both phenomena of the public world.'[14]

If there can be a false public realm, in which not freedom but other human possibilities are exhibited, there can as well be a false culture – mass culture itself. Both false culture and false politics emerge in the context of forms of organized living together which fail to realize the promise of sheer human togetherness, plurality, solidarity.

And if art manifests a capacity for thought that is neither cognition nor logical reasoning, so, as I suggested in chapter 1, does action, or politics. Is it possible that these manifestations can be grasped as such by those for whom art and action appear only by means of a mental capacity tied neither to work as the creation of use values (cognition), nor to labour as the production of goods for consumption (logical reasoning)? In other words could it be that the 'right love of beauty, the proper intercourse with beautiful things . . . has something to do with politics . . . that taste belongs among the political faculties?'[15] In my view Arendt does identify such a mental capacity. With regard to aesthetic matters, this capacity undergirds the exercise of taste, while with respect to political action, it informs our recognition of 'who' someone reveals him/herself to be. It is the faculty for judging.

As I will argue in chapter 6, judging plays a critical role in Arendt's account of properly political thinking; indeed it is the most distinctively political of our mental faculties. By examining this capacity in the context of a crisis in culture, Arendt wishes not only to illuminate its worldly character, but also to demonstrate its absence as a prime factor in the growth of false politics. The rise of mass society and the decline of judging go together and must be seen in their proper relation.

From the vantage point of culture and politics, the power of judging lies in its ability to inform 'the judicious exchange of opinion about the sphere of public life and the common world, and the decision what manner of action is to be taken in it, as well as how it is to look henceforth, what kind of things are to appear in it.'[16] According to Arendt, the thinker who came closest to recognizing the peculiar worldliness of judging was Immanuel Kant. For Kant, the capacity to judge requires and produces an 'enlarged mentality' (*eine erweiterte Denkungsart*). This enlarged mentality makes possible not merely the powers of discernment and discrimination with respect to art, but also political life itself, because in establishing the conditions for the exercise of judgement, it anticipates communication with others with whom one wishes to make an agreement. Judgement's 'claims to validity can never extend further than the others in whose place the judging person has put himself for his considerations.'[17] The activity of judging is at the heart of the consensus reached by those who seek to shape the world they have in common by ruling on the quality of those things in it. This consensus, which must be attained through persuasion and not force, is the basis and outcome of genuine political experience. In other words, judgement has a revelatory quality that suggests a kinship to action.

The role of judging in ruling on, and hence shaping, a common world suggests that it must have an objectivity that cannot be reduced to narrowly subjective 'preferences'. If the shape of the world as the objective forum for human action is determined by judgement, then the judgements themselves must have the permanence and stability of worldliness. That is, questions of quality, and not just truth, can be legitimate objects of rational insight. In this context taste works to discriminate among qualities. It situates the beautiful in a recognizably human world by introducing the specifically personal, an objective subjectivity, as a necessary element in the very structure of the beautiful itself – a beauty that is unmistakably human in its expression of our longings and capacities.

While both the beautiful and the political appear to exist, it is now clear that not simply any appearance will do. It is to judgement and taste that we must look for standards that determine the acceptability of what is made to appear. These standards are for Arendt 'humanistic': they must ultimately express some distinctively human purpose, an ontological commitment.

The issue of ontology is critically important here because of a peculiar and even disturbing quality of Arendt's account of the crisis in culture: the fact that all actors or creators of beautiful things, as well as the philistine as a historical figure, are or appear to be exclusively male.[18] This involves more than the semantics of using 'man' or 'he' to designate supposedly universal human properties. It also involves the question whether the very terms within which Arendt casts her arguments, notably taste and beauty, betray a necessary and uncorrectably male perspective, an aesthetics and politics of patriarchy. Arendt's favourable invocation of Pericles' defence of Greek culture as involving a love of beauty shorn of the 'vice of effeminacy' suggests a patriarchal perspective.[19]

Moreover, Arendt's most powerful defence of taste as a human capacity is that it 'sets its own limits to an indiscriminate, immoderate love of the merely beautiful . . . [It] debarbarizes the world of the beautiful by not being overwhelmed by it.'[20] But the notion of the 'barbarian' can carry uncomfortable implications of white European ethnocentrism at the least, if not outright racism itself.[21]

Thus the question: do Arendt's ideas about culture and its proper role betray sexist and racist assumptions? This is obviously vital because her account of a genuine politics is so intimately tied to her critique of mass society and its culture. If this critique is problematic in terms of gender and racial oppression, what then of her views of genuine political action, freedom and the public realm itself? It would seem that, in an era of increasing concern with gender and racial oppression, these would not be very helpful for a creative politics committed to humane and democratic values.

No doubt there is a troubling dimension to Arendt's account here. But just as the immanent logic of Arendt's position came to the rescue of her analysis of public and private in the face of Mary O'Brien's criticisms, so here too, I would argue, her arguments can be interpreted in a more expansive way than their specific formulation might at first glance suggest.

The question here, as before, concerns whether or not Arendt's concepts can play a role in other critical accounts of contemporary society. Put another way, are notions of beauty and taste simply white, male and European? I think that, from Arendt's perspective, the answer here would be 'no'. The capacity to articulate judgements based upon some sense of beauty or taste is a universal human property. This is not to say that specifically white, male and European ideas of these are or ought to be the only genuine ones (that Arendt may have thought this to be the case – and it is not clear that she did – is of no consequence here). Indeed Arendt's arguments imply something else. Notions of beauty and taste are contestable – perhaps, to borrow from Alasdair MacIntyre, essentially contestable and not least because pursuit of the beautiful to the exclusion of all else can have horrific implications: Arendt is acutely aware of the fusion of politics and aesthetics under Fascism. This is part of the reason why aesthetic terms have political implications.

Do feminists have their own conceptions of beauty? Do non-Europeans discriminate on the grounds of taste? I think the answers to both of these questions is 'yes'. Although the development of a specifically feminist aesthetic, one necessarily linked to feminist politics, remains incomplete (and perhaps incompletable on feminism's own assumptions about the necessity for a plurality of perspectives and the need to resist the affirmation of a single source of theoretical truth), efforts by feminist writers and scholars to retrieve from historical oblivion the works of female artists animated by alternative conceptions of form and structure indicate a vital interest in formulating an alternative account of beauty, and indeed art itself. And the increasing significance of art from the Third World in Europe and North America, much of it expressing Arendt-like demands for a genuine and indigenous public life freed from the bonds of imperialism, has brought with it a rising critical tide that has 'deconstructed' formerly dominant and unchallenged notions of artistic merit – precisely on the grounds of alternative conceptions of artistic worth. Significantly, both of these critical developments have at least called into question the way in which mass culture has functioned in Western imperial and Third World societies.

So I think there is a case to be made for reading Arendt's account of the crisis in culture as in principle open to a broad range of critical perspectives, and not simply as a defence of European standards. It is true that in her arguments, Arendt nowhere explicitly indicates a concern for victims of male domination or imperialist aggression. This raises the question of how justifiable it is to read Arendt in the way I have suggested; here lies one of those interpretative 'puzzles'. But something more must be said here. However much her account might accommodate contemporary critical currents of thought, there is no doubt that Arendt was no revolutionary in the sense of according a privileged political position to some putatively radical agent, be it women, people of colour or the working class. From her point of view, no one had a monopoly on either human virtue or human frailty; no one was in principle immune to the temptation to use beauty or taste, for example, in oppressive ways. Those inclined to defend the political credentials of a supposed agent are unlikely to find Arendt's political thought persuasive, however expansively it might be interpreted.

In a way, such criticisms from feminist and anti-racist perspectives parallel those which see in Arendt's analysis of culture an elitist disdain for the lives of ordinary people. But as I have tried to argue, this would be a serious misreading of both Arendt's intentions and her actual position. In her view, the incorporation of all strata of the populations of Europe and North America into a network of social relations geared to the cyclical demands of production and consumption has not been an unmixed blessing for those formerly excluded, even if, as she admits, it has raised their material living standards. As the domain of the social, that peculiar combination of public and private that effectively destroys both, mass society always threatens to overwhelm its members. It leaves them no place to 'hide'.[22]

Arendt's analysis of the crisis in culture is subtle and, potentially at least, far-reaching in its implications for a critical theory of politics.[23] Aside from the significance it accords to judging, her argument makes clear that philosophical and political debates about the character of modernity have significance not only for intellectuals or artists, but throughout the wider society as well. At the same time, it suggests that the conditions of mass society are to be condemned for the damage they do to large numbers of people and for the undermining of taste and judgement they enforce, and not for their mass character *per se*; certainly not for the ability of this society to provide an acceptable standard of living for more people than has ever been possible before in recorded history. Arendt's account calls to mind Walter Benjamin: 'Mass reproduction is aided especially by the reproduction of the masses.'[24]

II

Arendt's account of the politics of lying is another unique and powerful dissection of a phenomenon that both provides the basis for, and is one of the most potent expressions of, false politics in the contemporary era. If mass culture is the culture of people who exist together in space but not in a 'world', the politics of lying is a potent expression of the human capacity to act under conditions hostile to action. It is a kind of anti-political politics, a form of action which in the extreme can threaten the very possibility of acting itself.

It is no coincidence that for Arendt modern politics has increasingly been characterized by large-scale lying. As a distorted form of action, the deliberate falsehood, the systematic deception, has qualities which make it particularly suitable for an age of false politics. The crisis in culture involves the 'objective' conditions under which false politics has emerged. Political lying points to the 'subjective' basis of distorted action. It is a form of false revelation, an artificial verisimilitude. At the same time the existence of large-scale lying puts another matter on the political agenda: truth. Although Arendt is often said to have kept truth and politics, philosophy and public affairs, separate, her treatment of lying in fact demonstrates that this separation is far from absolute, that politics has a necessary 'moment' of truth.

It is in the nature of action that the very quality which makes it the embodiment of freedom and hence the basis of a genuine politics is fundamental to the equally unique human capacity to lie, 'this mysterious faculty of ours that enables us to *say* "The sun is shining" when it is raining cats and dogs.'[25] This quality is the imagination, our ability to say 'no' to existing reality by mentally removing ourselves from it. Since action, too, involves removing what is there to make room for the new, the denial of factual truth (lying) and the capacity to change the facts (acting) are closely connected. It is precisely the imagination which connects them.

The ability of action to create a new reality 'indicates that while we are well-equipped for the world, sensually as well as mentally, we are not fitted or embedded in it as one of its inalienable parts.'[26] The world exists as it does because humans have shaped it, and have consented to that shape. Once it has been created by human activity, the world does indeed assume an objectivity independently of those who inhabit it. But granting this, it is not inevitable that the world must be so and not otherwise. Social reality is a field of tension, perched between the actual and the potential; it is something more and other than the totality of facts and events. The affinity of lying with acting, and thus politics, is clear. The liar wants nothing more than that the world be other than what it is.

So much has been known for centuries. Arendt tells us that lies have always been important tools of the statesman's trade. What is distinctively modern about the current situation and requires explanation is first, the extent to which lying has become increasingly important in political life; and secondly, the forms such lying has assumed: the affairs with which it has been concerned, the people at whom it has been directed, the intentions informing its growth. To these questions and their theoretical implications Arendt devotes 'Truth and Politics', one her most remarkable essays. What she shows there is that modern historical consciousness, in league with certain other developments, has provided a hospitable environment for attempts at mass public deception.

It is of considerable importance that the concept of truth should come forward front and centre in Arendt's account of lying. This is not just because truth is the opposite of falsehood. As Arendt points out, this is the case only with respect to a specific kind of truth, although one relevant to her concerns here. Rather, she must confront the issue of truth in all its forms because lying is so closely related to acting. Since both seek to change the world, why is one morally defensible and the other not? Why is one form of acting labelled 'lying', with its associated connotations, at all? Obviously, Arendt acknowledges the baleful implications of lying for politics. Perhaps less obviously, although she explicitly argues the futility of abstract moral outrage in combating deception,[27] she is vitally concerned with the moral worth of politics as well: she wonders if politics is inherently deceitful. Political questions are inevitably moral questions. Arendt's treatment of lying demonstrates that this is so.

In the modern age people have tended to distinguish two kinds of truth: rational and factual. Rational truths are seen as the products of mathematics, philosophy and science. In opposition to factual truths, which arise out of and shape the realm of human affairs, rational truths are believed to possess an unchallengeable objectivity to which people must passively conform. Arendt is not completely comfortable with this distinction, but she finds it useful because it allows her to put the current relation of truth to politics in historical perspective.

Truth and politics have been in conflict since the emergence in ancient Greece of the Western tradition of political philosophy. For the ancients the conflict involved two competing ways of life, that of the philosopher and that of the citizen. Obviously shaken by the fate of Socrates, philosophers gloomily recounted the dangers befalling the truthteller in a world hostile to enlightenment about its real situation. Plato's allegory of the cave from the *Republic* is the most explicit and powerful expression of the philosopher's self-understanding.

But the truth under attack was the truth about eternal things which could provide governing standards for human affairs – in short, rational truth. There was no question of lying as the major threat. The challenge posed to truth by the public realm flowed from the very structure of this realm itself which, in its plurality, was the domain not of truth but of opinion. Opinion involves the kind of representative, prudential thinking which seeks to comprehend and mould the changing flux and flow of human events. It has a representative character: one forms an opinion by weighing an issue from a variety of perspectives. As a result, political thinking, understood here as the formation of opinions designed to shape the perceptions of others, 'is truly discursive, running, as it were, from place to place, from one part of the world to another, through all kinds of conflicting views, until it finally ascends from these particularities to some impartial generality.'[28] Such thinking can only be binding when others consent to the picture of the world it constructs, and this can only be brought about through persuasion.

These qualities stand in direct opposition to the character of rational truth which, in its concern for the enduring and unchanging, is not subject to the strains and shifts of opinions bound to the ebb and flow of politics. Such truth impresses itself upon the knower through the insight it gives into the fundamental nature of being. It is perceived by the eye of the mind (reason) and not acquired through the shared experience of public life. Because of the manner through which truth becomes known, it is always an individual and singular phenomenon, not a collective and plural one. For this reason persuasion, the stuff of politics, has no place in philosophy. People cannot be persuaded to recognize the truth and, once they have recognized it, cannot be persuaded to abandon it. In its peremptory claim to acknowledgement, truth coercively excludes the opinions of others altogether.

However, when a truth is brought into the marketplace of political opinion, it will likely be treated as simply as another opinion. Its compelling character will be lost, and with that its claim to being truth. The truthteller/philosopher faces two equally unpalatable options. She can witness mutely the disappearance of her or his truth amidst a welter of competing claims. Or, if without violence she can induce acceptance of that truth among the many, she could still see it reduced to the status of an opinion which, though predominant today, could be eclipsed by another tomorrow. For the philosopher, the urge to join knowledge to political power is potentially overwhelming. Of course it is this urge which Arendt finds so problematic in Western political philosophy, and which must be quelled if philosophy and politics, two distinct ways of life, are to be preserved.

But while the truths of philosophy may be opposed by illusions or opinions, they are not normally countered by actual lies. The conflict between rational truth and politics, even if it was, as for Plato, literally a matter of life and death, was nevertheless 'the perhaps inevitable tension between two ways of life within the framework of a common and commonly recognized reality.'[29] In the modern clash between truth and politics, however, it is precisely this common reality which is at stake. As such, the clash not only has consequences for politics, it is itself a political problem of the first order.

In the modern setting, the conflict between truth and politics involves factual truth, the stuff of human affairs. Unlike rational truth, which exists in isolation from the world of the many, factual truth is always related to other people, upon whom indeed it depends for its very existence. Such truth requires the witness and testimony of people together and, to be actualized fully, must be spoken or written about. It is thus political by its nature; hence although distinct, facts and opinions inhabit the same realm.

In a way this commonality is the source of the problem. That facts and opinions share the same relation makes it all too easy for one to substitute for the other – for fact to assume the character of opinion. What renders plausible the conversion of factual truth into opinion is the maddening contingency of all facts, a contingency rooted in the very capacity of specific facts to be other than what they are. It is tempting for people in political life to try and redo what has happened to make reality conform to their own interests.

It is by no means obvious that lying as a conscious policy should inevitably result from the confusion of truth and opinion. But factual truth shares with its rational counterpart the same coercive properties. It, too, demands acceptance without question and although it needs the plurality of individuals to survive, it has an objective quality not exhausted by the subjective confirmation of its existence. Historical facts have a stubborn obduracy impossible to overcome: no one could seriously claim that, in 1914, Belgium invaded Germany.[30]

Or could he? In Arendt's eyes the contemporary era has witnessed an alarming new phenomenon: organized lying, the attempt at mass manipulation of facts. For while the opposite of rational truth is illusion, the opposite of factual truth is most assuredly the lie.

Of course lies have always played a role in political life. But they usually involved state secrets, either factual truths which could not for reasons of security be made public, or intentions which in any event lacked the reliability of accomplished facts. These lies were intended to deceive only the enemy. The deceivers themselves, statesmen and diplomats, were both few in number and conscious of the truth. However, according to Arendt we have in recent times confronted large-scale attempts to deny the veracity of matters that are not secrets in the traditional sense, but are of public record. Under the circumstances, the teller of factual truths may be in no less danger than the philosopher in Plato's city. At least she encounters the same frustrating reception accorded the philosopher: what she has to say is treated as simply opinion. And precisely because it relies on the confirmation of others, factual truth may be even less self-evident than rational truth, and less secure. So indeed may be the teller of factual truth. In Hitler's Germany or Stalin's Russia, it was more dangerous to discuss concentration camps, whose existence was well known, than to utter heretical views at odds with the dominant ideology.

Under the conditions in which factuality undergoes siege, the teller of factual truth shares the anomalous position of the philosopher. The philosopher at least can politically validate the truth for which she stands through an exemplary action that draws its meaning from the philosophical principle itself. Factual truths express no such principles and a teller of factual truth, 'in the unlikely event that he wished to stake his life on a particular fact, would achieve a kind of miscarriage. What would become manifest in his act would be his courage or, perhaps, his stubbornness but neither the truth of what he had to say nor even his own truthfulness.'[31]

These considerations have become increasingly significant because of the change in the very purpose and character of lying. Attempts to promulgate not simply this or that lie, but an entirely different reality, even in defiance of one's senses, are the hallmarks of this change. And while totalitarian states have most obviously engaged in this practice, liberal democratic states have not been immune to it. Here, too, the dividing line between fact and opinion has frequently been blurred as whole chunks of history, past and current, have been refitted to meet the needs of politically dominant interests and purposes. The capacity to enforce new visions of the world, though far less arbitrary and brutal than totalitarian violence, can be ominously coercive none the less.[32]

The large-scale attempt to convert fact into opinion is a clear sign of the emergence of a qualitatively new form of lying. The presence of this new form joins for Arendt the issues of history and action, and so goes to the heart of the differences between genuine and false politics. To her, it is not surprising that the most flagrant examples of organized lying have involved efforts to rewrite the historical record, and she puts the concept of history itself in the forefront of her analysis. Ultimately, in its new form lying raises the question of the nature of historical interpretation. Since historical facts have an objectivity rooted in human activity, they cannot be considered apart from the human purposes out of which they arise, and which they in turn shape. Hence they cannot be divorced from an interpretative scheme which gives them meaning by fitting them into a story that can be told.

Yet the need for interpretation does not give licence to manipulate the facts any way one chooses. Every generation has the right to its own historical interpretations. But this does not give it the right to alter the factual material of history itself. Yet this is a threat we increasingly face; the historical record has become more and more vulnerable to systematic distortion. Arendt explores the qualities of lying that allow it such a profound impact on experience. These qualities emerge from the moral ambiguity of action whose capacity to negate and transform the given can be a source of both magic and horror. This ambiguity is crystallized in the intriguing figure of the conscious liar. Arendt's fascinating account of the liar as political actor is the key element of her argument.

By his or her nature, the liar is a person of action who wants things to be different from what they are, who wants to change the world. In this attempt to change the world, the liar has a pronounced advantage over the truthteller who, except under circumstances in which everyone lies about everything, is most assuredly not a person of action. Indeed for the truthteller to enter the fray on the side of a particular interest would be to sacrifice that impartiality which guarantees truthfulness in the first place. By its nature, truthtelling is not a form of action. Because it discloses the world as it is, it tends to acceptance of this world. It is thus clear why truthtelling is a form of action only when lying is thoroughly pervasive: only then is disclosure equivalent to change. (The relatively recent phenomenon of the bureaucratic 'whistle-blower' suggests that the current era may in fact be one in which truthtelling has become a form of action.)

That the liar is by his or her nature a person of action is not the only basis of his or her potency. The very essence of factual truth works in the liar's favour. In their contingency, facts have elements of unexpectedness and unpredictability. In fitting his or her 'facts' to meet the expectations of his or her audience, the liar eliminates the unpredictable. The resulting story thus has a greater apparent plausibility than the truth might possess. In effect the liar exploits the potential suppressed, but not in principle abolished, by the triumph of the actual. His or her action buries the old story and creates a new one in its stead. And once the liar has destroyed the real, he or she benefits from the 'existential illusion' that in historical perspective everything assumes a causal inevitability. The ability of the liar to create a 'false' history, so powerful because so close to the distinctively human capacity to act, poses for Arendt the central, frightening question: 'what is to prevent these new stories, images, and non-facts from becoming an adequate substitute for reality and factuality?'[33]

What prevents a tissue of falsehoods from becoming as real as the factual world it is meant to displace is the very quality which made the lie plausible in the first place, the contingency of all factual reality. As Montaigne noted, 'the reverse of truth has a thousand shapes,' and the liar's fabrication can be in principle be confronted with alternatives that are equally believable. She has opened up what was past by converting facts back into the potential out of which they had originally grown, and such a potential is literally limitless. The falsifier finds himself or herself floating aimlessly from one concoction of reality to another, always seeking ever-elusive certainty.

But lies 'can never compete in stability with that which simply is because it happens to be thus and not otherwise.'[34] The ground is pulled out from under everyday experience, which relies so heavily upon our ability to distinguish truth from falsehood. This, Arendt suggests, is the character of life under totalitarian domination, but as she makes clear that it can also take shape in democratic states – particularly among those practising deceit on a massive scale.

Indeed lying assumes political significance when the power of the state is deployed to establish and maintain a false world. Aside from conscious totalitarian attempts to rewrite history, there has emerged in recent decades what Arendt calls 'image-making' as a form of government policy. The tricks and illusions of sophisticated propaganda and slick advertising methods have buttressed campaigns to sell receptive publics prepackaged accounts of the political universe. Consumer sovereignty is no more real here than it is in the markets for other goods and services, as politically dominant interests armed with the latest techniques in opinion management strive to legitimize their versions of reality. In the process they create webs of deception by which whole nations may come to take their bearings. If deliberate lies were once intended to deceive only the enemy, an outside opponent, under contemporary forms of organized lying the enemy is us. (And it is of course a hallmark of the totalitarian state that it makes war on its own people.)

Because self-deception is so essential to the maintenance of the officially authorized picture of the world, a government tends to devote an increasingly large share of resources to maintaining the image, even if the purpose for which the image was established in the firt place is sacrificed. Under these circumstances the enemy becomes the truthteller who is then labelled a subversive, an enemy within. Prophetically ('Truth and Politics' was first published in 1967, just as opposition in the United States to the Vietnam War was beginning to crescendo), Arendt notes that 'the modern art of self-deception is likely to transform an outside matter into an inside issue, so that an international or inter-group conflict boomerangs onto the scene of domestic politics.'[35]

Those in the state apparatus who carry out the task of self-deception are for Arendt agents of 'defactualization'. They tend to be 'problem-solvers', eager to test reality against elaborate theories or 'scenarios' which assume that historical events are natural events which can be explained and predicted by reference to causal laws. Although Arendt does not write of false consciousness, she does note that such thinking itself requires self-deception and that the bureaucratic environment within which political managers operate is uniquely capable of shielding them not merely from the consequences of their actions, but from reality itself. Rational calculators all, these operatives evince a penchant for reversing Hegel by transforming quality into quantity: manageable mathematical calculations replace judgement based upon lived experience.

But experience takes its revenge. In the first place the liar is defeated by reality itself: the realm of fact is simply too large to cover over completely. However, the liar is also a victim at a more fundamental phenomenological level. The real world catches up with him 'because he can remove his mind from it but not his body.' In seeking to change our worldly habitation, the liar does more than rearrange the furniture. She seeks to mould the occupant. What the liar ultimately wants is not just a change in the human condition, but a change in human beings themselves.[36]

Because of the inevitable tension they create, exercises in mass deception are inherently destabilizing. The loss of the distinction between truth and falsehood, which under conditions of self-deception may extend to the liars themselves, in all cases threaten, and in extreme cases shatter, the very basis of the trust in what one's senses reveal that makes worldliness, and thus politics, at all possible. For this reason, however powerful the political and technical forces sustaining the desired vision of the world might be, members of the intended audience, especially the domestic population, are never fully convinced by the fabrications. If they comply, this is more the product of fear and (implied) coercion rather than persuasion. Individuals go along with whatever the powers that be demand, and credit no truth. They behave, in short, like the objects of nature-like causal processes that social science pictures them to be; here the issue of lying and the political context of science are joined. The roots of the cynicism of advanced bourgeois, as well as totalitarian, politics run deep.

Yet whatever the antagonism between truth and politics, Arendt believes that factual truth clashes with the political only at a low level of human affairs. Politics in a constitutional democratic state, however limited it might be in other ways, is not totally susceptible to the power of lying as a distorted form of political action. Institutions such as the judiciary and the university, which stand outside the public realm, are designed to engage in the disinterested pursuit of truth, and have frequently brought forth 'unwelcome' judgements and truths. Although always vulnerable to political pressure, these institutions nevertheless continue to function, as if the public realm recognized that it has a need for individuals and bodies over which it has no control. The greatness of the public realm is ultimately limited by those things that we cannot change; this is the sphere of factual truth itself. Truth provides the starting point for any attempt to change the world. But – and this is equally important – it should not be used as an excuse not to change the world. If I read Arendt correctly, truth in this respect *is* and *must be* contestable. If the facts themselves must be accepted, the need constantly to interrogate them must also be defended. That it is easy to confuse the two, and this is a human, all-too-human tendency, is the source of the problem.

The complementary relation of truth to a genuine politics is matched by that of truth to a genuine history. The very condition that reality is more than the facts suggests that facts only gain humanly comprehensible meaning when moulded into a story. Sorrow, and joy too, 'become bearable and meaningful for men only when they can talk about them and tell them as a story. To the extent that the teller of factual truth is also a storyteller, he brings about that "reconciliation with reality" which Hegel, the philosopher of history par excellence, understood as the ultimate goal of all philosophical thought.'[37]

The dynamic interplay of truth, history and politics establishes the unique combination of stability and change that characterizes the well-ordered and genuinely human public realm. The shifting properties of change and stability under specific historical conditions are reflected in the tension inherent in our relation to facts. We must finally 'tread the very narrow path between the danger of taking them as the results of some necessary development which men could not prevent and about which they can therefore do nothing and the danger of denying them, of trying to manipulate them out of the world.'[38] The pervasiveness of the politics of lying suggests that we are having considerable difficulty in treading this path.

III

In various ways all important manifestations of false politics exhibit the qualities of both the crisis in culture and political lying. That is, they incorporate and express the assumption of a quasi-natural social setting characterized by reason and truth, and they involve distorted forms of action which 'make sense' in the circumstances within which they are undertaken. Viewed from the perspective of false politics as a whole, the crisis in culture relates to the experiential milieu within which political institutions are constructed, while the prevalence of lying suggests the ways in which individuals, who as humans are necessarily acting and speaking beings, engage one another and their creations.

What is noteworthy about both phenomena, and by extension other forms of false politics, is that there is a genuineness to them. The entertainment which supplants culture meets a real need; lying changes the world. Arendt is not self-righteous in her criticisms. Mass culture destroys judgement, but it provides common standards of a kind which can orient people to a world that would otherwise be inscrutable and, arguably, uninhabitable. Lying destroys action, but puts into practice the hope, otherwise thwarted, that the world could be other than what it is.

This capacity to address real human purposes in a distorted and even destructive way is the hallmark of three especially powerful expressions of false politics: the modern state, ideology and political violence.

There is nowhere in Arendt's work a full-scale theory of the state.[39] But her awareness of the state as the central and incresingly pervasive bond which defines the meaning of collective experience, or citizenship, for large numbers of people shapes her reflections about the fate of action in the modern age. If mass society is the form of 'organized living together' which is established among people who have lost a common world and inhabit a social realm, then the state provides the skeleton for this new kind of body politic.

We have already seen how for Arendt modern (bourgeois) government is primarily concerned with the accumulation of wealth. Understood more comprehensively as the agent which regulates the entire range of social relations among individuals, the modern state is a bureaucratic apparatus which moulds and enforces a specific kind of human response to the social and political world: behaviour. Concomitant with the rise and triumph of *animal laborans*, behaviour is rule-governed human motion of the kind required by the demands of the cyclical labour process. It is necessity made into the content of freedom, one of the clearest indicators of the extent of world alienation. Behaviour, as a form of activity, and behaviouralism, the intellectual explanation and rationalization of this activity, both have their roots in the systematic organization and disciplining of human energies in the service of labour.

Critiques of behaviouralism in the social sciences have for the past three decades played an important role in critical and radical analyses of modern industrial societies, and in particular their attempt to demonstrate how behavioural science both legitimizes and reproduces inequality and domination.[40] While many of these analyses are pungent and lucid, they generally assume either that behaviouralism is descriptively inaccurate or, if descriptively accurate, ideological in its moral defence of the way political and social institutions function now, as opposed to how they might function if placed in the right hands and deployed for the right purposes. Arendt correctly perceives that the institutions of the administrative state both require and make possible only the kind of human response that the behavioural scientist, armed with an array of quantitative methods, is able microscopically to study and dissect.

As Arendt sees it, with the rise of the social realm, we have come to visualize political communities in the image of a giant family whose affairs require a kind of a giant housekeeping. As there is no place for action in the private household, so there is no room for it in the public household either. With its unpredictability and unmanageability, action is for our public housekeepers a threat to the smooth functioning of the administrative apparatus. As commitment to the dictates of necessity in the private sphere requires subservience to the rhythmic order of the life process, so the same commitment in the public realm requires, as Max Weber cogently demonstrated, submission to the calculable, ordered processes of the public household.[41] Deviance is 'irrational'. Thus society (and of course bureaucracy in particular) 'excludes the possibility of action, which formerly was excluded from the household. Instead, society expects from each of its members a certain kind of behaviour, imposing innumerable and various rules, all of which tend to "normalize" its members, to make them behave, to exclude spontaneous action or outstanding achievement.'[42]

To the extent that such normalizing tendencies work effectively and people 'behave', their activities can be treated causally. The laws of statistics can be applied to human behaviour because action and speech, with their inherent predictability, can be viewed as rare deviations from the norm of everyday life. Where this occurs, it is useless to look for meaning or significance in politics or history. In this causal universe conformism and automatism rule, and the statistically measurable uniformity that results is by no means benign: 'it is the no longer secret political ideal of a society which, entirely submerged in the routine of every day living, is at peace with the scientific outlook inherent in its very existence.'[43]

Under the circumstances, and here Arendt once more shows her debt to Kant, the operative philosophy of a social world in which freedom as the ability to act has been effectively banished is not rationalism but utilitarianism: Jeremy Bentham's calculus of pleasure and pain. Here the Benthamite claim that for the purposes of calculating aggregate pleasure or utility each is to count as one and no more than one takes on a frightening literalness. In the overall process of administration, each can in fact be *counted* while no one *counts*. This calculability, linked with the worldless subjectivism that results from the increasing propertylessness of the 'job holders' society, is at the heart of the basic utilitarian formula.

Given the character of the modern public realm, the utilitarian view of human nature is 'correct'. Moreover, with the growth of bureaucratized scientific innovation, backed by the state and capital, the great accumulators of power and wealth, modern society is, increasingly capable of 'acting' into nature by launching self-validating processes that create and in turn require more and more explicitly defined forms of behaviour. Such processes have the compelling urgency of the necessity in which they are rooted. While a totalitarian system clearly exhibits this tendency in its most highly developed and frightening form, all bureaucratic regimes 'tend to demonstrate that action can be based on any hypothesis and that, in the course of consistently guided action, the particular reality will become true, will become actual, factual reality.'[44]

Action that can be based on any hypothesis, and can validate this hypothesis as 'objective' truth, bears a striking resemblance to lying. The coincidence is no accident. The moral basis of political action is undermined by the absence of worldliness, of community. People without reliable cues by means of which to pose and answer questions of personal and public identity can at least find re-assurance either in the reliability of a methodical apparatus of cognition (with the collapse of tradition, for scientists this is scientific method itself; for most people, a common-sense scientism), or, as Bentham understood, the certainty of their pain. They can initiate processes by and through which they are able to interrupt everyday routines and inject themselves through deed and word into the affairs going on around them. The trouble is that the 'deeds' are the fulfilment of the necessaritarian demands of the bureaucratic apparatus; the 'words' are ideology.

IV

Behaviour and ideology share common ground for Arendt. Both possess a certain automatism; both provide reliability and predictability to everyday life. In other words, both address genuinely human purposes, even if in a distorted way. Both are forms of false politics.

In *The Origins of Totalitarianism*, Arendt defines ideologies as 'isms which to the satisfaction of their adherents can explain everything and every occurrence by deducing it from a single premise.[45] Ideologies claim the ability to control the historical process because they profess to have unravelled the mysteries of the historical past and present in a way that allows them correctly to predict and so determine the future.

It should be noted that, for Arendt, ideological thinking and historical thinking are not the same. For her, the problem of ideology is not that it is 'historical' as opposed to 'rational', some supposedly genuine mode of thinking uncontaminated by sensual, temporal experience. Rather it is the reverse: ideology is literally about logic, not content. Since logic concerns the adequacy of the relation between concept and object, thought and the world, the appeal of ideology becomes immediately evident. It serves to unify and render manageable a social universe which because of the loss of worldliness has become increasingly chaotic and incomprehensible to its inhabitants. To borrow from the Frankfurt School, ideology is identitarian: it abolishes difference in the interests of self-preservation or life.

Ideological thinking is so persuasive because of its intellectual consistency, and here lies its 'truth'. There is a quality of the human mind which demands structural consistency over mere occurrence. In a way this is the mental aspect of genuine worldliness because humans need to transform the chaotic and accidental into the patterned and explicable. In what Arendt calls a 'situation of spiritual and social homelessness', people will understandably be tempted by ideological solutions to their plight because these solutions promise at least a semblance of community.

And just as the liar is affected fundamentally by the demands of lying – in other words there is a formative process at work – those who fall prey to ideological reasoning are themselves 'formed' by it. This is particularly evident in totalitarian states, which incorporate ideological politics in its most extreme form. In discussing personal responsibility under totalitarian rule, Arendt argues that those most willing and able to stand up to the Nazi regime and its inhuman demands were not those who had well-developed and articulate value systems or who had an unshakeable commitment to norms and standards. These qualities bear the form of thought and judgement, but not necessarily the content – in short they are compatible with ideological reasoning. Rather, the sceptic able to think and judge for himself or herself is more likely to resist.[46] The difficulties in thinking and judging for oneself are, however, immense where there is no common world or stable location within it, no solidarity of people who are with, and not for or against, each other. In a sense, ideology is mass philosophy as consolation.

That a social universe shaped by ideology can create a false but 'real' home for people otherwise condemned to the abject isolation of an atomized existence is the primary lesson Arendt seeks to teach. In this respect her work links up with much of the contemporary critical discourse on ideology, a substantial body of debate and discussion about the complex ways in which thought is integrated into social processes.[47] This work has sought to move beyond the earlier critique of ideology identified either with 'official' Marxism, which emphasized false consciousness, or the sociology of knowledge, which juxtaposed 'ideology' to 'utopia'. To take one example, T. W. Adorno treats ideology as the 'exaggerated duplication and justification of already existing conditions, and the deprivation of all transcendence and critique.'[48] To take another, Claude Lefort argues that there is currently dominant in advanced industrial societies an 'invisible' ideology, a new 'logic of dissimulation' which infuses a comprehensive pattern of representations that seeks to move beyond both 'bourgeois' and 'totalitarian' ideologies and successfully obscure social divisions by unifying and homogenizing society through compromise and bargaining.[49] These accounts, and others, have been shaped by the industrialization of spirit which Arendt saw as underpinning the crisis in culture, and which reflects the quest for total control, or rationalization of social and political life – indeed, of history itself.

Thus Arendt's account of ideology and its claim to master history, in fact to make history a conscious creation, brings to the fore yet again the issue of balance among the elements of the *vita activa*. The confusion of acting and making which Arendt sees as crucial to the modern notion of history likewise attends the rise of ideological cognition. But the association of ideology and lying suggests that what is at stake is not only the *con*fusion of acting and making but the *fusion* of the two: in seeking to make history we have come to act in it in unrecognized and unpredictable ways. The dilemmas inherent in this state of affairs characterize the last phenomenon I wish to discuss: political violence.

V

In a way political violence provides yet another distinctive form of false politics. Like the crisis in culture and political lying, violence is both itself a form of false politics and an element of other forms. Both the state and ideology, for example, clearly involve the use of violence against people subject to them. Beyond these similarities with other forms of false politics, violence has two additional properties which deepen our appreciation of the complexities of false politics. One of these relates to the pattern of general reflection about violence in our culture; the other involves Arendt's own particular account of violence as it highlights the distinguishing themes of her political thought.

Violence occupies a peculiar niche in our political culture. At least since Hobbes, few have doubted that violence is a fundamental reality of political life. Fewer still have defended it. The solemn intonation of the virtues of moderation and the renunciation of the use of violence as a legitimate means of effecting political change are hallmarks of official power everywhere, while appeals to 'law and order' seem to be perennial staples of election campaigns. Violence is something hardly anyone approves of, while at the same time it is the first response many people are likely to recommend in the face of virtually every difficulty which appears to threaten the smooth and harmonious operation of the social and political system.

From Hannah Arendt's perspective, the common, rather contradictory, conception of violence is a fundamental reflection of its very nature. She believes that violence is quite capable of threatening the public realm and inflicting immense suffering. But she also believes that, properly understood and applied, it can play a useful, if limited, role in politics. However, this role is quite distinct either from the role violence actually plays in political life, or from the role common opinion normally allows it.

Violence thus differs from other forms of false politics inasmuch as it has a certain authenticity these others lack: a properly organized political realm might well have a legitimate place for it. Yet as hypocritical as it might often be, the condemnation of violence can strike such a responsive chord because for most people it indicates a failure of community, a breakdown in the structures of organized living together. In Arendt's terms it involves a threat to plurality. The key to a sensible analysis of violence is to grasp both its appeal and its limits, to see how and why people resort to it, to fathom its 'reasons'.

Violence takes on such a complex character in our political culture because is often confused with another phenomenon: power. The concept of power occupies a place in Arendt's thought almost on a par with freedom, action and the public realm; in fact as Arendt sees it, power is what keeps the public realm together.[50] I have raised the issue of power here, rather than earlier on, for two reasons. In the first place, 'power', like 'violence', is widely but misleadingly used, the degree of misunderstanding varying directly with the extent of its use. In the second place, what Arendt sees as its genuine character is most sharply evident when it is contrasted with violence. However much they might be confused, the gulf between them is immense. To put it another way: political violence provides a powerful summation of the main qualities of false politics because power is so often, and so wrongly, seen as the fundamental element of actually existing political forms. Getting clear about violence helps us understand genuine power and thus appreciate the limits to our existing public life.

From Arendt's point of view, at the heart of the confusion of power and violence is the assumption that power is a commodity, that it can be owned and measured. Violence, which relies upon strength or instruments if it is to be carried out, can be treated as a property capable of being possessed. But genuine power cannot be so possessed. It is a quality of individuals acting and speaking together. It can only exist collectively. Its proper home is the political realm, but one that must have the character of the polis:

> Only where men live so close together that the potentialities of action are always present can power remain with them, and the foundation of cities, which as city-states have remained paradigmatic for all Western political organization, is therefore indeed the most important material prerequisite for power. What keeps people together after the fleeting moment of action has passed . . . and what, at the same time, they keep alive through remaining together is power.[51]

Because of its character as a potential inherent in the existence of a plural world, because it 'springs up between men when they act together and vanishes the moment they disperse' and thus 'can only be actualized but never fully materialized', power possesses an elusive quality which can never be completely reified. For this reason people are tempted to substitute force or violence, which relies upon measurable and possessable implements, for power.[52] In a world in which the commodity form, the labour process, the supplanting of action by labour and work, have triumphed this temptation is very strong. Yet force can only destroy power, it can never replace it. In a nutshell this is the problem with modern political violence.

The assumption that violence and power are the same is widely held, even among many on the political left who call for a radical democratization of existing states and societies. Thus it is not surprising that Arendt's conception has not been clearly understood or has been dismissed as incoherent. Yet with so many traditional notions of politics now in question, this might be changing. To take one example: in a well-known article in 1977, Jürgen Habermas criticized Arendt's notion of power for ignoring the strategic dimension of power, that is, the element of force that it must acknowledge if it is to be effective. On the whole he shared in this essay Arendt's favourable view of power, even though he had a somewhat different conception of it. Yet in his more recent work, Habermas has identified power as a 'steering medium' which, along with money, anchors the political and economic systems as these increasingly threaten the communicatively structured lifeworld.[53] His assessment of power seems to have changed but his concept of it has not. Yet in reality he has moved closer to Arendt on this point, not further away. What he appears all along to have understood as power is precisely what Arendt calls force or violence. What he now defends as a freely negotiated, normatively meaningful way of life outside the reifying structures of state and economy is in fact much closer to what Arendt calls power. As dissatisfaction with prevailing forms of state and economy increases, Arendt's notion of power may offer an insightful new way of looking at alternative modes of political organization.

But whatever the future might hold, violence, whether called 'power' or not, continues to obsess us and now plays what Arendt considers a destructive role in political life. Its stature as a form of false politics remains undiminished.

As we have seen, Arendt originally viewed violence as historically an element of the private sphere, a means of dealing with the demands of necessity. Because it involved the objectification of people and things, it allowed for no reciprocity and hence was inherently anti-political.

Although the logic of Arendt's position was evident enough – she sought to establish the distinction between freedom and necessity – her rather sweeping and unnuanced analysis exposed her to Mary O'Brien's charge that she was oblivious to the political dimension of violence. But Arendt did not rest with the account of violence she provided in *The Human Condition*. In response to the political upheavals of the 1960s, which saw widespread revolt against state institutions and political practices, she sought explicitly to examine the role of violence in public affairs. And while she continued to hold that at its core violence was unpolitical, she also made clear that given the character of the contemporary public realm, its appearance might not be unexpected – nor even always and in every case would it be immoral or indefensible. The backbone of her argument is her distinction between power and violence and her critical assumption that, where genuine power is absent, violence may emerge to fill the gap. Ultimately her argument raises the issue of the relation of power to the modern state. For Arendt it is no accident that the contemporary significance of political violence is closely linked to ongoing problems of political legitimacy.

It is vital here to recognize what for Arendt may be the most perniciously anti-political assumption of modern political thought and practice: that the fundamental quality of the political relationship is obedience, and the key political question is 'who rules whom?' Children may be required to obey until they are able to act for themselves. But when adults in the political arena are said to obey, they are in fact giving support. If this support is unwilling, this is evidence of coercion, but still does not constitute obedience, which is based upon a temporary differential in the capacity for rational autonomy. In effect Arendt makes a radical claim: the true citizen does not obey. She may acknowledge the right of others to decide public matters in accordance with the rules of accepted institutional arrangements. But this is a matter not of obedience, but of authority, itself the product of agreement about the nature of a common world and what is required to maintain it. That obedience and authority have come to be so widely confused itself further testifies to the decline of worldliness and a concomitant crisis of authority in contemporary political life.[54]

The importance of violence, then, is that it clearly puts into focus what is required in order to establish the viability of a politics which does not equate power with rule or command. However, Arendt is aware that it is easy to equate power with both of these and with violence because for most people politics is the same as government – which, to borrow from Max Weber's famous definition – has the legitimate monopoly on the use of force as a last resort in support of the existing structure of formal political power. Yet while power is the essence of all government, violence is not. Even those governments which rely overwhelmingly upon force to sustain social cohesion cannot fall back on it alone: even a totalitarian government requires not only implements of violence but networks of informers and secret police officers who form a kind of community, a power base.

Nevertheless, totalitarian governments are only the most extreme example of a more widespread phenomenon, namely the increasing tendency for states to substitute violence for power as if they were the same. The consequence has been a developing crisis of political legitimacy almost everywhere. This is because, in Arendt's eyes, only power but never violence can create legitimate authority; power requires no justification but demands and produces legitimacy, while violence may be justifiable but never legitimate. Thus power and violence are opposites: 'where the one rules absolutely, the other is absent. Violence appears where power is in jeopardy, but left to its own course it ends in power's disappearance . . . Violence can destroy power; it is utterly incapable of creating it.'[55]

For Arendt the obsession of both governments and citizens with violence goes hand in hand with the growth of structures of command and obedience, and the entrenchment of relations of hierarchy and rulership as the essential qualities of the modern state. In other words, violence and administration are yoked together. And because the administrative state has both emerged in tandem with, and helped make possible, the growth of modern science, violence has taken its contemporary form in a social universe increasingly shaped by scientific possibilities, and the natural and human energies thus unleashed.

The connections linking the state, science and violence lead Arendt to the discomforting conclusion that in a sense contemporary violence is 'rational' – rational because practised by a supposedly rational state using methods perfected by that most rational of modern institutions, science.

By its very nature violence is uniquely suited to scientific rationalization. As distinct from power, force or strength, violence requires implements if it is to be effective. Indeed the utilization of implements may be at the heart of violence itself. Arendt notes that violence is ruled by categories of means and ends much more appropriate to fabrication, with its implication of the thorough and sudden transformation of the material worked on, than to action. This being the case, violence is more fully and explicitly determined by changing historical circumstances than are other elements in the realm of human affairs.

The context within which the contemporary concern with violence has emerged has thus been shaped by the rapid scientific developments of the twentieth century and the challenge these have posed to theories of inevitable progress. Any consideration of the role and purposes of violence must take into account the seemingly incontestable fact that the means of violence have become so potentially destructive that no political purpose could plausibly justify their use. 'Hence warfare – from time immemorial the merciless arbiter in international disputes – has lost much of its effectiveness and nearly all of its glamor.'[56]

Hence the problem of violence is linked with a larger problem, the relation of moral to scientific progress. In an argument that links her with a tradition of critical analysis stretching back at least to Rousseau, Arendt claims that we can no longer assume that the two forms of progress are directly connected; indeed the term 'progress' itself no longer gives us a meaningful standard by which to assess social change. In these circumstances the appeal of violence, and its confusion with power, become understandable. To many people, it may seem that in the modern administrative state only violence can interrupt what would otherwise be automatic processes. In other words, violence can be a substitute for genuine action.

As a substitute for genuine action, violence can be especially appealing to precisely those groups who are striving to open up or reconstitute a public realm which would facilitate genuine action and thus be a home for freedom. As examples here, Arendt uses the student movements of the 1960s which transformed politics both East and West. But more recent oppositional forces, such as Polish Solidarity and the Western European peace movement (whose emergence

Arendt would have lauded), make the point just as well. On occasion such movements resorted to violence to further their political aims. Arendt is more sympathetic to this violence because unlike official violence, it strives to remove barriers to free action. However in the end even this more defensible form of violence is self-defeating. For what those seeking a transformed political reality actually desire is of course power, the realization through collective action of a common, rationally determined purpose.[57]

At the core of this sympathetic criticism of those practising civil disobedience is an extraordinary claim, not fully acknowledged by Arendt herself. In effect, while violence can be a form of action – it interrupts processes that would otherwise proceed automatically – power is not. By keeping the public realm together, power makes action possible. But it cannot itself be a form of action without in the process undermining its own preconditions and the public realm which it needs as much as this realm needs it. The attempt to convert power into action, which comes about when it is confounded with violence, is in fact the hallmark of sovereignty. For sovereignty seeks to embody or represent the principle of unity, which binds a body politic together and can truly exist only in the intersubjective activities of the members of this body, in a single locus of authority. As we have seen, for Arendt sovereignty effectively destroys a public realm, it does not create or sustain it. To be truly powerful is to be non-sovereign: the failure to recognize this is in a sense what false politics, whatever form it takes, is all about.

In light of this distinction, the motive for what might be called defensible political violence becomes even more compelling, if no less self-defeating. Where there is no genuine public space and thus no possibility for action, who can worry about power, even if without it violent action cannot achieve its purposes? This dilemma is made all the more poignant by another way in which violence relates to human experience, and here Arendt's powerful if largely hidden ontology is brought out with unusual clarity. As she puts it, under certain circumstances violence ('acting without argument or speech and without counting the consequences') is the only way to achieve justice. Such violence and the rage which may accompany it are in these cases human and natural, and we would not be fully human if we were to live without them.[58]

However, the tendency in our culture is to cover this over. At the heart of this tendency is the separation, in both theory and practice, of emotion from reason, a separation which mass culture in particular strongly reinforces. To Arendt nothing is so destructive of a meaningful analysis of violence than this dualism.

Arendt begins by setting out the problem of rage as an explanation for violence. She challenges the view that rage is only and in every case irrational. In fact rage is not even necessarily aroused by misery or suffering as such. Only where our sense of justice is offended, where we suspect things could be other than what they are and we can change them, is the kind of defensible rage Arendt has in mind likely to emerge.

What is most notable about Arendt's argument is that while rage and violence can and do occur together, they need not. Nor, if they do, is the violence that ensues necessarily irrational. In other words it is not the presence or absence of rage, but the purpose and context of violent acts, that determine their rationality. Arendt suggests that it may be rational to react violently to the use of appearances to deceive and words to conceal. Violence only becomes irrational when it is in fact *rationalized*, 'that is the moment the re-action [in response to injustice] in the course of a contest turns into an action, and the hunt for suspects, accompanied by the psychological hunt for ulterior motives, begins.'[59] Measured and studied, such violence finds a niche in the arsenal of techniques for the manipulation of people as objects that has always been the essence of modern, bourgeois politics.

The irrationality of rationalized violence in turn illuminates the split between emotion and reason in modern life. Arendt sharply criticizes the most commonly formulated expression of this dualism: the view that rationality and emotion are fundamentally at odds.

Absence of emotion neither causes nor promotes rationality. 'Detachment and equanimity' in view of 'unbearable tragedy' can indeed be 'terrifying', namely, when they are not the result of control but of an evident manifestation of incomprehension. In order to respond reasonably one must first of all be 'moved' and the opposite of emotional is not 'rational', whatever that may mean, but either the inability to be moved, usually a pathological phenomenon, or sentimentality, which is a perversion of feeling.[60]

This is a powerful and important observation. It provides a phenomenological basis for Max Weber's fear that industrial society was fated to come under the reign of 'sensualists without spirit and voluptuaries without heart'. It indicates the ghostly quality of that form of experience once removed which provides the stuff of human behaviour in advanced industrial society. And it makes clear why contemporary forms of violence that are in fact products of the organization of society are read back into human nature: violence suggests a hidden rationality, the instrumental rationality of social control.

In view of the complex character of modern political violence, and especially the possibility of its justification, Arendt concedes that, given the character of society and the state, violence can have a political use. (And one can think of the opposition to the South African state, which in an exaggerated form manifests the worst qualities of all states, in light of this consideration.) It can sometimes allow those seeking change to 'ask the impossible in order to obtain the possible.' In other words, to the extent that violence expresses a humanly necessary, but socially denied, connection between emotion and reason, it can have a defensible if limited place in politics.

Yet in the end, violence can only promote certain limited goals, ones which may be essential for human life in a given social order, but which are not synonymous with establishing a genuine public realm. In other words, violence is at best a weapon of political reform. This suggests that the limitations on the role violence can play in public affairs are built right into its very structure. As an adjunct of the life process, violence serves the needs of life, not the world. Violence aims at change, and this is why it can be a form of action, but not fundamental change, change rooted in the recognition of what must be done to bring social institutions in line with the claims of genuinely human purposes. In the absence of the demand for a new order of things, violence affirms the institutions and practices of the existing society, even if it may threaten certain elements of it. This is true not only in the sense that violence is the logical product of a society whose overwhelmingly dominant passion is the fear of violent death, but also in the sense that, given its reliance on implements, violence is 'dumb'. It neither presupposes nor makes possible inter-subjective agreement, discussion and persuasion.

Thus violence will be counter-productive if, when confronted by it, the established authorities meet it with relatively trivial reforms. If under such circumstances violence is the only basis for demands for change, and the only mode through which change is sought, the failure to achieve change will leave only violence itself; the world will become in turn more violent but no more political. By its nature violence is not immoral. But even given its reformist uses, it is indeed likely to be anti-political.

However, recall that Arendt in effect makes a distinction between popular and official violence. She is a partisan of neither, but while the popular violence of those seeking change can at least under certain circumstances point toward something authentically new in the realm of human affairs, official violence has a different focus and function. More precisely the ability of the modern state to maintain support for its institutions, that is, legitimacy, depends not upon force of arms, but agreement among its citizens. In opposition to contemporary conservative arguments, Arendt suggests that if we are confronted with an increasing impotence of power, political violence is not the culprit. It is the collapse of stable political structures, the withering of spaces of appearance, that breeds violence, not the other way round. In these circumstances the increasingly overcentralized, unaccountable and unresponsive bureaucratic state will be tempted to use violence to stabilize itself 'because those who hold power and feel it slipping from their hands . . . have always found it difficult to resist the temptation to substitute violence for it.'[61]

This sober assessment indicates that violence crystallizes in particularly sharp fashion the tensions and ambiguities of false politics. As a form of distorted action it provides outlets for a human capacity otherwise denied expression. And it reveals clearly the need for new modes of political thinking: the contradictory and potentially misleading character of terms such as 'power', 'force', 'sovereignty', 'government', even 'violence' itself, suggests that in contemporary political life we frequently do not, and cannot, mean what we say or say what we mean.

Yet whatever the 'truth' of violence in the existing state of affairs, its radical distance from a public life grounded in solidarity, from that at which action aims, means that it can be readily turned into a bulwark against a genuine politics and a prop for a repressive state – a prop that can even be used in the very name of freedom, or democracy, or civilization. It can, in other words, be used to support an inverted public sphere, and the more completely it is so deployed, the more fully perfected will be this inverted world. As we will see, the paradigm of the inverted public sphere is totalitarianism.

In this chapter I have sought to show that where outlets for genuine political action are absent, false politics, vehicles for distorted expressions of the capacity to act, will emerge. The forms of false politics that Arendt discusses have a real appeal for people. Thus entertainment and mass culture are essential for social and individual life; lying may well be in the service of the quest for a stable 'home'; ideology makes sense of the senseless; the state is a functioning political organization, for its subjects eminently preferable to the alternative of statelessness, total isolation from an identifiable community.

Yet the ultimately unsatisfactory character of these modes of public life means that there is always the possibility that people will rebel against what could become intolerable conditions. This rebellion need not lead to the establishment of a new public sphere, a genuine space of appearance. It could in fact lead to a more ruthless assault upon those human qualities which require a public sphere if they are to be expressed and developed at all, to the point at which the denial of these qualities, still evident in the forms of false politics discussed here, might not even be recognized as such. It could lead to totalitarianism.

4 Totalitarianism

The most decisive historical development in Hannah Arendt's life, and the most profound influence on her political thought, was – and how could it have been otherwise? – the triumph of National Socialism in Germany. As a Jew, Arendt had to come to terms with the existence of a regime which set as a main purpose the destruction of her people and grimly succeeded in destroying a large part of it. Only one of those fortunate and terrible accidents of fate which respected no specific living person spared Arendt from her own destruction at the hands of the Nazis. As a thinker, she had to come to terms with a reality which exploded all the received philosophical categories she and so many others had taken for granted, categories which had seemed an indelible part of the very society and culture which produced Adolf Hitler and the Nazi movement.

A society in which the claims of reason had defined the intellectual culture more completely than anywhere else succumbed to Nazism and its horrors. Did this make rational reflection itself impossible, a murderously bad joke, poetry in the shadow of Auschwitz? For Arendt the task was clear. Whatever its contribution to the general horror, reason, or mind, or thought was indispensable. However plausible or tempting, the view either that totalitarianism was beyond rational explanation, or that reason itself was a chimera, had to be rejected. In her quest to understand this radically novel political form, Arendt remained steadfastly committed to reason and its demands.

These demands led in some interesting directions. While totalitarianism itself was radically new, its origins were rooted in commonly accepted motives, purposes and practices. The ways in which the familiar crystallized into the novel is an important theme in Arendt's treatment of totalitarian domination. For example, both the suggestion that proto-totalitarian features characterized all states and the startling claim that totalitarian leaders like Hitler and Stalin were in the last analysis relatively insignificant, historical non-persons little deserving of the attention lavished upon them, reflect this fundamental dimension of Arendt's account.[1]

But Arendt's main claim is that this novel form of government in a perverse and profound way meets human needs. Totalitarianism is, after all, the product of human beings, only some of whom could be considered 'abnormal'. If reason can help grasp the nature of totalitarianism, this means that the phenomenon itself somehow shares in this reason. In Hegelian terms, it is in a manner of speaking 'justified'. In spite of her deep reservations about philosophy, Arendt held fast to this fundamental assumption of the German philosophical tradition: that there is a necessary relation of mind to the world that is both the basis and the outcome of thought as a consequential human pursuit, that nothing is merely 'accidental'.[2]

However, to justify in this way is not passively to accept. Reason does not simply register in a coherent and logical fashion the reality of an existing state of affairs; it is not simply a matter of logic. Reason judges the world in terms of its range of possibilities for a more fully adequate human life.

This normative dimension of reason, frequently unacknowledged or unrecognized by her critics, suffuses Arendt's account of totalitarianism. Although she herself tended to downplay or even deny it,[3] her treatment of total domination is the most explicitly and powerfully ontological of her writings. It is the most thoroughly concerned with the human essence and its status under specific historical conditions.

Totalitarianism as radical and mundane at the same time; totalitarianism as a novel species of government which exhibits the form if not the content of rational political relations – this new arrival on the historical stage is the ultimate form of false politics. Neither demonological attack nor fatalistic acceptance grants access to its inner structure or its experiential meaning.

And the lure of both these approaches is very powerful. Although the concept had been in general circulation at least since the Second World War, the 'new' Cold War of the 1980s saw a marked revival of interest in it, largely as a rationale for the military build-up in the West against the 'threat' of the 'totalitarian' Soviet Union. With the evident end of this Soviet 'threat', the concept may well pass out of view once again. From Arendt's perspective this would be a serious error. This is not because she was an inveterate cold warrior – *The Origins of Totalitarianism* is not a Cold War tract – but because for her the concept had relevance beyond its use in analysing Hitler's Germany or Stalin's Soviet Union. The 'origins' of totalitarianism were found in many states, not simply these two. More importantly 'totalitarianism' was designed to account for a new arrival on the world stage which, once here, might recur in many different, and even surprising, contexts. Its use as an ideological weapon in struggles for power on the world stage ironically undermines its moral significance even though it has been invoked precisely for 'moral', that is condemnatory, purposes.

It is highly ironic that what Arendt intended as a contribution to a much needed new way of thinking about politics should instead have come to be used widely in support of a conventional theory and practice of power politics (that is, the politics of force and violence) which totalitarianism not only has required us to reconsider but whose practice in a post-totalitarian world carries immense dangers for everyone. Even after the smoke has cleared in the wake of Hitlerism and Stalinism, we are perhaps even less able to see our way clear politically than before: the fate of 'totalitarianism' suggests the depth of our need to develop a new understanding of genuine political thinking, a way to get out from under the debilitating effects of false politics.

With these concerns serving as a context, in this chapter I first explore Arendt's account of totalitarianism, and offer a brief assessment of it. I then examine contemporary attempts to deal with the phenomenon by three thinkers strongly influenced by Arendt's political thought: Claude Lefort, Cornelius Castoriadis and Agnes Heller. I seek to show that their accounts are seriously flawed, largely because they fail to appreciate the novelty of Arendt's position, that is, they fail to recognize sufficiently her attempt to recast what it means both to think and act politically. Finally I discuss Arendt's most controversial work, *Eichmann in Jerusalem*. This work, the sequel to *The Origins of Totalitarianism*, sharpens and deepens the argument of the larger study by detailing the context of everyday experience within which totalitarianism could appear 'normal'. Included in this context are what we still consider desirable political and moral standards, and Arendt's account of these forms the real and surprising core of the book. That this has been overshadowed by the controversy over her interpretation of the role of Eastern European Jewish political, social and cultural organizations in the Holocaust reflects the unwillingness or inability of many both to recognize the distinctive character of Arendt's position and to undertake the difficult task of rethinking what it means to think and act politically.

I

The Origins of Totalitarianism is a remarkable work. It is an astonishing attempt to crystallize into its essential elements 200 years of Western European history which culminated in the planned destruction of an entire people. Its purpose is to demonstrate that, as radically new as it is, totalitarianism has roots in historical forces which by a century or more pre-existed the rise of Hitler and Stalin.

Scholars and thinkers other than Arendt have obviously noted such forces. Arendt imaginatively weaves seemingly disparate phenomena – the 'problem' of the Jew in the early days of modern society; the peculiar career of Benjamin Disraeli; the Dreyfus affair in France; the economic basis of imperialism; the development of racist ideology – into a striking account of a political movement which pursued the twin aims of global rule and the total domination of the individual. It is a genuinely tragic tale of a world that has lost its bearings. As Margaret Canovan notes, Arendt's book 'is worth reading because it is a very considerable work of art.'[4]

Not surprisingly, a work of this sort has generated significant differences of opinion about its ultimate nature and worth. Because of its narrative approach and its reliance upon historical evidence to support its case, Arendt's account has often been treated as straightforward political history or political sociology and assessed, often unfavourably, in these terms. Agnes Heller, for one, states flatly that 'Arendt's approach to totalitarianism is strictly historicist.'[5] Even those who detect a theoretical purpose not reducible exclusively to the elements of the historical account are inclined to make the historical dimension primary and to equate perceived historiographic deficiencies with theoretical inadequacies. Thus Arendt has been reproached for failing to get at the essential character of Nazi Germany or Soviet Russia as new types of state forms, for lacking a coherent account of how its supposedly distinctive character can emerge and why it emerged in some states but not elsewhere, and even for stating or implying that it is *sui generis* and cannot really have understandable 'origins' at all![6]

To be sure Arendt's use of history seems at times selective, if not arbitrary. And there are occasional lurches in the argument, jumps in reasoning and logic, that are not easy to follow. But it would be a serious mistake to judge the work on these grounds alone. It is sometimes claimed, particularly be those intrigued by Arendt's interweaving of historical evidence with literary analysis (most notably in her treatment of Joseph Conrad's *Heart of Darkness* as a signal account of early twentieth-century Europe's imperialist mentality), that, for good or ill, *The Origins of Totalitarianism* is highly suggestive or allusive rather than analytically precise. In my view this quality is not merely accidental, it is integral to Arendt's approach. Neither historicist nor rationalist, neither empiricist nor essentialist, *The Origins of Totalitarism* is not only an attempt to think and write about a radically new and unprecedented phenomenon. Although not explicitly metatheoretical, it is also an attempt to think in a new way about the political by focusing on a phenomenon which neither the conventional historical record, however extensive, nor conventional rationalist political concepts, however precise or radical (for example, 'class'), can ever fully illuminate.

The Origins of Totalitarianism is best read as an ontologically informed account of a distinctive and frightening political reality which threatens in a powerful and unprecedented way our human status as political beings. This account uses historical evidence in a manner which strives to respect the balance between, on the one hand, taking historical facts as 'the results of some necessary development about which [people] can therefore do nothing', and on the other, 'trying to manipulate them out of the world'. The concepts used to understand totalitarianism are drawn from Arendt's own unique arsenal and relate to her perspective on the political nature of genuine human capacities. Thus, although she deploys notions commonly used to analyse the phenomenon, such as 'state', 'power', 'violence', 'class', even 'capitalism', and although she relates it, as do others, to racism, imperialism and bureaucracy, Arendt in the final analysis seeks to account for totalitarianism in terms of worldlessness. Totalitarianism is rooted in and reinforces two critical developments: the attack on plurality and the increasing pervasiveness of atomism and loneliness. In Arendt's view, this radically new political form builds upon a human sense of desperation whose character has not been sufficiently understood.

Underlying the attack on plurality and the consequent destruction of a body politic with at least some measure of solidarity was the decay and decline of the modern nation-state, the severing of people from the worldly ties that characterized the nation-state as a distinctive political form. This decay was the product of what Arendt calls 'the political emancipation of the bourgeoisie': the achievement of political as well as economic power by the bourgeois classes of European states.[7] While historically indifferent to formal public life, the bourgeoisie in late nineteenth-century Europe was compelled by a deep-seated crisis in the process of capital accumulation to assume a more active political role. This class turned to the state to help it out of its economic difficulties, and in particular sought to use state power as a vehicle for expanding capitalist market relations beyond the now limiting confines of national political and economic boundaries. The most powerful expression of this was modern imperialism – one cornerstone of totalitarianism.

While her position here is broadly Marxist, and in particular is indebted to the ideas of Rosa Luxemburg, Arendt takes the account in a fundamentally different direction from that taken by Marxist orthodoxy. The concentration and centralization of political and economic power that resulted from this development was seen by Marxists as progressive and necessary because these would pave the way for the transition to socialism by establishing the economic foundations of a new community, a new solidarity. In Arendt's view the outcome was exactly the opposite. Imperialism provided a proving ground for the perfection of forms of social control that were ultimately to penetrate and wither the political realm of the imperial state itself – and thus undermine any possibility of a new community. The emergence of the bourgeoisie as a political ruling class ushered in a distinctive type of politics. This politics turned on a fundamental political principle: unlimited accumulation of power for its own sake.

The accumulation of power and the accumulation of capital are but different sides of the same coin, namely, the expansionist dream of a capitalist market society. From its vantage point as the economically and now politically dominant class, the bourgeoisie screened all phenomena through the requirements of the creation of wealth. It came to see clearly the utility of political power as a prod to further wealth creation once the limits of a strictly national capitalism had been reached. When the national interests of European states came to be identified more and more exclusively with the economic interests of a small group, the deployment of power in the direct service of capital was inevitable. Expanding abroad to protect the property of owners of superfluous capital seeking a profitable outlet for it, the nation-state through its instruments of violence – the police and the army – could actively create and apply the 'laws' of capital accumulation.

In applying these 'laws', the expanding state apparatus developed new and lethal techniques of rule that ultimately distinguished imperialism from other historical forms of domination, such as colonization and ancient and medieval empire-building. These new techniques and their supportive institutions bound together the dominator and the dominated in the context of certain ideological and institutional peculiarities of the nation-state that, according to Arendt, immensely complicated the process of imperialist expansion.

The most significant and lasting institutional development to come out of the era of imperialism was the creation in imperial states, and in particular Britain and France, Arendt's primary models, of separate colonial administrations, and the consequent distinction between 'domestic' and 'foreign' policy. As Arendt sees it, the basis for this separation lay in the fact that without a fundamental transformation, the nation-state is unsuited to a politics of unlimited expansion. This is because the nation-state is founded on the consent of its members (a consent broadened in the nineteenth and twentieth centuries by increased democratization). Consent cannot be stretched beyond certain limits without destroying the *national* character of the state, and it cannot be readily won from conquered peoples without deception or force. Moreover, the claims of the nation-state to uniqueness, of its people and its laws, flies in the face of the demands of imperialist rule, which must be predicated on the subordination of the 'inferior' culture and society of the conquered to the 'superior' purposes and institutions of the imperial power.

The result was an inner or secret government within the more public and ostensibly accountable one. Relying increasingly upon government by decree and operating independently of any institutionalized popular consensus, colonial administrators developed new mechanisms of power and policy formation based upon the extension of bureaucratic relations and technical or administrative rationality. As I argued in chapter 3 administrative rationality involves treating people as abstract, 'behaving' mechanisms to be managed rather than as willing co-participants in a public realm. This could be carried out with particular ease and ferocity in colonial affairs because subject peoples were viewed as mysterious, 'alien', not fully human inhabitants of the 'heart of darkness'.[8]

To be sure these developments did not go totally unchallenged. Arendt notes that there was in the imperial state political conflict between those committed to the values of justice and liberty supposedly enshrined at home, who believed their colonies should be governed by these values, and those charged with the management of colonial affairs, who ruthlessly implemented imperial decrees. In the course of this conflict, 'the colonial services never ceased to protest against the interference of the "inexperienced majority" – the nation – that tried to press the "experienced minority" – the imperialist administrators – "in the direction of imitation", namely, of government in accordance with the general standards of justice and liberty at home.'[9]

In the face of political opposition (which Arendt suggests was anchored in the late nineteenth century by a politically conscious working class at the peak of its influence), as well as the evident 'success' of colonial policies in fostering the expansion in the service of capitalism, it was a short step to the conversion of domestic politics into a species of imperial politics, in effect the pursuit of internal colonization. If the 'people' could not understand the harsh realities of the world, for their own good they had to be controlled by the 'experienced minority'. The ethos of the colonial office, particularly its celebration of apolitical administrative decisions as the substance of political rule, was increasingly to shape domestic affairs as well.[10]

The transformation of domestic politics into an extension of the colonial office was in turn facilitated by the effects of capitalist expansion on the home front. The same problem that produced the need for expansion abroad – the presence of excess capital without profitable outlets for investment – drastically altered the domestic social structure of the imperial state. The human expression of the crisis in capital accumulation was the marginalization of increasingly large numbers of people deprived of a livelihood within the existing economic order. This was because 'the tremendously increased wealth produced by capitalist production' was created 'under a social system based on maldistribution'.[11] The other side of surplus capital was surplus people who no longer had a stable place in society and who thus lost 'all natural connections with their fellow men'.[12] These people formed a new and frightening social force in capitalist society: the mob.

What for Arendt made the mob such an ominous presence in a now decaying bourgeois social structure was that far from providing a source of opposition to the politics of accumulation responsible for its plight, the mob became an ally of capital; there developed a connection between organized economic power and the socially marginalized. This connection was of critical importance to the imperial state because it could provide some measure of social cohesion in the face of the consequences of the maldistribution of property, which threatened to overwhelm society as the gulf between the wealthy and the dispossessed broadened.

In these circumstances the mob, which was composed of the refuse of all classes, was not merely a body of people which stood outside, while remaining related to, the realm of social reproduction as did the owners of superfluous capital. It also expressed an existential stance toward questions of human association. In increasingly class-divided societies, the mob served as a perverted expression of a community no longer possible under conditions of continuous accumulation. Precisely because it consisted of the refuse of all classes, it could plausibly appear that 'the mob and its representatives had abolished class differences, that those standing outside the class-divided nation were the people itself (the *Volkgemeinschaft*, as the Nazis would call it) rather than its distortion and caricature'.[13] Imperialism, which linked surplus money with surplus individuals, seemed to be the antidote to the divisive effects of social conflict: in the colonies people could see themselves as English or German, whatever their social positions at home. A common imperial interest could substitute for the lack of real national cohesion. If the development of capitalism was destroying the fabric of the nation-state, imperialism could prop up its failing institutions, although, for Arendt, this particular cure was to prove as fatal as the disease it was designed to combat.

II

The triumph of the mob as a political force and imperialism as a political project spelled the end of the nation-state as a stable and rational political form because the vehicles of citizenship which were central to its historical development were to all intents and purposes destroyed. Or to put it another way: the connecting links, the 'mediations' by which people developed political identities and could inhabit some location in the world relative to others were seriously eroded, if not swept away. In the bourgeois nation-state, the political answer to the question 'what is a human being?' was: a citizen who possessed inalienable rights. Capitalist expansion and the accompanying social marginalization thoroughly undermined the possibility of citizenship in this sense by destroying the worldly basis of political community. Increasingly, larger and larger numbers of people could no longer rely on a stable and determinate framework within which to pursue rationally their interests and purposes. Social class itself as a stable location in the world with its own communitarian ties, and the traditional political party, shaped by organized class-based interests which possessed rational content, were in Arendt's view among those institutions which in the new order of things came to lose much of their worldly significance, even as they continued nominally to exist.

This collapse of mediating institutions and the consequent undermining of stable, politically guaranteed identities took place in complex relation with two other developments which helped define the visible character of the post-imperial state, even as the worldly character of this state was being sapped. One of these developments saw the decline of the commitment to what Arendt calls the 'rights of man': universal values rooted in the assumption of a general human solidarity which transcended the evident differences among particular groups and individuals. For Arendt, the disintegration of the nation-state and the collapse of human rights as an effective political standard went together, because only the nation-state had been able to provide the institutions of citizenship, conditions of membership in an organized political community, through which human rights could be actualized. In other words, 'universal' standards require embodiment in particular, identifiable social and political practices if they are to have any genuine content. Where there are no political structures and relations which help define the limits of human activity in society the connection between political life and the normative demands of standards such as the 'rights of man', or 'justice' or 'freedom' is lost.[14] When one becomes simply a 'human being' without such ties, he ends up 'representing nothing but his own absolutely unique individuality which, deprived of expression within and action upon a common world, loses all significance . . . It seems that a man who is nothing but a man has lost the very qualities which make it possible for other people to treat him as a fellow-man.'[15]

The second development was the attempt by the nation-state itself to establish social equality. For Arendt this is not necessarily regrettable; she understands it as a plausible implication of the claims of modern, post-Enlightenment citizenship. And she also knows that it did not entail economic equality; the maldistribution inherent in a capitalist economy took care of that. But the pursuit of equality was not chimerical; it had real consequences. However, because it went hand in hand with the undermining of mediating institutions and a common world, it took on some peculiar characteristics. In Arendt's eyes, equality can only work when it is a principle of political organization in which otherwise unequal people have equal rights. But this can only be accomplished if concrete differences themselves are organized into the political realm; in a manner of speaking their very organization equalizes them (there are clearly echos of Arendt's notion of the 'who' in this). However, where this cannot occur, the achievement of equality can only result in an attack on difference itself. In these circumstances the 'more equal conditions are, the less explanation there is for the differences that actually exist between people; and thus all the more unequal do people become.'[16] People are distinguished not according to the standards of an equality within difference but rather according to an ominous new criterion: whether they are 'normal' or 'abnormal'.

At this point Arendt's ontological assumptions come once more into play. If people cannot be bound together in worldly ways, they will be bound together in an unworldly fashion; some kind of ersatz community will emerge, one organized on some alternative principle

to that of the nation-state. For Arendt the new principle of organization in the face of the collapse of the nation-state and the developments associated with this was racism.

As the political status of human beings, and hence their social
identities, was being increasingly threatened where not destroyed
outright, there ironically developed an almost lurid fascination with
human nature. The success of the natural sciences and the newly
developing social sciences in unravelling nature's secrets triggered a
profusion of doctrines which sought simultaneously to define 'scientifically' the truly human and to provide an understandable account
of the dynamics of a society that to its members was becoming
increasingly difficult to understand. A bizarre combination of rationality and mysticism, enlightenment and myth, emerged both in official
intellectual quarters and in the culture at large. Hand in hand with
the triumph of science went a fascination with the mysterious and
the occult. Many sought feverishly the hidden 'key' that would unlock
the secrets of a history whose human hand had become virtually
invisible. Without worldly ties and a meaningful public life, people
lacked a stable basis for judging things. Political events and developments could be explained with reference to almost any imaginable
cause or explanation as long as these made 'sense'.

For Arendt the most significant product of the coalescence of the
rational and the irrational, the scientific and the mystical, the 'logical'
account of events in terms of historical and social trends, and the
revelation of a hidden hand orchestrating all that happened, was
racism. The most visible form of racism was anti-semitism.

While anti-semitism itself was hardly new, the form of it which
emerged in the imperialist period was novel. This was 'social' as
opposed to 'political' anti-semitism, and it took root alongside the
more general development of race-thinking among large masses of
people. Race-thinking made supposedly ineradicable physiological
and psychological properties of groups of individuals the grounds
upon which their human status and social and political positions were
established. The changing and ambiguous position of the Jew in the
nineteenth century European nation-state reflected the working out
of these developments. What was ultimately to emerge was a new
kind of community established according to the principle of racial
exclusion, with the Jew as the threatening outsider in defence against
whom the people had to band together.

The 'new' anti-semitism was a consequence of the emergence of the
social in Arendt's sense of the fusion of the public and private realms.
It is, in other words, a product of a labouring or consumers' society
and thus indelibly linked to an expanding capitalism. In a sense the

full and ominous meaning of the triumph of the social over the political became clear for Arendt in the changing character of anti-semitism: there is a line connecting the rise of society to the establishment of the Nazi death camps.

A clear indication of the emergence of social anti-semitism was the tendency, among both Jews and non-Jews, to distinguish between Judaism and Jewishness. Parallelling the absorption of the political by the social, Judaism, with its explicit political and religious content, was transformed into Jewishness, a socio-psychological condition. In a number of respects this was highly ominous. In the first place, whereas Jews could escape Judaism by conversion to Christianity, there was no escape from the indelible condition of Jewishness. In the second place, Jewishness was a non-rational, essential quality of the Jew's nature, amenable to study only through a rationalized social 'science', psychology, whose very character as a science gave its findings an unchallengeable necessity. The growth of Jewishness as a category of serious social and political analysis indicated the most bizarre dimension of nineteenth- and twentieth-century race-thinking: its tendency to link outrageous social claims with the apparently most advanced methods of science.

All this was for some time largely hidden by the increasing integration of Jews into the mainstream of European society and the fascination of non-Jews with Jewish life, a manifestation of a more general concern with the 'exotic'.[17] But integration itself was to set the stage for the growth of social anti-semitism. Because of their importance to the fiscal health of the nation-state, many Jews were granted social and political rights, with the ironic consequence that this tied them to the institutions of this state just as it was beginning to decline. Arendt argues that the assault on the nation-state in the late nineteenth century inevitably focused on the Jews, who comprised the one group visibly associated in the public mind exclusively with the state apparatus.

With the nation-state no longer able to provide a home for the increasingly large number of marginalized people created by the dynamics of capitalism, in a world in which race-thinking had become respectable, national or patriotic consciousness gave way to race consciousness. The most important bearers of such consciousness in the pre-totalitarian era were the pan-national movements of Central and Eastern Europe. For such people, race seemed to provide a principle of communion, one based upon distinctions among people who seemed palpably to differ in fundamental respects, but who had been accorded by the nation-state political and social equality. And with the collapse of the nation-state, a 'community' based on race could even seem more natural than the discredited nation-state because 'scientifically' verifiable differences among people were visible to all in a way that the abstractions of a rights-based account of human beings were not.

In this context Jews were doubly damned. Not only did they seem privileged by virtue of their association with a state with which fewer and fewer people could identify (hence their equality seemed onerous and unjust), but they were also involved with institutions which increasingly operated according to 'reasons of state', to the principle of secrecy. If governments behaved secretively, then Jews could be seen as the mysterious force at work in them.

These developments were for Arendt evident in both the political career of Benjamin Disraeli, who embodied the ambivalent perception of the Jew as both central to the functioning of society and as an outcast operating as a *deus ex machina*, and in the Dreyfus affair in France, which revealed the political importance of the mob and the political possibilities of anti-semitism as the foundation of perverted solidarity. Such phenomena demonstrated the increasing presence of racial questions in everyday life. And of course not just European Jews were targeted. So, too, were the colonized peoples of the developing empires.

The fate of Jews in late nineteenth- and early twentieth-century Europe was a precursor for the emergence later on of large numbers of stateless people, who were stripped not only of rights but also the right even to have rights. But in a fundamental sense, the condition of statelessness came to be shared by more and more people who, while nominally citizens of legally recognized states, nevertheless lacked a share of a genuine common world. With the virtual disappearance of a public realm and the emergence of a hidden public life from which the overwhelmingly large majority of people were excluded, these people more and more fully became objects of a bureaucratically organized sovereign power. While not exterminated literally like so many of the stateless were to be, the increasingly depoliticized citizens of the nation-state suffered their own unique expulsion from the human community. Their fate was to be an awful loneliness and isolation upon which totalitarianism could feed: 'What prepares men for totalitarian domination . . . is the fact that loneliness, once a borderline experience usually suffered in old age, has become an everyday experience of the evergrowing masses of our century. The merciless process into which totalitarianism drives and organizes the masses looks like a suicidal escape from this reality.'[18]

Expelled from a meaningful political community, individuals could plausibly assume both that the world was run by mysterious and ineffable forces and that they had no responsibility for its shape. Instead they came to identify their fate with the need to go along with the secret forces of history and necessity. The sense that they were swept up in the currents of history and would only count if they pushed the right way rendered people politically irresponsible. In these circumstances they were all too willing to follow others who promised to decipher the historical process for them and not only give them the 'truth', but also create a new home for them in a political movement which could control history by going along with it.

III

As a political force in the twentieth century, totalitarianism built upon these 'origins': the continuing crisis of capitalism, the emergence of imperialism and the growth of race-thinking and anti-semitism. In Arendt's view, the most important features of totalitarianism – the pivotal role of the masses and their organization into a movement, the central place occupied by ideology and terror and, ultimately, the concentration camp – can only exist where the collapse of public life has produced a population of atomized and isolated individuals no longer able to relate to each other as true political equals sharing a common world.

The cornerstone of the totalitarian state is its mass support. Arendt sees the origin of the masses in the same processes that created the mob in the nineteenth century, namely the breakdown of mediating institutions, and in particular social class, which gave people a stable place in the world. The masses 'are not held together by a consciousness of common interest and they lack that specific class articulateness which is expressed in determined, limited and obtainable goals.'[19] In other words they are apolitical people, 'job holders and good family men', as Arendt puts it.

In fact she goes further. She argues that in contrast with the mob, which consisted of people who behaved in a manner consistent with their marginal status, that is, they exhibited vice and criminality, mass individuals tend to be 'normal' adherents of conventional, bourgeois morality whose main desire is to fit in. In other words, they are philistines who, as we saw in the previous chapter, lack the means and opportunity to develop taste and judgement, and thus to exercise personal responsibility.

It is already becoming clear why for Arendt totalitarianism is such a troubling phenomenon to account for, even beyond the acknowledgement of its horrific effects. For while the totalitarian state is a criminal state, the vast majority of its people are not criminals. In their irresponsibility and lack of judgement, they willingly fulfil prescribed roles in society and little question what they do. For this reason they are in fact more reliable than actual criminals. About Nazi Germany Arendt notes: 'For the ruthless machines of domination and extermination, the masses of co-ordinated philistines provided much better material and were capable of even greater crimes than so-called professional criminals, provided only these crimes were well-organized and assumed the appearance of routine jobs.'[20]

In melding this lot of atomized but 'normal' individuals into a cohesive body, the totalitarian movement utilizes an array of techniques and mechanisms whose rationality admirably serves the irrational aims to which they are directed. The effectiveness of these techniques and mechanisms relates directly to their capacity to provide a surrogate alternative to a genuine community in solidarity as a response to the isolation of the members of the mass. In particular it provides an outlet for political action where no public realm exists. Totalitarianism seeks to transfer the thwarted potential for action from responsible citizens to an apparatus which combines them and their capacities together and assumes the initiative for action, while reinforcing the very depoliticization that created the conditions for the emergence of this apparatus in the first place. Since, no matter how relations among them might be structured, only real people can act, what results is precisely the irresponsible responsibility which the disintegrating nation-state of the late nineteenth century had generated. People act in unacknowledged and uncomprehending ways; they do not think what they are doing.

It is for this reason that, if I read Arendt correctly, totalitarianism as a political force first assumes the form of a movement, rather than a traditional political party. In this respect, the relation of party to movement roughly parallels that of power to violence. Both party and power presuppose and sustain a stable public realm in which people share literally their inter-ests, the spaces of appearance between them; these provide means of acting. By contrast, like violence, a movement is a form of action itself which produces continuous change without this being anchored in worldly arrangements or purposes. The dizzying speed with which things move, the permanent mobilization of the population at first within, then without, the structures of the movement, are essential to the movement's very being.

Hence, once a totalitarian movement captures the state, in a real sense it destroys it – for Arendt there is, strictly speaking, no real totalitarian form of government. While adopting 'normal' political forms, a totalitarian movement must remain unworldly. It is for this reason that, once in power, such movements set out immediately to create parallel organizations which eventually take over and shape to their aims their counterparts in the state system. This is the fusion of party and state noted by virtually all students of political theory and totalitarian rule. This fusion guarantees that the totalitarian state remains a machine geared to continuous expansion, continuous movement.

If the totalitarian movement and the totalitarian state bind people together in a coherent way, what substitutes for the worldly ties of a truly public realm? Arendt's answer is that propaganda (and the ideology with which it is intimately associated) and terror, the most visible elements of totalitarianism, fill this role. More than simply by-products of totalitarian rule, they are central to its very character. This has profound consequences for our understanding of it.

Given the chaotic quality of life for members of the mass who enjoy no worldly ties with one another, totalitarian propaganda thrives on the escape it provides from reality into fiction, from coincidence into consistency. It 'establishes a world fit to compete with the real one, whose main handicap is that it is not logical, consistent and organized. The consistency of the fiction and the strictness of organization make it possible for the generalization eventually to survive the explosion of more specific lies.'[21] What gives this strictness of organization its substance is the practice of terror. Hence Arendt's view that terror, utilized increasingly with the aid of ever more refined, scientifically grounded techniques, maintains a false world.

Propaganda thus goes hand in hand with ideology, the actual attempt to construct a false world. As I argued in chapter 3, ideology, too, presents a consistent and logically ordered picture of a chaotic world for individuals otherwise condemned to a totally arbitrary existence. However, between propaganda and ideology there exists a crucial difference. Propaganda has a coercive character that proves increasingly effective in securing compliance with the official version of the truth. But it still presupposes the existence of another, real truth that cannot be totally obliterated. The horror of life under totalitarianism is that political power is used to construct and maintain a thoroughly ideological world. In this world the elements of the dominant ideology – racism under the Nazis, the Bolshevik version of class struggle under the Communists – become literally true, no longer matters for debate or discussion. As built into the fabric of reality itself, the dictates of the ideology must be heeded and accepted as real and necessary by all seeking to make their way in the (false) totalitarian universe.

The structure of the totalitarian movement is designed to turn ideology into reality. Arendt suggests that the major 'contribution' totalitarianism makes to political practice is organizational. The totalitarian organization effects the delicate balancing act by which those in the movement are insulated from the pressures of the world outside, while at the same time the outside world is led to perceive the movement as normal, or at least not beyond the range of acceptable political alternatives.

Thus the ubiquitous front organizations whose presence has been noted by all students of totalitarianism play a central role in the movement. These organizations provide 'a bridge to normalcy' for the fanatically committed of the movement's adherents. They serve ultimately to mask the irrational purposes for which the entire organizational structure has been created.

Beyond and behind the front organizations, the totalitarian movement is organized into a hierarchy which is characterized at successively higher levels by increasing cynicism and contempt. At the peak stands the office and person of the Leader. Surprisingly, unlike most analysts of totalitarianism, Arendt devotes little attention to Hitler or Stalin themselves.[22] The reasons for this are complicated and even controversial. In part, as noted earlier, Arendt de-emphasizes the Leader because in her eyes Hitler and Stalin, quintessential products of societies undergoing the breakdown of worldliness, were in a manner of speaking non-persons. This means or, I think, that each had no 'who': there was nothing to reveal. In Hitler's case in particular, modern image-making and sophisticated techniques of mass political manipulation created an appearance that sustained the willingness of millions of people to believe that he was in control, not only of the state but of history itself.

A more fundamental reason why the Leader figures so little in Arendt's account relates to the structural position he occupies. The supreme task of the Leader 'is to impersonate the double function characteristic of each layer of the movement – to act as the magic defence of the movement against the outside world; and at the same time, to be the direct bridge by which the movement is connected with it.'[23] In an uncomfortable resemblance to Machiavelli's Prince, who in a world of appearances must remain free of the appearances he thrusts up so that he can change as circumstances dictate, the Leader must be able both to make claims and to avoid responsibility for them when they do not pan out. He is helped out here by the structure of the totalitarian movement itself, which, in a memorable metaphor, Arendt compares to an onion. Because each level in the hierarchy of the movement views those levels below it with contempt, the organization ironically stays afloat in the world outside the totalitarian lies. It is this sliver of reality in an organization built on ideology and terror that allows sympathizers not in the movement's inner circles to remain credulous and gullible, and thus lets the Leader and those around him escape responsibility for living up to their claims and pretences. In this way the Leader can shift his ground according to the requirements of totalitarian domination. Thus the 'real mystery of the totalitarian Leader resides in an organization which makes it possible for him to assume the total responsibility for all crimes committed by elite formations of the movement *and* to claim at the same time, the honest, innocent respectability of its most naive fellow traveler.'[24]

The idea that in a movement and state notorious for its highly visible and supposedly all-powerful Leader, this figure in a real sense abjures leadership may seem perversely paradoxical. But consider the structure of an onion. Peel off its layers and at its core there is nothing, indeed there is no core itself. I think what Arendt is getting at is that in a fully realized totalitarian movement and state, leadership is a kind of absence at the centre – in other words the Leader is a 'non-person'. Yet the onion as a layered structure has depth, reality, existence. The totalitarian movement is a structured vehicle for action in which no particular component of it assumes responsibility for the actions that are undertaken. It is in this sense a functioning inverted public world.

Hence the Leader truly represents the movement: he 'leads' while simultaneously (and correctly) absolving himself of the responsibilities of leadership. He initiates things while at the same time seeing himself as, and presenting himself as, a simple executioner of the demands of history. He is the ultimate ideologue.

If I understand Arendt correctly, this is clearly a difficult position, perhaps another 'puzzle'. Yet I think that she here defines the extreme terms of totalitarian domination; she sets up a limiting case, one for which, however, we have ample support at least from Nazi Germany. Under more 'normal' circumstances leadership as more conventionally understood plays a prominent role politically.[25] Indeed Arendt argues that once in power, totalitarianism encounters a fundamental problem. Seizing power is the obvious goal of a totalitarian movement, but acquiring it is not an unmixed blessing. If the twin aims of totalitarian rule are total domination and global rule, the exercise of state power always carries the threat that total domination will turn into just another form of absolutism and the drive for global rule will be transformed by the limits of national boundaries into simple, aggressive nationalism in competition with other nationalisms. In other words, ideology can not completely or indefinitely keep the outside world totally at bay. When the outer world collides with the total state, 'normal' patterns of power and responsibility can reassert themselves – which is why many in the Nazi hierarchy made plans to either flee or die in case of military defeat, even as they behaved as if they were above or beyond the claims of the world.

Thus, the totalitarian movement/state politicizes or institutionalizes the situation of the liar who finds it increasingly difficult to square fiction with reality. The source of the unlimited pursuit of expansion which undergirds its twin aims of total domination and global rule lies in the need for the total state to maintain the ideological world it has created. Like the liar who attempts to reconvert the past into the field of infinite possibilities from which it had originally emerged, the Leader and the movement he heads work to institutionalize infinite possibility as a permanent state of affairs. The idea that not only is everything permitted, but that everything is possible, is for Arendt the most distinctive characteristic of totalitarian domination. It is so powerful a claim that even those in the movement who believe neither in its ideology nor its Leader are swept up by it, and thus go along with the movement's demands.

As a consequence of this, totalitarianism at its most extreme is profoundly nihilistic: anything goes, nothing has any sense or can last. The fact that everything has become possible is subtly transformed into the idea that everything possible is necessary. In its search for ideological consistency, the totalitarian state/movement acts simultaneously on the view both that everything is within its control and capacity to manipulate, and that it is, at the same time, simply an agent of an inexorable historical process.

This nihilism assumes a number of forms. In the first place, it gives totalitarianism a profoundly anti-utilitarian character. The leadership acts ultimately in a way that sacrifices the real interests of the nation to the fanatical pursuit of ideological purposes and the maintenance of the organizational hierarchy. The 'terrible efficiency' of totalitarian organization can easily mislead us in this respect. Its success lies as much in its ability to act in disregard of material factors as it does in its efficient functioning.[26]

Secondly, totalitarian nihilism sustains the view, which owes its origins to the nineteenth-century expulsion of people from polity and economy, that individuals are superfluous. One expression of this is the peculiarly totalitarian notion of the 'objective enemy', and the terrible belief that 'every crime the rulers can conceive of must be punished, regardless of whether or not it has been committed.'[27]

Eventually, as society becomes more fully totalitarian, even the idea of an objective enemy and the logically possible crime is abolished, and victims are chosen completely at random. No one is free of suspicion. Everyone is potentially guilty independently of his or her specific behaviour. Once the judgement is made that someone is unfit to live, it is only a short step to the belief that he or she never deserved to exist – and thus all evidence of his or her existence must be eliminated.

The other expression of the dispensability of individuals is the concentration camp. For Hannah Arendt the concentration camp is not an accidental outgrowth but an essential institution of totalitarian rule.

The concentration camp is a surrealistic inferno whose 'gruesome crimes' take place 'in a phantom world which, however, has materialized, as it were, into a world which is complete with all sensual data of reality but lacks the structure of consequences and responsibility without which reality remains for us a mass of incomprehensible data.'[28] The chilling world is created by the establishment of total domination, and ultimate destruction, of the individual.

The destruction of the individual proceeds in three stages. First, the 'juridical person' is killed off by stripping an individual of the protection of the law, and then by confining him or her to a concentration camp which operates outside the normal penal system and thus beyond any recognizable judicial procedure. In this way the individual is stripped of fundamental human dignity as a responsible being; in fact most people in the camps were neither criminals nor political opponents, but were detained for no particular reason at all. What follows is the elimination of the moral person. This is accomplished by making the death of an individual anonymous: whether an individual is dead or alive at any point in time is impossible to discover. Death is thus robbed of its meaning as the end of a fulfilled life. To complete the destruction of an individual's inner moral sense, he or she is made an accomplice in the deaths of others. Finally, with the moral person destroyed by the blurring of the distinction between the murderer and the murdered, there comes the actual destruction of the unique identity of the physical person. This is more and worse than just death itself. It involves the elimination of all that is specifically human in the individual save for the most elementary, animal-like reactions. In this the camps were laboratories for experiments in human nature, demonstrations of how far it is possible actually to produce a new kind of human fit for totalitarian rule. This is a person prepared to fill the dual role of executioner and victim, to carry out the dictates of an ideology which claims both to master the movement of history and to prepare people to play a predetermined role in it – including the leadership itself.

The experience of the camps makes clear why we must see totalitarianism as a horribly new arrival on the world scene. For Arendt, the existence of the camps points to the presence of what she calls radical evil. This is an evil so immense in its scope and outrageous in its underlying assumptions that it mocks both just retribution and rational justification as the precursor of some ultimate good. In Arendt's terms it can neither be punished nor forgiven, and is thus a form of action which can never be brought to a conclusion by the only means available for reconciliation with its otherwise infinite consequences. Nothing in the history of political life so completely undermines our human status as political beings.

IV

Not surprisingly, Hannah Arendt's account of totalitarianism has been both highly praised and strongly criticized.[29] I do not intend here to deal with these assessments, but rather to suggest, in line with my overall argument about her attempt to clarify the nature of the political, what I think is the most productive way to read her analysis. I will then proceed to examine more recent efforts to develop further her position.

I suggested at the beginning of this chapter that 'totalitarianism' has come to be widely used in ways that are at odds with Arendt's purposes in developing the concept. My claim is that if totalitarianism is the ultimate form of false politics, then it must be understood in terms of Arendt's implicit ontology. This means that it must involve freedom, action and the public realm as these have been shaped by the vicissitudes of history and citizenship. Because Arendt employs these concepts in a highly distinctive way in terms of which she self-consciously distinguishes herself from prevailing currents of thought, her treatment of totalitarianism must also share this quality. If I am right in my account of her key concepts, then her treatment of totalitarianism is radical – it gets at the roots of the phenomenon – rather differently, and I would argue more completely, than other explanations with which it is often lumped, and in terms of which it is criticized.

To put it another way, freedom, action and the public realm – the political, or public life, broadly understood – do not fit easily within the framework of capitalism, socialism or democracy, at least as these have been used as dominant categories in political analysis. In one way or another these concepts have informed virtually all accounts of totalitarianism. Totalitarianism has frequently been seen as a inevitable result of a misguided attempt to change human nature and eliminate diversity, economic liberty and political freedom, in the pursuit of a chimerical equality; the particular target of this account has usually been the Soviet Union. On the other side, it has been understood as the attempt by a reactionary ruling class, confronting a powerful, potentially revolutionary movement of the subordinate classes, to consolidate its position by wiping out all opposition, that is, by abolishing political freedom in the interests of the economic freedom (that is, power) of the ruling strata. Here the focus has tended to be on Nazi Germany. In each case totalitarian domination has been seen to involve the absorption of society by an all-powerful state in the hands either of revolutionary demagogues or the big bourgeoisie, with the smashing of democracy as a consequence (although each of course entails a different conception of democracy).

Partisans of either position can find in Arendt support for their stand. On the one side, as we have seen, she is highly critical of the pursuit of social equality by the nation-state and the tendency for this to produce a numbingly ominous conformity. In support of her view that totalitarianism institutionalizes the nihilistic view that anything is possible, she suggests that the concentration camp was a laboratory for the attempt to remake human nature, a vehicle for 'the engineering of human souls'.[30] On the other side, she was profoundly critical of the dynamics of capitalism as these undermined and then ultimately destroyed the worldly ties that bound people together, and so promoted atomization and loneliness. This combination of 'capitalist' and 'socialist' criticisms should be no surprise given that she viewed both capitalism and socialism as anti-worldly regimes of expropriation. In other words, Arendt was no cold warrior, but this tended to get overlooked in the heated ideological climate of the forty years after the Second World War.

Complicating this state of affairs was a related, but distinct, set of circumstances. Following the turbulent 1960s, which saw widespread challenges, East and West, to unaccountable bureaucratic authority (a development which strongly influenced Arendt at the time), came the political disillusionment and economic decline of the 1970s and 1980s. Accompanying this transformation, and simultaneously reinforcing it, were new paradigms of political analysis and corresponding ideological currents in the political cultures of Western states as a whole. Neo-conservatism, the view that the capitalist market should wherever possible replace the state in meeting social and political as well as economic needs, was the most visible and successful of these new currents. But the overall intellectual climate could broadly be characterized by an expression used widely during this period to describe popular economic prospects: the lowering of expectations.[31]

A fundamental element of this new intellectual reality was an increasingly explicit critical reassessment of democracy itself, a value to which everyone had at least in principle been committed in the post-Second World War era. On the political right, this was most cogently expressed by the so-called 'ungovernability' thesis. According to this thesis, the popular and growing demands for economic security associated with the postwar liberal democratic welfare state had to be checked if the state was successfully to manage the capitalist economy, the only genuine source of wealth. For this to occur the state had to be insulated from 'excessive' democratic pressures by means of, among other things, the restoration of the authority that had come under siege during the 1960s. At the same time a state with renewed authority could more successfully meet the 'threat' of Soviet totalitarianism which had grown in strength because of supposed Western weakness in the face of New Left challenges to liberalism. Hence the 'ungovernability' thesis contributed to the ideology of the 'new' or 'second' Cold War.[32]

That intellectual and political voices on the right should develop this sort of outlook was no surprise. What was more surprising was that a variant of it took shape among many who saw themselves, or had seen themselves, on the left. This outlook went beyond the classical Marxist view, supposedly undermined by the success of the welfare state, that capitalism and democracy were inherently incompatible, and sooner or later one or the other would go (although there were those who advocated this position). Rather, it expressed its own diminished expectations, in this context about the possibilities of radical or revolutionary change. It reflected an increasingly conservative sense that the left in the twentieth century had everywhere gone terribly wrong and that certain cherished left values, especially democracy, could be part of the problem. Something about the attempt to realize a radical democracy based upon a supposed absolute equality was seriously amiss.

The rethinking about democracy involved a reconsideration of the merits of a previously discredited liberalism, at least as this related to its alleged reservations about political power and the need to control it. Here the increasing interest in the ideas of John Rawls or Ronald Dworkin, for example, is illustrative. But the reconsideration of democracy also produced a confrontation with the ideas of thinkers such as Tocqueville, Montesquieu, Hegel or Burke, who do not fit easily into the liberal tradition, but who were seen to have much to say that was relevant to a contemporary mass democratic politics, and particularly its perceived tendency to become statist, authoritarian and even totalitarian. In short, what increasingly came under scrutiny was modernity itself and the Enlightenment project of a thoroughly rational society.[33]

It was in this context of widespread doubt and pessimism that not only was totalitarianism reaffirmed as a central theoretical and practical problem, but Arendt's ideas came for the first time under extensive and serious examination by the left – including of course her account of totalitarianism. For those shaken by the realities of existing socialisms, but unprepared to embrace wholeheartedly free-market capitalism, Arendt clearly has a good deal to offer. But does she share the same reservations about modernity? Is the reading in this light of Arendt's treatment of total domination a replay of the 1950s, that is, is it an ideologically coloured misreading? What exactly is the relation in Arendt's work between totalitarianism and modernity?

In this respect it is well to recall that in her seminal essay 'Tradition and the Modern Age', Arendt is quite clear that the decline of tradition, a central element of modernity, was by no means a one-sidedly negative development. It prepared the way for much-needed new thinking about politics that would better equip us to live with a reality in which history and science had come to play such decisive roles. This outlook is carried forward in Arendt's account of totalitarianism. There is no doubt that totalitarian rule is a modern phenomenon. But are its roots found in certain difficulties to which democracy is allegedly prone, notably an always potentially dangerous conflict between freedom and equality, which requires that democracy must be cautious, must limit itself? Is it the case, in other words, that '[F]rom a political point of view, the questioning of modernity means the questioning of democracy'?[34]

In my view, Arendt's answer is: not necessarily. One of the most powerfully argued parts of *The Origins of Totalitarianism* is a withering assessment of the political thinker whose ideas most fully presaged for Arendt the main elements of totalitarian ideology. This thinker was not Rousseau or Marx. It was Thomas Hobbes, a primary architect of modern liberalism, and certainly no democrat. In Arendt's eyes, Hobbes, 'the only great philosopher to whom the bourgeoisie can rightly and exclusively lay claim', articulated a theory which put an ever-expanding power for its own sake at the core of politics, and with ruthless logic drew from this insight proto-totalitarian positions. For Hobbes, the price of security in a world of potentially murderous antagonisms between self-seeking individuals was the ceding of all political rights to the commonwealth in return for safety in the exclusive pursuit of private satisfactions. The state's monopoly of power is secured by making those who come together to create it thoroughly powerless. Under such circumstances, people yield not only their political but their social responsibilities as well. The state assumes the burden both of protection against criminals and of care for the poor. Thus the distinction between criminal and pauper breaks down. Both are outsiders and both are freed from any obligation to a society that does not take care of them. They are liberated to pursue without limit their own desire for power. Thus 'Hobbes foresees and justifies the social outcasts' organization into a gang of murderers as a logical outcome of the bourgeoisie's moral philosophy' – an early anticipation of the mob. The joint presence of powerlessness and criminality are the nodal points of a society that simultaneously whips up and thwarts antagonistic passions. The inherent result is the instability of a social structure geared exclusively to the continuous acquisition of power for its own sake.[35]

Thus for Arendt not modernity as such, but its bourgeois dimension, is largely the culprit in the rise of totalitarianism.[36] Of course, as we have seen, she does not accept the Marxist solution to the problems of bourgeois modernity, viewing this as rather more of the same and thus not as radical in its critical intent as is assumed. Yet elements of Marxism are from Arendt's perspective more attuned to what is needed to resist totalitarianism than are other currents of thought. For example, although she has little sympathy for socialism she does argue that the ideology of the workers' movement in late nineteenth-century Europe, democratic, cosmopolitan and rationalist, at least for a while inoculated the organized working class against the viruses of racism and anti-semitism.[37] In the ranks of the workers' movement itself were found the 'true representatives' of those people 'whose revolutionary actions had led to constitutional government'.[38] On another front Arendt is also clear that eliminable human deprivation and suffering, 'of which there has always been too much on earth', provides a fertile ground for totalitarian solutions, especially whenever it seems impossible 'to alleviate political, social and economic misery in a manner worthy of man'.[39] That the pursuit of material improvement can tighten the stranglehold of a labouring society does not mean that we should not seek such improvement.

Could it be then that democracy as the opening of public space to equal participation in the exercise of genuine power in a milieu of widespread material security might be an antidote to totalitarian threats? Arendt's arguments suggest the need at least to consider this. Post-Marxist leftists might well agree. But I think Arendt parts company with them, and this involves once more her distinctive, ontologically informed, conceptual framework. For example, power is for Arendt the antithesis of the power that post-Marxist leftists argue must be cautiously fenced in by a self-limiting democratic polity. This power is Hobbes' power, and for Arendt leaving it as the centrepiece of actual politics is ultimately self-defeating: it would not help knit people together in solidarity in pursuit of a common purpose, it would rather reinforce the fragmentation that breeds the conditions for total domination in the first place. Understandable as this might be, given the horrors of this century, this democracy, or more accurately this conception of the nature of the political, is shrivelled and crippling, resembling nothing so much as the prudential calculation of the cautious bourgeois – whose baleful role in culture and politics we have already examined. In this sense, from Arendt's perspective, post-Marxist political theory has failed to break with its Marxist forebear. Both are highly conservative, fundamentally wedded to the very culture with which they are supposedly at odds.

In other words, Arendt is prepared to consider the possibility of revolution, which almost no one these days, least of all on the left, wants to discuss. (Significantly, Arendt wrote *On Revolution* not before but after *The Origins of Totalitarianism*.) In the next chapter I will examine the complexities of her account of revolution. Here it is important to note that for Arendt a fundamental change in the human social situation is required if the threat posed by total domination is to be successfully confronted. This is not a change in human nature of the sort totalitarian regimes sought to enforce. It is, however, no less thoroughgoing for that, consisting as it does in providing forums for the capacity to act which as an inverted public realm the totalitarian state amply demonstrated. In this respect Arendt is helped out by the way in which the apparently inevitable and unchangeable has been almost magically transformed, and always in a manner that surprises us; such is the nature of action. Hand in hand with the horror and threat of totalitarianism is the prospect of a genuine public realm – and of course vice versa. The disappearance of ostensibly totalitarian states should not occasion the jettisoning of the concept, any more than the existence of totalitarianism itself should stifle the quest for a radically reconstituted public life.

To put it polemically: while in the 'first' Cold War, the right and most of the left stood more or less opposed to one another, in the 'second' Cold War much of the left in effect made common cause with the right. The consequences for the left have not been positive. Not only was the post-Marxist left wrong about the stability of the Soviet Union, from Arendt's point of view it necessarily had to be wrong: regardless of its pretensions it was insufficiently radical. Reading Arendt's account of the 'origins' of totalitarianism in light of her distinctive concepts and against the backdrop of the need to reconsider what political thinking can mean – and not the 'causes' of totalitarianism, which both left and right have thought they could ascertain – demonstrates in my view how this could be so.

V

The above considerations help put into perspective the ideas of three contemporary thinkers who have not only sought to analyse totalitarianism but have also acknowledged a debt to Hannah Arendt. Writing during the 1970s and early 1980s, Claude Lefort, Cornelius Castoriadis and Agnes Heller outlined an account of the Soviet Union as a stable and expanding totalitarian power which represented the major threat to freedom and democracy in the world. They saw Arendt's position, as presented in *The Origins of Totalitarianism*, suitably modified to take into account developments or issues that Arendt did not or could not treat adequately, as an important cornerstone of their own efforts. While insightful in many ways and interesting as attempts to relate Arendt's arguments to contemporary political affairs and to show the continuing relevance of her work, all three suffer from serious difficulties that reflect a failure to grasp adequately the novelty of Arendt's position.

It should be noted here that although all three have turned out to be rather dramatically in error in their assessment of the strength and status of Soviet totalitarianism, and, at least in the case of Castoriadis and Heller, mistaken in their specific predictions about the political dynamics of Soviet-style societies, this is not primarily why I believe their analyses to be flawed. After all, as Arendt herself understood, it is the nature of the future that it cannot be predicted; no one can be totally 'correct' about it, although we all have the need to try to make sense of what might happen (this of course is the origin of the faculty to make and keep promises). Rather, certain assumptions at the very core of their analyses were both at odds with Arendt's own perspective and as a consequence made the sorts of errors into which they fell less avoidable than they might have been. Putting it contentiously, had they actually been more attuned to what I have suggested is Arendt's position, they might not have taken their accounts in the direction they did.

All three writers are former Marxists who still claim some identity with the left. This being the case, for all three the status of Marxism itself is in large measure at issue. In their writings generally they have contributed to the frequently agonizing reappraisal of Marxism and socialism by radical intellectuals and activists confronted by the realities of Stalinism and of 'actually existing' socialist states. In breaking with a Marxism that has ossified into an apology for domination, they have sought to show how, at the level of its basic assumptions, Marxism has come to betray its most fundamental commitments and values. The betrayal is not the sort that can be overcome by salvaging an ostensibly genuine Marxism from its historical 'distortions' (a tactic that is itself idealist and hence antithetical to Marxism's own claims). The problem rather emerges from the kind of thinking Marxism is: an attempt to render society completely transparent by means of categories that are allegedly the cognitive expression of the 'real' movement of social life, itself understood as an historical totality. For Lefort and Castoriadis in particular, this is a rationalist illusion rendered all the more lethal by what it entails: that because Marxism is not just an external intellectual vantage point from which reality is defined and assessed (that is, not just another 'philosophy'), it has the irresistible and potent force of the given (science, production, law, power) behind/beneath/through it. In these circumstances, the transformation of Marxism into a justification for domination is an immanent possibility tragically realized in the historical experience of socialism in the twentieth century.

Lefort, Castoriadis and Heller open up further Marx's crucial insight into the social nature of being and thought. They seek not just to explore the social basis of Marxism itself, but also to deepen and enrich the critique of the social itself, and in particular its symbolic or 'imaginary' moments.[40] Clearly this task involves following Arendt in taking seriously what an earlier generation of Marxists called the 'superstructure', and especially ideology, as constitutive of 'reality' itself. Very much like Arendt, Lefort and Castoriadis (Heller is less inclined to this view) see totalitarianism, in its zeal to sacrifice the material interests of the people, as fundamentally anti-utilitarian and thus a product of forces not restricted to the 'infrastructure' alone.

For his part, Lefort brings to his analysis of totalitarianism the resources of historical political theory, in particular eighteenth- and nineteenth-century liberal and democratic thought. In Lefort's eyes, both modern liberalism and democracy emerged in a historical context shaped by a sensitivity to the nature, extent and legitimacy of political power. Institutionalized in the modern state, power was split off from other social domains, specifically law and knowledge. The modern 'democratic revolution' (Tocqueville) took place within this post-feudal setting. It expressed at the level of legitimizing symbolism the disarticulation of formerly integrated social spheres, the breakdown of an organic body politic.

This break down, which may be thought parallel to Arendt's conception of the decline of tradition in the modern age, established immense possibilities for a new mass politics, and grave dangers. With no directing centre through which the affairs of society could be co-ordinated and arrayed hierarchically, social life became pluralistic. Individuals came increasingly to see before them expanding possibilities for determining the direction of their lives – including their lives as citizens. In this context political power could no longer be viewed as 'embodied' in the figure of the monarch, for example. Rather, power had to be represented as an 'empty place' which can never be occupied by anyone without destroying it in the process. Keeping the place of power symbolically 'empty' was the animating drive behind liberal and, later, democratic notions of citizenship.

However, conservatives and radicals alike viewed much more ominously this fundamental change in the dominant representations of the nature of society. They saw not the expansion of individual autonomy, but the collapse of community as such. In the face of what were seen as powerfully disintegrative forces, there developed an understandable yearning for a new social cohesion, a restoration of the lost organic unity.

According to Lefort, modern democracy stands at the intersection of these conflicting forces and concerns. For its promises to be realized, it must successfully mediate both the quest for autonomy and the yearning for integral unity.[41] It can do so only if it enshrines both the sovereignty of the people and the denial of power as an object possessed by any group or individual. Failure to achieve this balance threatens the unique qualities of democracy as a radically open and indeterminate social order able to provide space for the realization of the diverse projects of free and equal individuals, a social order willing to embrace the contingency of history.

For Lefort, democracy involves the preservation and deepening of the division between civil society and the state – in Arendt's terms, between the private and public realms. This means on the one hand that the place of power must never be *absolutely* empty because 'then those who exercise it are perceived as ordinary individuals, as forming a faction at the service of private interests'.[42] On the other hand, if the image of the people is actualized, if a party claims to identify with it and to appropriate power under the cover of this identification, then it is the very principle of the distinction between state and society . . . which is denied; and, at a deeper level, it is the very principle of a distinction between what belongs to the order of power, to the order of law and to the order of knowledge which is negated. The economic, legal, and cultural dimensions are, as it were, interwoven into the political. This phenomenon is characteristic of totalitarianism.[43]

The claim that, at the level of fundamental representations, totalitarianism emerges out of the tension-laden dynamics of modern democracy is the controversial core of Lefort's argument. In this respect Lefort is a powerful exponent of a post-Marxist scepticism about democracy, a political theory of diminished expectations. This underlies his view that the left's uncritical embrace of the notion of 'substantive' democracy [and he includes Arendt in his criticism here[44]], which is opposed to its merely 'formal' counterpart, has shorn the left of a meaningful conception of the political, and hence prevented it from developing a sensible analysis of political events, especially in the so-called 'socialist' world.

If Claude Lefort uses eighteenth- and nineteenth-century political thought to develop his account of totalitarianism and democracy, Cornelius Castoriadis draws upon classical political philosophy as a basis for analysing contemporary political dilemmas. His work seeks to examine the implications of the Greek inheritance for the future of freedom and democracy in our own societies.[45] As for Arendt, so for Castoriadis: this legacy has both practical and ontological dimensions. These dimensions bear an inherently complex and tense relation to one another. Nature is the standard by means of which things human are to be judged, but nature can only become this standard by means of nomos, convention. There can be no escape from the act of instituting society in its imaginary significations ('justice', 'equality'). There can be, in other words, no escape from the demands and dilemmas of what, in Arendt's language, is action. This is the essence of the political.

Castoriadis lodges his account of totalitarianism in his treatment of the historically grounded 'imaginary institution of society'. He is concerned particularly with changes in this process that accompanied the emergence of modern society and the rise of capitalism. At the level of instituting symbolism, modern society is a self-created entity given over to the rational mastery of nature and history, with both seen as providing horizons of infinite possibility. The form of life incorporated in modern society is universal and encompasses both capitalist and socialist states. The continuing strength of Europe's own bureaucratic-capitalist legacy is the primary source of the *internal* threat to democracy. The *external* threat was the Soviet Union, which, according to Castoriadis, had the bureaucratic, but not the democratic, inheritance. During the Stalin era, the Soviet state was fully totalitarian in Arendt's sense, particularly with regard to the role of the Leader, the presence of mass terror, the 'total disregard for efficiency' and the dominant role of ideology.[46] But like Arendt, Castoriadis views 'classical' totalitarianism, particularly in its Soviet variant, as inherently unstable. He thus saw the Soviet Union as having entered a post-totalitarian phase in its development.

Arendt had argued that the totalitarian state always confronts the threat of being transformed into a 'normal' tyranny, ominous enough to be sure. She saw it occurring in the Soviet Union following the death of Stalin. For Castoriadis, there was a similar transformation. This transformation, a mutation of the total bureaucratic capitalist regime, produced 'a new type of social-historical formation': the stratocracy, or rule by the military.[47] What Castoriadis called 'the military sub-society' was in his view the only successfully functioning element of Soviet society. In its ability to command resources, establish economic priorities and in general determine the nature and pace of overall social and cultural development, the Soviet military was much more and other than the military arm of the state. Its role exceeded even that of a classic military dictatorship. Rather, it was the carrier of 'the only project which holds the Russian regime together'. This project, monstrous enough even if that of a regime no longer fully totalitarian, was 'domination by Brute Force, and for Brute Force's sake'.[48] It is this project which, in the eyes of Castoriadis, required stout resistance by Western liberal democracies, even as they sought to realize their own democratic impulses against their ruling capitalist oligarchies.

As Castoriadis saw it, in the early 1980s this struggle was threatened by then current political conditions in the West. These included, among other things, the ostensibly deeply rooted tendency of the European peace movement to make sheer survival above all else its primary political project, to avoid war at all costs – including successful Soviet expansion.[49] In Arendt's language, Castoriadis sought to defend action against the imperatives of a labouring society.

Agnes Heller stands somewhere between Lefort and Castoriadis in her specific assessment of totalitarianism and its application to the Soviet Union. Like Castoriadis she saw the Soviet 'threat' as real and pressing. But unlike Castoriadis, she believed that the term 'totalitarianism' remained the most accurate description of the regime and its aims. The Soviet Union had successfully achieved the complete totalization of society, by which she appeared to mean the destruction of all free political space and the absorption of society by the Party/state, a process that extended to everyday attitudes and experiences. And this regime was stable:

totalitarianism knows no temporal limits. Once sedimented and re-produced in accordance with functionalist patterns, a totalitarian society can continue to reproduce itself smoothly . . . Contemporary Soviet totalitarianism, which has left its revolutionary birth-pangs behind, is an entirely conservative society, a legitimized and, at least for the time being, a well functioning one. Unfortunately, all hopes of a near collapse of this social structure seem as misguided as hopes for its eventual thoroughgoing social reform.[50]

Those spheres of law, power and knowledge which Lefort claimed had to be kept distinct were on this view clearly fused. In the Soviet case the only way they could have become disentangled was 'by a predictably cruel revolution'.[51]

Heller situated her account of contemporary totalitarianism explicitly in the context of Arendt's. She sought to update that analysis by relating it to developments in the Soviet Union after Arendt's last edition of *The Origins of Totalitarianism*. In Heller's view, Arendt had been too hasty in arguing the demise of totalitarianism in the Soviet Union after Stalin. But Heller did not restrict her focus to the Soviet scene alone. Taking seriously Arendt's claim that proto-totalitarian forces existed wherever certain initial conditions were present, she attempted to extend the analysis to Third World states that could be considered totalitarian: Iran after the Islamic revolution; Kampuchea under Pol Pot; China, particularly during Mao's Cultural Revolution. She also drew attention to certain contemporary developments in Western Europe where she detected a 'detotalization process' at work, even in the face of certain social features which in other circumstances had led to totalitarianism: disillusionment with traditional political parties, the emergence of 'grand' issues in lieu of interest-based conflict, the continued massification of society. What seemed at bottom to be common to these otherwise distinctive phenomena, and which justified considering them in light of Arendt's analysis, was that all involved 'a new kind of modernity'. The Soviet Union represented a unique 'triad' of 'functionalism, totalitarianism, industrialization'. The Third World states featured 'anti-modernization on the one hand, and a religious ideology as an instrument of totalization on the other hand'. Meanwhile detotalization proceeded in Western Europe presumably because states there embodied an alternative type of modernity, namely 'capitalism, democracy, industrialization'.[52] Clearly Heller's position here was very similar to that of Castoriadis, although she viewed the rise of social movements in Europe, the main consequence of the decline of political parties and class-based politics, much more favourably.

Heller felt that for the foreseeable future, totalitarianism would remain a threat, particularly in the Soviet Union. She did, however, express the hope that, just as some of Arendt's earlier prognoses had proven in error, so too might her own.

The attempts by Lefort, Castoriadis and Heller to deepen and extend the insights of Hannah Arendt within a framework shaped by Marxian ideas have a good deal to recommend them. They properly understand totalitarianism as vital to Arendt's overall thought. For his part, Lefort promotes the extension of the distinction between the state and civil society as the basis for a political power that would not simply be a means of oppression, in this respect touching base with some of Arendt's more important concerns. Castoriadis shares Arendt's concern with classical political philosophy; while our problems may be 'modern', the classical foundations of them should not be forgotten. And Heller, whose debt to Arendt here is perhaps the most powerful, in line with Arendt's position accepts that Western colonialism and imperialism have remained pivotal for the political pathologies of the Third World, and that the rise of new social movements in Europe show that even in the face of proto-totalitarian pressures, totalitarianism is not inevitable: 'instead of the passivity of the atomized masses, we see a rather active populace ready to fight out issues directly' (although she adds that we should be cautious in our optimism about this).[53]

Yet all three accounts are in my judgement seriously, perhaps fatally, flawed. As social prognoses they have been undermined by events. As examples of Arendt-like reflections, they miss what is most powerful and distinctive in her work. At no point do they confront Arendt's notions of worldliness, freedom and action, particularly the latter in all its complexity. Yet these are utterly decisive for the argument Arendt makes in *The Origins of Totalitarianism*, even if they were developed for the most part after that work was first published. Instead these accounts attempt to assimilate Arendt's concepts to frameworks which in my view are singularly inappropriate.

The worst offender in this case is Heller. I have already suggested that she (incorrectly) sees Arendt's approach to totalitarianism as 'historicist'. She compounds the problem by arguing that Arendt was an 'evolutionist' who attributed a certain inevitability to a sequence of historical events. But this is precisely the kind of causal thinking Arendt abhorred and warned against. Heller then proceeds to claim that it is possible to detect in Arendt 'two ideal-types of modernity: the democratic and the totalitarian'.[54] Quite apart from Arendt's scepticism about ideal types as such, this claim is simply without foundation. If there are ideal types in Arendt, they are more of the order of worldly public spaces/realms versus mass societies and states. Since we have had in Arendt's view unfortunately very few examples of the former – the most notable being the council form of government that as we will see in chapter 5 has popped up during all modern revolutions – modern states have rather more elements of the latter. This is of course why conditions for totalitarianism can be found in all modern states, including supposedly 'democratic' ones. To draw the kind of distinction entailed by Heller's categories is to court ideological misrepresentation, which is exactly what happened in the context of the 'second' Cold War.

In his distinction between two forms of bureaucratic capitalism, and the contrast with the classical democratic legacy, Castoriadis at least comes rather closer to Arendt's own Aristotelian concerns. But if Heller's distinction is in a sense too sharp, that of Castoriadis is not sharp enough. For Arendt, totalitarianism was not simply a form of capitalism, however responsible capitalism was for the growth of total domination. In any event Castoriadis does not really tell us how the conflicting legacies in the Western heritage can be reconciled, East or West.

In the end, while obviously critical of the politics of existing liberal democratic states, none is particularly clear about the barriers there to freedom and democracy. (This is especially true of the United States which is treated, if at all, with a surprising naivety and lack of depth, although it is at least arguable that 'Pentagon capitalism' is the American equivalent of Soviet central planning, with similar structural consequences that are rapidly becoming more apparent.) In Castoriadis' terms, it is unclear how deeply entrenched the Greek democratic heritage actually is in contemporary Western societies.[55] Put otherwise, neither Lefort, nor Castoriadis nor Heller examines sufficiently the importance of recent and current movements *away* from the realization of democracy, however conceived, in Western states, particularly as a result of the rise of neo-conservatism and changes in the nature of contemporary capitalism. These forces have brought about, among other things, dramatic increases in the working time required to sustain a 'normal' standard of living, a redistribution of income from labour to capital and an assault on the welfare state. These developments have had not only economic, but also social and cultural consequences. In light of this, it is unclear what would constitute the democratic political health of European – North American states; Castoriadis, for one, came perilously close to equating the strength of democracy exclusively with the willingness to face the Soviet threat.[56]

Ironically it is Arendt, the supposed political 'purist', with her concern for the ability of material deprivation and loneliness to undermine a genuine politics, who is more helpful in this respect. In other words, there seems no equivalent in the writings considered here of Arendt's complex account of the rise of the social realm and the consequent decay of the nation-state, a failure especially evident in Agnes Heller's claim that, 'to our everlasting historical fortune', the nineteenth century 'took a turn towards parliamentary liberalism, rather than an early form of totalitarianism.'[57]

And of course, although all three thinkers acknowledged that neither the Soviet Union nor its satellites were monolithic societies, and that revolts against the Party-State were highly likely, none was able to foresee the speed or extent of the collapse of Soviet hegemony, nor indeed of the Soviet state itself – until now, at least, with minimal violence and as a consequence of action, frequently popular action. To be sure, this does not automatically forestall such violence in the future or guarantee that a democratically organized civil society will result. But Arendt herself would never have claimed that it would. After all, not just freedom and equality, but hatred and jealousy can be principles of freedom and political action.

In the final analysis they missed the implications of Arendt's conclusion to the original and subsequent editions of *The Origins of Totalitarianism*. She argues there that the total state contains the seeds of its own destruction because, among other things, every birth of a new human being is a beginning, and with it comes the chance of establishing something new, something which can testify to the reality of genuine human capacities. It is in the context of these concerns that Arendt is able to show both the formidability and the frailty of totalitarian rule. This is the reverse mirror image of the formidability and frailty of a genuine public realm and the power which knits it together. In other words, what is involved here is false politics, a theme for which there appears no room in the writings of Lefort, Castoriadis and Heller.

Moreover, there is another dimension of totalitarianism which Arendt strikingly and powerfully illuminates and which is also by and large absent from the accounts considered here. This involves the experiential nature of totalitarian rule (an issue Heller raises but does not develop): how do people see themselves and conduct themselves in a totalitarian state, one which subverts all accepted notions of rationality and decency? From Arendt's perspective this means confronting the reality that for people in desperate circumstances, a totalitarian political universe can become meaningful, 'normal', even legitimate.

It is well known that Arendt's analysis of the trial of Nazi functionary, Adolf Eichmann, *Eichmann in Jerusalem: A Report of the Banality of Evil*, gives precisely an account of the experiential nature of totalitarianism (although surprisingly little is said about it in most treatments of totalitarianism, including those considered here). It is evident from the reception this book has received that there is wide recognition of this theme as critically important for Arendt. Thus there has been considerable debate about Arendt's portrait of Eichmann, and in particular whether she had exculpated him of his crimes. And the expression 'banality of evil' itself has become almost a cliché. Yet, at the same time, exactly in what the 'normalcy' of totalitarian rule experientially consists has not been extensively examined, and because of this the significance of Arendt's contribution to political theory has not been fully appreciated.

At stake here is not merely the character of totalitarianism as a form of society, but also the nature of a human and humane alternative. Agnes Heller, for example, defends as an 'ideal' regime 'the Great Republic', in which the rule of law guarantees a 'just procedure' under which all social and political conflicts are addressed, if not resolved, by discourse or negotiation. This model is developed 'so as to secure the reproduction of relations of symmetric reciprocity and to block the re-emergence of social domination.' A healthy measure of civic virtue is vital to ensure that people make workable the checks and balances which could prevent the growth of unaccountable power and domination, and can do so on the basis of adequate knowledge and the right to participate equally. This model is also self-limiting in that it says 'something about the citizen's way of life, but nothing, or very little about the way of life of good persons'. The tendency to impose some conception of the good life, supposedly inherent in popular sovereignty, is thereby restricted.[58]

While Heller identifies Rosa Luxemburg and Hannah Arendt as carriers of the tradition of the Great Republic, its primary source is Immanuel Kant, and Kantian regulative ideas of freedom and justice suffuse her account. In other words, the ideal regime draws upon conceptions of duty and morality that have been central to the Western tradition of political thought, ancient and modern, from Plato down to Kant and his inheritors. Yet as I have argued Arendt was wary of the impact of the tradition of political philosophy on public life, in large measure because of its particular moral content. Analytically her critical scepticism involved her particular conception of political action. But I want to suggest that the experiential complement to this scepticism lay in certain characteristics of Adolf Eichmann, the person, and the milieu within which he lived and worked. It is Hannah Arendt's troubling claim that without a rethinking of both political thinking and political acting, we are unable to understand the most disturbing quality of Eichmann and totalitarianism: that he and others like him might in carrying out their murderous tasks, or in supporting those who do, in some way be consciously living in accordance with, and not against, the standards of the Western tradition of political philosophy, the very standards that supposedly characterize the humane alternative.

VI

It is ironic that *Eichmann in Jerusalem*, which may turn out to be Hannah Arendt's most memorable work, is not likely to be recalled for its theoretical qualities. The book is now largely remembered for the heated passions it has aroused since it was first published as a series of essays in *The New Yorker* magazine in 1963. Many have seen in it, and still see in it, not only an exculpation of Eichmann but also an attack on Jews who perished in the Holocaust as willing contributors, through the behaviour of their leaders in co-operating with the Nazis, to their own massacre – claims that seem difficult to reconcile with what Arendt actually has written.[59]

While I think the debate raised important issues,[60] in my view it presupposed certain assumptions about Arendt's account of Eichmann that were not made explicit, but which have profound implications that go beyond the debate itself. I want to get at these by examining *Eichmann in Jerusalem* as a work of political theory, that is, as an account of human nature and its relation to political institutions.

In fact there is ample evidence to support the claim that the work is primarily, if not exclusively, a work of political theory. It addresses at length the classic question of justice, and in this light makes a specific proposal for institutional changes that would more adequately comprehend the realities of the modern human condition.[61] It deals with the structure of modern bureaucracy and the capacity of bureaucratic imperatives to displace politics and so undermine citizen responsibility and autonomy. Here Arendt notes that 'the essence of totalitarian government, and perhaps the nature of every bureaucracy, is to make functionaries and mere cogs in the administrative machinery out of men and thus to dehumanize them.'[62] And it emphasizes the importance of judging as the essential quality of citizen rationality and autonomy, and the reality that the capacity and willingness to judge is everywhere under siege, including in liberal democratic states. Thus: 'about nothing does public opinion everywhere seem to be in happier agreement than that no one has the right to judge somebody else. What public opinion permits us to judge and even condemn are trends, or whole groups of people – the larger the better – in short, something so general that distinctions can no longer be made, names no longer named.'[63] Ironically, only if people are willing to judge and in the process show *themselves* to be capable of autonomous agency can the full magnitude of Eichmann's crimes be appreciated. In this respect a source of hope comes from the very fact that Eichmann was judged in a court of law. For this reason Arendt supported the trial and the actual judgement itself, something which has sometimes been forgotten in the controversy over the book.

As important as these questions are in *Eichmann in Jerusalem*, in my view her main contribution can be found in chapter 8, entitled 'Duties of a Law-Abiding Citizen'. Applied to Eichmann, this title is ironic, even satiric. Yet, instructively, this chapter follows one which discusses the notorious Wannsee Conference in January 1942, where the bureaucratic details of the Final Solution were worked out. Arendt's claim is that after 1942 the Nazi state became fully totalitarian, and both created and reinforced the conditions under which its murderous plans could become a matter-of-fact part of everyday life. In this context the irony turns in on itself. For what Arendt suggests in chapter 8 is that in a criminal state, certain rational categories can support the self-understanding of those whose actions are required to sustain the state, without these categories being used in a consciously hypocritical way.

The key to Arendt's analysis here is the notion of 'conscience'. She advances the admittedly provocative idea that a distinguishing quality of Adolf Eichmann throughout the conduct of the Final Solution was his continuing adherence to the demands of his conscience, even as the Nazi regime began after 1944 to crumble and the Final Solution itself started to come unstuck. It was his conscience, suggests Arendt, that told Eichmann, who in the latter stages of the war helped orchestrate the mass murder of Jews in Hungary, that even as others in the state apparatus began to make business deals with representatives of the Hungarian Jewish community under which the lives of some Jews were spared in return for cash or even ownership of abandoned assets, he must continue vigorously to prosecute the Final Solution because that was what the will of the Führer demanded.

What made the matter of Eichmann's conscience so difficult and

important was that it involved for him questions of moral consciousness and duty. For Arendt this turned on a distinction Eichmann
himself drew even if he was only dimly aware of its implications.
According to the accused, he always sought to be a law-abiding
citizen who did his duty, which meant that he not only obeyed his
military orders, he obeyed the law. The claim that Eichmann could
not be tried for his role in the Final Solution because he was only
following 'superior orders' was never advanced by Eichmann himself.
While he claimed that he knew that he participated in 'crimes
legalized by the state', this did not make him any the less willing to
follow his conscience and obey the admittedly criminal laws.

In obeying the law, Eichmann argued that he was living up to what
he understood to be the precepts of Kant's moral philosophy. When
asked to clarify this apparently absurd remark – mindless obedience
to obviously criminal laws is clearly at odds with Kant's conception
of practical reason upon which the ability to act morally depends –
to everyone's surprise, Arendt's included, he produced a reasonably
accurate interpretation of the categorical imperative: 'I meant by my
remark about Kant that the principle of my will must always be such
that it can become the principle of general laws.'[64] He claimed further
that after the Final Solution had got under way, he had stopped
living according to this moral-political standard, but Arendt insight-
fully suggests that in fact Eichmann had distorted the imperative to
read that one should act as if the principle of one's action was the
same as that of the legislator of the land – Hitler himself. The will of
the Führer, and not the practical reason of the individual, thus became
the basis of the law and correspondingly one's actions under it.

In one sense Arendt defends Kant against the use to which Eichmann had put him. Eichmann's was a bastardized Kantianism, a
version 'for the household use of the little man', to use Eichmann's
own expression. Yet at another level I think the effect of this upon
Arendt cannot be underestimated. To hear the precepts of a giant of
German humanist philosophy quoted with considerable accuracy and
with no hint of hypocrisy left an impression on her that profoundly
affected her subsequent work, and in particular *The Life of the Mind*,
where she explicitly acknowledges that a primary intention of those
reflections was to justify the term 'banality of evil'.[65] And she does
go on to note in *Eichmann in Jerusalem* that Eichmann certainly
followed Kant in his commitment to enforce the law in its universality, without exceptions. In doing so, she suggests, he had proof
for himself that 'he had always acted against his "inclinations",
whether they were sentimental or inspired by interest, that he had
always done his "duty".'[66]

So too, according to Arendt, did millions of others in this criminal, totalitarian state struggle to avoid their 'inclinations', the temptation to go against their consciences and the law of the land: 'Many Germans, and many Nazis, probably an overwhelming majority of them, must have been tempted *not* to murder, *not* to rob, *not* to let their neighbours go off to their doom . . . and not to become accomplices in all these crimes by benefitting from them.' She concludes with masterfully bitter irony: 'But, God knows, they learned how to resist temptation.'[67]

Since, for Arendt, Eichmann's sincerity was never really in doubt, or rather was no more in doubt than any 'normal' person's might be under the circumstances, Arendt concludes that Eichmann was neither stupid nor immoral but thoughtless, banal. To be sure, his inability to think was masked by his apparently thorough command of formal logic, but this is utterly consistent with the logicality of ideological reasoning. Unfortunately this quality of thoughtlessness was missed by most people because of the deeply rooted tendency in our culture to resist judging. This expressed itself in two ways. First was the attempt to present Eichmann as an inhuman monster, for Arendt an example of judging in terms of trends (that is, thinking ideologically) and thus not truly judging at all. To see him in this way would be in fact to exculpate him as an unconscious agent of a suprasensual process and there would be no point in trying him. Secondly, the unwillingness to judge was expressed in the idea that there is 'an Eichmann in every one of us', yet another form of judging in terms of trends or groups. Arendt not only denied this, she took issue with the hopelessness and pessimism it implied by arguing that the trial itself showed that although under siege, judging still did exist. As long as the capacity to judge was not totally destroyed, totalitarian horror could be resisted. It might still be possible to call things by their true names.

In the end the unique power of Arendt's position, and the distance that separates her from Lefort, Castoriadis and Heller, is nowhere more visible than here. There is a reason why Arendt argued that the Soviet Union after Stalin was no longer totalitarian, and this involves more than optimism about Khrushchev's reforms. Could it be said that the masses of Soviets had undergone the transformation in moral consciousness that Arendt identifies as a quality not only of Adolf Eichmann but also at least of the majority of Germans? Is not the presence of this transformation evident in the apparent unwillingness of many Germans to acknowledge in the wake of Nazism's collapse the nature of the regime or their complicity in it, or to condemn those who were its architects? Put another way, will the past be as 'unmasterable' for the people of the former Soviet Union as it has proved to be for the people of Germany?[68] On the other side, if it is possible to live according to 'decent' moral and political standards and commit evil, can we not find evidence of totalitarianism in our own non-totalitarian states, and might this not get worse in the post-neoconservative, post-Cold War world? These are difficult questions, but in my view they must be posed in the context of the contemporary use of 'totalitarianism', and Arendt's account of it.

Maybe Charles Taylor put his finger on what is at stake here when he noted recently that most modern moral, and thus political, thought has been concerned with the question of what it is right to do, rather than what it is good to be.[69] Perhaps we cannot get clear about some fundamental matters unless we pose the second question, that is, unless we 'say something about the way of life of good persons', unless we judge. Arendt's greatness may lay here: she provides us a means, certainly not easy or unproblematic, of confronting the second question, without denying plurality and falling prey to a kind of ontological sovereignty. And she sought to explore the equally difficult political form within which this question might be pursued not just as a matter for the *vita contemplativa*, but also for the *vita activa*: revolution.

5 Revolution

Arendt concluded the second edition of *The Origins of Totalitarianism*, published in 1958, with an analysis of the abortive 1956 revolution in Hungary. She saw in it vindication of her final argument in the first edition, which emphasized the possibility for a new beginning that inheres in every birth, and hence the capacity for women and men to challenge threats to our human status as political beings, including of course the threat of totalitarianism.

If in the modern age we have seen in totalitarianism an unprecedented threat to human plurality, we have also seen the emergence of a unique expression of the human ability to begin anew, to act in freedom, to create a genuine public realm. For Arendt, this is the phenomenon of revolution.

Arendt's treatment of revolution was her last extended exercise in political theory (her posthumously published *Life of the Mind* and her lectures on Kant were philosophy with political implications). To be sure, she continued to write frequently about politics after the publication in 1963 of *On Revolution*. Such essays as 'Truth and Politics' and 'On Violence' came later, and are not without substantial theoretical interest and merit. But in a real sense, *On Revolution* provided the logical and chronological conclusion to her political thought. If Arendt is concerned with the fate of a genuine politics in the modern age, then revolution as the peculiarly modern attempt to reclaim our political 'inheritance' establishes the historically determined form of, and prevailing limits on, the re-creation of the polis. Revolution, then, is about acting individuals, spaces of appearances, genuine power, freedom itself. It is therefore also about hopes and possibilities, and not just social, political and historical forces, or states, parties and classes.

If revolution is about freedom, action and the public realm, and thus the possibilities of citizenhsip, then like its reverse mirror image, totalitarianism, it is not only a historical but also an ontological phenomenon. It deals with the content of a genuinely human existence; it is about what it is good to be and not just what it is right to do. But if this is the case, then it is, like the capacities which it draws upon and expresses, risky. It can deny these very capacities in the attempt to realize them. It can produce its own form of false politics.

But the false politics that revolution-gone-wrong can generate – and Arendt believes all modern revolutions have in one way or another gone wrong – is very different from the other forms I have discussed, including totalitarianism. These forms stand more or less explicitly opposed to the elements of a genuine politics, even while in various ways partly realizing them, and even while justifying themselves in terms of them (for example, freedom). This is evident in the concepts and phenomena with which false politics is associated: violence, propaganda, terror, lying et al. To be sure, revolution as false politics can and does involve these. However, since its goal is to realize a genuine politics against institutions and practices that thwart public life, its 'falsity' has not only a distinctive character but a poignant one as well. As Arendt understood the great revolutionaries, and her discussion of Robespierre in *On Revolution* is decisive here, they were motivated by some powerful and wonderfully human qualities and purposes which directly involve important ways in which people can live with one another. Here she grasped something very significant and far too often missed: that people become revolutionaries because they feel revulsion at affronts to human decency, and not because they understand surplus value.

But – and again we see the uniqueness and difficulty of Arendt's thought – the motives that impel people to revolt are not the same as those which should find their place in the structure and maintenance of a public realm. In this respect, Arendt's clearest statement about the qualities of a genuine public *and* private realm, and the necessary interrelation between the two, is in *On Revolution*, not in *The Human Condition*.

However, modern revolutions and revolutionaries have been unavoidably shaped by the same circumstances that produced false politics: the rise of history and historical consciousness, the growth of science, the triumph of the social. Revolutionaries have by and large understood themselves in the light of all three, and this has profoundly affected not only their intellectual outlook but also their human, all too human, motives. In seeking to establish a genuine community, they have ended up undermining their very quest. Or to put it another way, what they were aiming at – a public realm, a vibrant public life, *res publica*, was not what they achieved.

Given that the modern situation remains our situation, is there any possibility of creating a genuine politics? Should we try? Are such efforts doomed to recreate the very conditions against which they are directed? In light of such issues, I argue in this chapter that Arendt's concern with revolution is not so much with the historical details of revolutionary upheavals, but rather with two other things: the historical 'openings' for political action in a world inhospitable to it; and the ontological foundations of both the explosion, always unpredictable, of revolutionary action and the contradictory forces set loose during revolutions themselves. These reflections are framed by what I take to be Arendt's response to modern revolutions with all their fearsome problems and ambiguities: that the failure of revolution is in a way a greater tragedy than the 'success' of totalitarianism. Is this a counsel of despair, a throwing up of one's hands in the face of historical inevitability? Here I agree with Karl Jaspers' assessment, in a letter to Arendt, of *On Revolution*: 'On the whole, your vision is, finally, a tragedy – which does not leave you without hope.'[1]

I

For Hannah Arendt, revolution is tied above all to the growth of historical consciousness. That is, it involves the idea of the sudden unfolding of a new and unprecedented course for history, a new story, a bright future. Since not all political upheavals are revolutions, what distinguishes revolution is the presence of people who view themselves as historical beings capable of shaping the future, of creating something new or novel.[2]

Since Arendt is highly critical of modern historical consciousness, this entails a serious problem: how can the creation of a public realm of freedom, the very core of revolution, be reconciled with a historical consciousness which, according to Arendt, undermines public life? And Arendt is convinced that the main impetus to revolution, even in the face of historical consciousness, *is* the desire for freedom. While the roots of this desire can be traced back to the Greek polis itself, it gained a new foundation in the experiences of revolutionaries who, as self-consciously historical beings, also at the same time felt the human capacity for novelty. Because this sense of novelty – or as Arendt elsewhere puts it, the sense of being caught between past and future – entailed such a rupture with previous conceptions of time and human purpose, it carried with it a certain pathos, a kind of wondrous apprehensiveness in the face of the demands of a future to be shaped. This could only create a complex consciousness in revolutionary actors, and this complexity is a central element of revolution itself as a political pursuit: '*only where this pathos of novelty is present and where novelty is connected with the idea of freedom are we entailed to speak of revolution.*'[3] Of course, free action is about novelty, the bringing forth of something new into the world. The question is: what kind of novelty?

The problem confronting the first revolutionaries was the relative absence of conceptual tools by means of which they could forge an understanding of events and their role in them. For, according to Arendt, what they proposed to do was radically unprecedented, namely, to create a new kind of political order in which subjects ruled themselves. While there were terms in pre-modern political language to describe uprisings against existing rulers, there were none capable of comprehending this novel reality. In search of the appropriate means both to express and to shape this novelty, revolutionaries looked to another human activity that was undergoing momentous transformation: natural science. Fittingly, the sense of pathos in the face of novelty was at first felt most acutely among scientists and philosophers who confronted a cosmos which could no longer be explained by classical conceptions of motion. Only later did it shape the world of the many, that is, become politically relevant. Thus the way in which men and women came to understand change and movement in their *social* universe continued to bear traces of its origins in the early modern efforts to grasp the truth about the *natural* universe.

Indeed the term 'revolution' itself had originally been an astronomical category which designated the regular, lawfully revolving motions of the stars. Hence, at first glance it would seem that the term was inappropriate for the experience it was used to illuminate. 'If used for the affairs of men on earth, it could only signify that the few known forms of government revolve among the mortals in eternal recurrence and with the same irresistible force which makes the stars follow their preordained paths in the skies.'[4]

However, 'revolution' carried an additional connotation that was ultimately to prove decisive in the the course of actual revolutionary upheavals. It suggested a process of irresistible movement according to fixed laws that operated beyond the control of human beings. On *this* meaning, it became possible in the midst of revolutionary activity for individuals to see themselves as swept along by the inexorable stream of historical events, whose logic they might comprehend but not actually challenge or transform. Acting individuals who sought to create something new in the context of a future unfolding before them came to misunderstand their own roles in the world. The one modern political act which demonstrated the reality of human freedom came to be understood as the product of a rigid, lawlike transcendental process.

This (mis)understanding on the part of revolutionaries, the product of the decisive role of modern historical and scientific consciousness, in turn generated a false understanding of freedom itself, even in the face of its authentic presence in revolutionary action. As I argued in chapter 1, what history and science share in common is an emphasis on necessity. Freedom, too, came to be understood in the image of necessity, and this affected the way it was related to real events and political experiences. For Arendt genuine freedom 'is participation in public affairs, or admission to the public realm.'[5] As I noted in chapter 2, this suggests an affinity with what is often called 'positive' liberty: the ability and right of individuals to participate actively in public life, exercise a role in determining the decisions which govern them, and so develop themselves as enjoyers and exerters of their human capacities.

By contrast, freedom conceived in terms of necessity, with the implication of passivity in the face of the inexorable, has a clear connection to 'negative' liberty, or the removal of barriers to activity. The most powerful account of negative freedom is that of Thomas Hobbes, for whom such freedom involves the absence of impediments to the motion of beings themselves impelled by their irresistible desires – in short by the demands of necessity. Arendt does not deny the importance of this condition, inasmuch as it involves the absence of oppression. She does deny, however, that this is freedom. Instead it is what she calls liberation. 'And since liberation, whose fruits are absence of restraint and possession of the power of locomotion, is indeed a condition of freedom . . . [it] is frequently very difficult to say where the mere desire for liberation, to be free from oppression, ends, and the desire for freedom as the political way of life begins.'[6] But as difficult as it is, we must keep the two distinct if the meaning of revolution as the establishment of a domain of freedom is to be preserved.

However, the relation between freedom and liberation is complicated by the presence of the third dimension of the modern age which, along with history and science, has profoundly affected revolutionary consciousness and action: the triumph of the social, that fusion of the private and the public, economics and politics, which signalled the elevation of the labour process as the dominant element in the *vita activa*. The confusion of freedom and liberation is for Arendt the expression of the social in revolutionary upheavals. Her analysis of 'the social question' in revolution forms the provocative core of her position in *On Revolution*.

II

By the 'social question', Arendt means the problem of poverty, the economic context within which two of the three great modern revolutions, the Russian and the French, have been undertaken. (The American Revolution was largely spared the troublesome effects of the social question, the main reason why Arendt sees it as the most successful revolution.)[7] Because of the presence of the social question, the distinction between liberation from oppression and the establishment of a realm of freedom was lost. The consequences of this loss have been considerable: revolution as the establishment of freedom became revolution as the fulfilment of the harsh demands of necessity.

This tension at the heart of both the theory and practice of revolution is expressed powerfully in the thought of the two thinkers most closely associated with the Russian and French Revolutions respectively: Marx and Rousseau. The tension is also found in the lives and actions of the two great leaders in these revolutions: Lenin and Robespierre. This parallel is significant. For Arendt, the problems of modern revolution reflect not only the distorting presence of the social question, but also the pitfalls of a certain relation of theory to practice, of political thinking to political acting. In this context, Arendt's argument in *On Revolution* is, ironically, a kind of immanent critique of the claim that political and economic matters must be kept separate. In revolutionary upheavals the social question conditioned the relation of theory to practice. Perhaps a world in which material deprivation has been sharply reduced might bring about a different, more satisfying relationship.

This I think is evident from the way in which Arendt treats the social question in revolutions, even as she feels compelled to condemn its baleful effects. Although critical of the attack on poverty as a primary goal of revolution, she is not indifferent to the plight of the poor, nor does she believe that poverty is ineradicable. In fact she is remarkably sensitive to the effects of poverty on individuals, to the reality that it is not just a state of material deprivation but also a dehumanizing assault on their capacity for freedom.[8] She also argues that the real impetus to the introduction of the question of poverty into the public sphere was in fact political, even if in the end the social question undermined public life itself.

It is in light of these views that Arendt treats Marx as a theorist of revolution. She sees Marx here, as in his account of labour, as contradictory. On the one hand, she claims that Marx saw mass revolutionary uprising as involving not just the end of material deprivation but also the pursuit of freedom: 'If Marx helped in liberating the poor, then it was not by telling them that they were the living embodiments of some historical or other necessity, but by persuading them that poverty itself is a political, not a natural, phenomenon, the result of violence and violation rather than scarcity.'[9] It is clear that Arendt herself agrees with this. On the other hand, by the end of his life Marx was equating revolution not with a revolt against dehumanizing conditions and on behalf of freedom, but with the unfettering of the productive forces. Revolution became the pursuit of abundance. In Arendt's view, the result was a surrender of freedom to necessity.

To this point Arendt has essentially repeated her earlier arguments in *The Human Condition* about the 'distressing alternative' in Marx between productive slavery and unproductive freedom. But she adds a third point that complicates her argument about the negative effects of the social question on revolution. She argues that 'Marx's efforts to rewrite history in terms of class struggle was partially at least inspired by the desire to rehabilitate posthumously those to whose injured lives history had added the insult of oblivion.'[10] This is powerfully put and suggests not only the complexity of Arendt's account of Marx, but also of the social question itself. For Arendt the attack on a poverty which is the product of human will and not natural scarcity may provide an opportunity for political action in pursuit of freedom. She does note, although often forgetting it, that freedom requires liberation, although it must not be confused with it.

Marx, the theorist of social revolution (in Arendt's sense of the social) *par excellence*, had a profound effect upon Lenin, and Arendt sees Lenin's complex role in the Russian Revolution as reflecting this influence. In his claim that the revolution would consist ultimately of electrification plus the soviets, Lenin expressed from Arendt's perspective the proper relation of economics to politics. While electrification would help answer Russia's social question – it would treat economic matters as they should be treated, namely, as technical and administrative ones – the real achievement of the revolution would be the creation of soviets as the foundation of a new body politic. To be sure, Lenin consistently subordinated the role and power of the soviets to the demands of economic development. Nevertheless, his position demonstrated 'one of the not infrequent instances when Lenin's gifts as a statesman overruled his Marxist training and ideological convictions.'[11] In a nutshell this captures Arendt's sense of the relation of Marx's revolutionary theory to the practical context within which the attempt to realize it took place. The Revolution self-destructed when it failed to sustain the soviets, the public spaces, it had thrust up, and not primarily because of pressures from hostile capitalist powers.

But if the social question played a significant role in the Russian Revolution, it was most powerfully present, according to Arendt, in the French Revolution. Pressed by the ineluctible mass demand for salvation from misery, French revolutionaries substituted the drive for relief from poverty for the pursuit of freedom from tyranny. They did this for very specific historical reasons: 'The inescapable fact was that liberation from tyranny spelled freedom only for the few and was hardly felt by the many who remained loaded down by their misery.'[12] The masses required a double liberation from both the demands of necessity and the yoke of tyranny. The confusion of the former with the latter was in the circumstances understandable. Yet as understandable as it was, the rise of *le peuple* as a political force entailed the introduction of necessity as the sole content of public life. The hold of necessity on the vast majority of men and women, far from being loosened, was tightened and extended to all.

For Arendt the substitution of necessity for freedom in the name of freedom, in effect the confusion of liberation and freedom, can be traced in the political thought of Jean-Jacques Rousseau, a thinker with considerable, if diffuse, influence on the French Revolution.[13] Arendt interprets Rousseau's conception of the general will as the unanimous and sovereign will of the people itself, which admitted no division and brooked no dissent. Rousseau saw the general will as that which bound the many into one, and further believed that a common experience could provide an existential ground for it. Such a will could be based upon the recognition that when in the everyday world two conflicting interests were opposed equally by a third one, they would come together in opposition to what was in effect a common enemy.

In Arendt's view, the logical consequence of this was a continuous state of war against a permanent enemy whose presence required constant vigilance. Moreover, Rousseau in this view went even further and located the enemy within the citizen him/herself. It was the particular, selfish interest of the individual whose presence called forth its antagonist, the general will. Rousseau's *âme déchirée* provided the most solid basis possible for the permanent state of war that produced the conditions under which the general will could emerge. In light of Rousseau's position, revolutionary virtue came to be identified with selflessness, 'and it is this equation which has put, as it were, its indelible stamp upon the revolutionary man and his innermost conviction that the value of a policy may be gauged by the extent to which it will contradict all particular interests, and that the value of a man may be judged by the extent to which he acts against his own interests and against his own will.'[14]

We have here again the problem of sovereignty as a kind of repressive denial which, as we have seen, Arendt finds so pernicious for modern political theory and practice. Obedience, violence, ruling and being ruled – all these elements of a false politics coalesce here. The sovereign will excludes any exchange of opinion and ultimate agreement on that basis; it is hostile to consent with its implied notions of choice and persuasion. In this notion of the will, with its basis not merely in external events but also in the structure of the individual, can be found the seeds of revolutionary terror.

And Arendt associates the celebration of the sovereign, general will with a powerful current both of the Enlightenment and political philosophy as a whole: the rule of reason. In particular she notes suggestively that revolutionary leaders, and she includes here the American Founding Fathers, understood government as the collective equivalent of the rule of reason over the passions which characterizes the well-governed individual. In this she sees a 'facile and superficial equation of thought with reason and rationality'.[15] That thinking and reasoning are not the same is a theme I will explore in the next chapter. Here it is worth noting that Arendt seems to claim that in a sense all modern revolutions have at some level been revolutions of reason, of philosophy – not of politics. She does not, unfortunately, develop this view and it leaves us with another 'puzzle'. Thinking is not simply rational cognition, and this leaves open the question whether it has some sensuous foundation. If this is indeed the case (and Rousseau, for one, thought that it was, a dimension of Rousseau that Arendt appears to miss)[16] then in what might this consist? Could it have something to do with the social question and could identification with the poor help provide this basis, however much the social question has undermined revolutionary action? In other words, have revolutions failed because, in spite of their professed aims, they have undermined rather than reinforced solidarity?

These matters loom large in Arendt's account of the French revolutionary leader, Maximilien de Robespierre. Her powerful portrait is a tragic one which is designed to show how in the historical context within which revolutions have taken place, certain very powerful and desirable human qualities became ultimately the basis not of freedom, but tyranny. These qualities – compassion, love and the identification with others these involve – far from being revolutionary, are in fact anti-political.

For Arendt, Robespierre is the model of the selfless revolutionary who came to judge himself and others by the extent to which they acted against their own interests and their own wills. This in turn was closely linked to Arendt's provocative claim that what French revolutionaries sought was not power as the organizing principle of a public realm, but rather absolute goodness. In Arendt's view, the social question was decisive here. The sheer magnitude of suffering that revolutionaries in France confronted, and the bodily necessity that drove it on, could not fail to impress itself upon intelligent people who reacted in a perfectly 'natural' way, that is, with sympathy for the suffering many and outrage at the vices and selfishness of the rich few. In response to the grinding presence of poverty, human compassion became the supreme political virtue.

As powerful as it is, and as understandable as it is in the face of human suffering, for Arendt compassion is anti-political because it abolishes the worldly space, the inter-est, that simultaneously divides and unites people. Because it is a kind of empathy which abolishes distance, it is without those qualities that can spring up only in the spaces between individuals, in particular the capacity for speech. Thus compassion is incapable of 'all kinds of predictive or argumentative speech, in which someone talks *to* somebody *about* something that is of interest to both because . . . it is between them.'[17]

In all this, compassion is very much like love: both are intimate experiences properly belonging to the private realm as the realm of intimacy, a sharing that can only take place when and as distance is abolished. And like love, compassion is expressed most forcefully in the language of gesture and glance. It can never be established discursively; in a sense it is mute. In this respect it has much in common with violence, and it is no coincidence that Arendt notes a close affinity between absolute goodness, so closely associated with compassion, and absolute evil. Both share 'the elementary violence inherent in all strength and detrimental to all forms of political organization.'[18] Because neither absolute good nor absolute evil can 'speak', each can meet the other only with violence.

Compassion is anti-political because it cannot be generalized to more than an immediate few without being transformed into pity, a perversion of compassion. What makes pity so lethal is that it is what compassion becomes when it enters the public realm. Where compassion shares, pity objectifies. It turns suffering individuals into mere functions of abstract categories such as 'the suffering masses'. What under all circumstances transforms compassion into pity is that pity is a sentiment, and can thus restore the psychic distance that compassion abolishes. But the restoration is a false one, the very opposite of the genuine solidarity of people who share a common world that unites while simultaneously separating them. Pity has a vested interest in preserving individuals as objects and not fully as autonomous agents, subjects or actors. It thus seeks to maintain them in a state of suffering, for without such conditions, pity has no basis. Thus 'Robespierre's glorification of the poor, at any rate, his praise of suffering as the spring of virtue were sentimental in the strictest sense of the word, and as such dangerous enough, even if they were not, as we are inclined to suspect, a mere pretext for lust for power.'[19]

And since sentiment is by its nature boundless, not only Robespierre but also those revolutionaries who have come after him, have been largely insensitive to real individuals and quite prepared to sacrifice them to some larger force, be it principle, history or the revolution itself. This, suggests Arendt, is the basis of that faithlessness which plays such a central role in revolutions gone sour, as revolutionaries are prepared to sacrifice anyone, even their closest followers and supporters, to some ulterior purpose. It is the close affinity of compassion with love, and both with goodness, that makes absolute goodness ultimately outside the bounds of, and hence incapable of being expressed within, the political realm.

On the other hand, the rage at injustice, unearned privilege and the luxuries of the rich in the face of the horrors of poverty fuels the obsession with hypocrisy, which Arendt sees as standing side by side with compassion as the most profoundly influential human response to emerge during revolutionary upheavals. To make hypocrisy a political vice, to see the enemies of the revolution as hypocrites above all else, is to see them as throwing up a veil of appearances behind which lurk suspicious motives. Another ominous consequence of elevating private matters to public scrutiny becomes clear here. A fundamental property of human passions is that 'they are certainly located in the human heart.'[20] These qualities need to be hidden, private, if they are to flourish; they are not meant for public display. Once the motives forged in the darkness of the heart come into the light of the public world, they become objects of suspicion, behind which there could only be ulterior aims and purposes. The universe of limitless suspicion surrounding Robespierre which led to The Terror has its basis here. Pursuing the 'same sad logic of the human heart, which has almost automatically caused modern "motivational research" to develop . . . into a veritable science of misanthropy,' the search for motives, 'the demand that everybody display in public his innermost motivation, since it actually demands the impossible, transforms all actors into hypocrites; the moment the display of motives begins, hypocrisy begins to poison all human relations.'[21] The normal doubts about one's innermost motives, which develop because without confirmation by others we can never be certain about what only we ourselves know, generates the utter lack of trust in anyone that so infected Robespierre's behaviour.

Because the passions reside ultimately in the privacy of the human heart, revolutionary aims based upon them, and Arendt here makes happiness the prime target of her criticism, are inherently destructive of a genuine politics. Her position is linked to her more general claim about the fusion of the private and the public in the social in the modern world. To the extent that private/social concerns alter the character of what Arendt calls *public* happiness – the desire for political freedom – revolution fails to realize its purpose. With the triumph of the social realm, freedom has, as Arendt had argued in 'The Concept of Freedom', become a private matter, and moreover something which had to be defended against public power. Hence, 'Freedom and power have parted company, and the fateful equating of power with violence, of the political with government, and of government with a necessary evil has begun.'[22] It was the social question, which saw the presence on the public scene of the ineluctable demands of necessity on a frightening mass scale, which laid the basis for these fateful equations.

III

So for Arendt, the link is complete. The existence of poverty and the compassion it arouses in people who want to establish a new body politic, but cannot avoid the social question, shatters the mediate bonds of a shared world and replaces them with the immediate relations of people who share only the desperate urges of necessity. The revolution is seen to fall under the sway of an inexorable course of events of which the revolutionary activists serve, in a frighteningly literal way, as executioners. Since the suffering and compassion which fuel the revolutionary drive are singular and essentially uncommunicable experiences, they can only become politically relevant when transformed into pity, whose objectifying gaze reproduces and enhances in *social* terms the status of suffering men and women who are merely mute objects of *nature*. And since the reality of suffering is communally generated, a form of political thought based on it assumes surreal dimensions. Purity of motive, never unambiguously determined, becomes the basis for political choices, including the choice of who is to live and who is to die. The endless search for real motives lurking behind the mere appearance of things keeps the revolution going. But the revolution has lost its real object: the establishment of a public realm in which being and appearance are one and where trust in what one's senses reveal is guaranteed. What is finally lost is the distinction between liberation from tyranny and freedom to found a public realm.

Modern revolutions have thus witnessed the confrontation of the social in its most extreme form – mass poverty – with the political in its most extreme form – the attempt to build from the ground up a *res publica*, a *novus ordo saeclorum*, as Arendt calls it. There is a genuinely tragic conflict here between two powerful sets of distinctively human attributes. On the one side are passions such as compassion which, although incapable of finding a place in public life, clearly must be part of a fully human life. On the other side is the quest for freedom, the capacity for acting and speaking beings to come together in a public sphere, which Arendt sees as essential if we are to become 'who' we are. Some important questions come from this. Has the general triumph of the social in modernity made the establishment of a truly public life impossible, even as false politics has made it necessary? In other words, do revolution and totalitarianism form the twin political expressions of the crisis in history, the limiting conditions that define our situation as potentially acting beings?

Arendt appears to see the matter in such grave terms. Certainly the fate of revolutions in the modern world highlights for her in a very powerful way the failings of both philosophy and science in showing us the way through our difficulties; indeed both have contributed to these. In a very complex and suggestive argument, Arendt attempts to show that our conceptual failings have had practical consequences, that all modern revolutionary theory has been unable fully to comprehend the novelty of what revolutions have been about. Although not dealt with explicitly here, Marxism is very much in the forefront of Arendt's account. In a way, *On Revolution* completes her coming to terms with Marxian ideas, and it reinforces the argument that runs like a red thread throughout her work: that Marxism emphatically sustains rather than challenges those forces in bourgeois society that tighten the stranglehold of necessity and undermine freedom.

But not only Marxism is the target here. Even the American Revolution, which Arendt otherwise exempts from her criticisms of the French and Russian Revolutions, is seen to suffer from flaws in their own way as fatal as the effects of the social question were to be for its European successors.

The inability of revolutionary theory conceptually to grasp the phenomenon it sought to explain and justify is not a trivial matter because concepts are a fundamental part of the very experience they conceptualize, which is why 'thinking what we are doing' is the hallmark of Arendt's entire political thought. This is because thinking begins with remembrance, and such remembrance can only be secured if incorporated within a framework of concepts which can in turn sustain the continuing exercise of it.

This is especially true of political thinking because what secures 'the affairs of mortal men from their inherent futility is nothing but the incessant talk about them, which in its turn, remains futile unless certain concepts, certain guideposts for future remembrance, and even for sheer reference, arise out of it.'[23] And these affairs are not about inanimate objects in space, or other living beings. They involve 'who' people are, their identities. Conceptualizing what these agents were about has a profound impact upon how we see ourselves as at least potentially acting beings.

The failure of political philosophy to illuminate new experiences is of course for Arendt an old story. This story has its origins in the aftermath of the Periclean age in Athens, when 'the men of action and the men of thought parted company and thinking began to emancipate itself altogether from reality, and especially from political factuality and experience.'[24] But in the modern age, as we saw in chapter 1, modern science, which has displaced classical philosophy as the locus of legitimate knowledge, has done its part to foster misunderstanding of our political possibilities. Modern scientific understanding cannot and does not concern itself with questions such as 'what is the nature of man and what should be his stature?' or 'what is the goal of science and why does man pursue knowledge?'[25] Modern science, from which, after all, revolution has derived many of its conceptual underpinnings, seeks to uncover what stands behind things as they appear to humans. Reflecting the Cartesian 'school of suspicion' out of which it arose, science is in effect engaged in its own search for 'hypocrisy'. Since only things, but never people, can be so probed successfully, scientific research comes most fully to fruition in modern technology and its ability to command the forces of nature. Humans adopt an instrumental attitude towards nature which ultimately comes to include them as well. In the process, they come to see themselves passively as merely observers of the universe in its various manifestations. Eventually as an observer, the human being is integrated into this observable system as one of its determinate parts. 'It is as though Einstein's "imagined observer poised in free space" – surely the creation of the human mind and its power of abstraction – is being followed by a bodily observer who must behave as though he were a mere child of abstraction and imagination.'[26]

The result of this is the attempt to convert practical questions into technical ones. For Arendt, this development is clearly evident in the tendency for revolutionary movements to mould their activities according to the demands of an ideology, a 'science' of ideas. This 'science' comprehends a process of historical inevitability, with events unfolding according to the determinist logic of the idea. Only the experience of necessity seems overwhelmingly to confirm this sense of the inevitable. The world of things comes to assume a permanence and stability that the world of individuals, shorn of the tradition that had once guided it, can no longer provide. Revolution is both a historically specific challenge to the increasing erosion of a genuine politics rooted in freedom, and an embodiment of those forces that have been responsible for this erosion. In other words, revolution has become possible only as large numbers of men and women have become conscious of their capacity to inaugurate a new order, but this capacity itself is grasped in technical and not practical terms. Given the problems of mass poverty in most revolutionary settings, the result has been the submergence of the pursuit of freedom that is at the heart of revolution itself.

Thus a tragic flaw of all modern revolutions has resided in the failure of post-revolutionary thought to remember the revolutionary spirit, the spirit of freedom, action and the public realm. This failure of thought has been matched by, and reinforced by, the inability of revolutions to establish lasting institutions that testify to these qualities of a genuine politics. The principle of public freedom and public happiness has remained 'the privilege of the generation of founders . . . but has haunted all revolutionary thinking since.'[27] The invasion of the public realm by the private concerns of necessity, which shaped freedom in its image, has its conceptual representation in political categories that have had their content redefined in social terms.

It is around this point that Arendt makes a fundamental criticism of the American Revolution. Arendt is a staunch defender of the American Revolution and the institutions that emerged out of it. She finds much to admire in *The Federalist Papers*, the famous justification of the American constitution which in its treatment of federalism and democracy is rightly considered a landmark of modern political theory. She favours John Adams, a key 'Founding Father' of the constitution, as a political thinker who for her combined the proper relation of theory to practice. Above all, she sees the American Revolution as by far the most successful of modern revolutions because by and large it successfully avoided the pitfalls of the social question, although as she admits this came about because the issue of slavery was evaded, with long-term implications for the legitimacy of the American state.[28]

But in recent decades, more than a few cracks have developed in the edifice. The divisive war in Vietnam and the Watergate scandal, which saw a president driven from office for unconstitutional and criminal acts, have revealed the extent to which the original spirit of foundation has been sapped and ideological illusion, cynicism and corruption have become endemic.[29] The civil rights and student movements of the 1960s showed the extent to which many had been excluded from the American constitutional consensus.[30]

For Arendt, the source of decay lay in the failure of Americans to remember that the United States came about through a deliberate attempt to found a realm of freedom, and not as the result of some historical necessity. This failure to remember the real origins of the American polity has had momentous consequences. It has undergirded the counter-revolutionary outlook of both the American people and their governments which in turn has supported the use of American power to maintain corrupt and unpopular regimes. Not only has this undermined American prestige in the world, it has also led people to overlook or dismiss the generally positive example of the American Revolution itself and to identify revolution exclusively with the French Revolution. Coupled with the lethal confusion of freedom with 'free enterprise', the widespread American fear of revolution and blind commitment to the *status quo*, domestically as well as in foreign affairs, have had a profoundly destructive impact on American political culture as a whole.[31] The revolution which was the most conscious of its basis in the foundation of freedom seemed finally most vulnerable to the corruption of that basis by the demands of the market.

But there was another way in which the foundations of the American polity were sapped by historical developments. Here Arendt zeroes in on the way in which even where revolution has succeeded, it has, until now at least, been unable to sustain its achievements.

IV

As bleak as Arendt's account of revolution may at times appear, at no point does she dismiss it as a human possibility or as a goal that political actors under the right circumstances should seek. This is because we have evidence from the revolutionary upheavals themselves of authentically revolutionary goals and institutions, whatever their ultimate fate historically. We can, in other words, detect in all revolutions echos of a truly public life. Without some evidence of this, we would be unable either to recognize the essential character of revolution as a phenomenon, or appreciate the tragedy of its failure.

The impact of the social question and the failure of revolutionaries and their inheritors to conceptualize adequately the novelty of what they have achieved are the two main reasons why, according to Arendt, revolutions have gone sour. But she suggests another, deeper reason why revolutions have been thwarted in the realization of their aims. There is a radical discrepancy between the experience of revolutionary activists, on the one hand, and their intentions, on the other: 'The act of founding the new body politic, of devising the new form of government involves the grave concern with the stability and durability of the new structure; the experience, on the other hand, which those who are engaged in this grave business are bound to have is the exhilarating awareness of the human capacity of beginning, the high spirits which have always attended the birth of something new on earth.'[32] The question here for Arendt is the same one posed for Machiavelli in his reflections on Livy's history of Rome: how is it possible to preserve in a stable set of institutional arrangements something of the spirit of foundation, as the Romans had done, without the tradition that had successfully bound the Romans to their past?

The existence of this split between the act of foundation of a body politic and the creation of institutions that could preserve the spirit of foundation, with the associated problem of how the 'founders' should relate to their creations, subtly transforms the tenor of Arendt's treatment of revolution. It suggests that even where the social question has been solved, or revolutionaries adequately and fully understand the real significance of what they are attempting, revolution might falter or fail. It means that revolution cannot definitively resolve the problem of how individuals can live together in solidarity, much less serve, as Marx claimed, as the transition from human prehistory to a history in which people would self-consciously set the terms and conditions of their association and live according to them. Revolution does not do away with politics because the harmony that is supposed to result from it makes politics irrelevant. Revolution is rather the beginning of politics. In a way this whole problem parallels the difficulty of relating private motives to public purposes, a difficulty that played so decisive a role in the French and Russian Revolutions.

How the problem of relating foundations to institutions has affected all revolutions shapes Arendt's account of the fate of a genuine public realm in the revolutionary and post-revolutionary period. In one way or another all modern revolutions have sought to institutionalize the essential elements of what has come to be called the bourgeois public sphere, 'a realm of our social life in which something approaching public opinion can be formed . . . a realm of private individuals assembled into a public body who as citizens transmit the needs of . . . society to the state in order, ideally, to transform political into "rational" authority within the medium of this public sphere.'[33] Particularly important for Arendt is the relation of interests (a phenomenon of a group) to opinions (the province of individuals). The deliberative organs of the public realm make it possible for people possessed of worldly interests – men and women joined by, while simultaneously separated by, a common world – to develop politically relevant and discursively effective opinions: ideas about public matters 'formed in the process of open discussion and public debate'.[34] It is with respect to this classical bourgeois concept of opinion, and not the manufactured notions of a commodity culture, that Arendt repeats the injunction of the authors of *The Federalist Papers* that all government is based finally on opinion. And the basis in opinion of authority is never more evident than under the impact of a revolutionary upheaval, when what was once accepted without question becomes the focus of discursively redeemable validity claims.

For Arendt, this state of affairs speaks of both the strengths and limits of revolutionary practice and theory. As she puts it, 'opinion and judgment obviously belong among the faculties of reason, but the point of the matter is that these two, politically most important, rational faculties had been almost entirely neglected by the tradition of political as well as philosophical thought.'[35] In light of this situation, Arendt focuses on the efforts of revolutionaries to provide a space, a set of institutions, within which freedom could be exercised. It is here that, taking place under conditions more ideal than in France or Russia, the American Revolution suffered its most significant setback. In the wake of the Revolution, Americans created institutions which in their very make-up facilitated the tranformation of a potential sphere of freedom into an actual realm of necessity. The politics of an 'extended republic' came ultimately to serve expansionism at the expense of republicanism, the needs of economic growth over the demands of a genuine public life.

Critically important to this process has been what Arendt sees as a highly troubling issue of modern politics: representation. As the institution by means of which someone absent is somehow simultaneously to be made present, representation incorporates the contradiction built into the very fabric of bourgeois politics. This contradiction is rooted in the fact that individuals under the power of Leviathan must at one and the same time both pursue their self-interested mechanical strivings in an unimpeded fashion and yield the right to act to the sovereign, whose self-interest is the preservation of all.[36] Representation uneasily maintains harmony between the conflicting imperatives of bourgeois public life – but ultimately at the expense of what is truly political. The bourgeois public sphere self-destructs. Arendt puts the matter forcefully: 'political freedom, generally speaking, means the right to be a participant in government, or it means nothing.'[37]

Among American revolutionaries, it was Thomas Jefferson who most pointedly and poignantly grasped the character of political freedom and its relation to revolution. Arguing for the creation in the new body politic of 'small republics' in the form of a ward system, Jefferson underscored a fundamental truth. If the end of the revolution was freedom and the creation of political space where freedom could appear, then only small participatory bodies, wards or 'elementary republics', would suffice. The constitution of the new state should have provided for such spaces, and protected them. For only here could people, by sharing in public power, truly enjoy both public freedom and 'public happiness'.[38]

Yet the American Revolution failed in the task of creating a public space of freedom. As Jefferson himself knew, only the 'representatives of the people, not the people themselves, had an opportunity to engage in those activities of "expressing, discussing and deciding" which in a positive sense are the activities of freedom.'[39] More ominously still, the failure of the Revolution came at the very pinnacle of its success, namely, the creation of the American Constitution. The Constitution cheated Americans of the gift of freedom because it provided a public space only for representatives of the people, not the people themselves. To compound the problem, the Constitution not only failed to deal with the cancer of slavery, but also brought into existence a new and powerful form of the social question. As both a framework for law and a policy document, the Constitution facilitated not economic prosperity as such, but 'a rapid and constant economic growth, that is, of a constantly increasing expansion of the private realm'.[40] By giving power to the people solely in their private capacity, not in their capacity as (potential) citizens, that is, co-participants in the formulation of the laws under which they were governed, as actors and republicans, the Constitution failed to achieve the political breakthrough the revolution had promised. The institutions of representative government reintroduced the old conflict between rulers and ruled, and so for the vast majority of people, politics became what it had always been: an external force operating on them from without and from above.

The extinguishing of public freedom under the American Constitution colours dramatically what is perhaps the most utopian and visionary of Arendt's writings: her account of the emergence in the course of all modern revolutions of a new form of government, the council system. Whether in Paris after 1789 and in 1870–71, Russia in 1905 and again in 1917, Berlin and Munich in 1918–19, or in Hungary in 1956, revolutionary governing councils, soviets or *räte*, 'sprang up as the spontaneous organs of the people, not only outside of all revolutionary parties but entirely unexpected by them or their leaders.'[41] The councils represented 'the amazing formation of a new power structure which owed its existence to nothing but the organizational impulses of the people themselves'.[42] For Arendt the always unexpected appearance of the council system demonstrated that revolutions are never made by revolutionary leaders, or follow the path prescribed by revolutionary ideologies, but can spring up wherever and whenever large numbers of men and women come together in common purpose and inject themselves through word and deed into events going on around them.

These councils served as agents of radical democratization. They 'consciously and explicitly desired the direct participation of every citizen in the public affairs of the country, and so long as they lasted, there could be no doubt that every individual found his own sphere of action and could behold, as it were, with his own eyes his own contribution to the events of the day.'[43] Above all, they abolished the distinction, so central even to the revolutionary party, between those who know and those who act. The councils were structured on the assumption that the average citizen possessed the capacity to form his or her own opinion and to act on it. In this sense they expressed the important truth that where knowing and doing part company, a space where freedom can flourish is lost. The separation between knowing and doing undermines both.[44]

It is here that the status of economic life and the social question becomes central for the organs of freedom. Revolutionary councils, as these evolved in France, Russia, Germany or Hungary, were not workers' councils centred in the factories. Nor could they be if they were to function successfully. On this point rests the nub of Arendt's claim that politics and economics remain irreducibly distinct. The difference between them is the difference 'between participation in public affairs and the administration or management of things in the public interest'. It is the difference between *politics* and *administration*. The consummate political actor and the successful administrator are not only not the same person, they generally cannot be. This is because 'the one is supposed to know how to deal with men in a field of human relations, whose principle is freedom, and the other must know how to manage things and people in a sphere of life whose principle is necessity.'[45] The victory of the revolutionary party, organized according to a division of labour between those who know and those execute, signals the triumph of necessity. The autocratic structure of the party is aptly suited to the demands of industrialization and economic growth that in all cases have come to supplant explicitly political concerns.

Thus even where revolutions have succeeded in kindling the spark of freedom and founding a home for it in the form of wards or councils, they all have failed to preserve what Arendt calls their 'lost treasure'. The political consequences of this failure of revolution have reverberated throughout all contemporary Western states, and not just those that have undergone revolutionary change. The concepts and institutions of liberal democratic political systems have been infected by the legacy of revolution's subordination to the demands of the social question.

Of considerable significance here is the fate of the term 'elite'. Arendt argues that the 'elementary republic' which would form the key institution of a truly revolutionary polity would be composed only of those who are concerned about the state of the world, and not just their private happiness. However, such an elite would not be identical with a social, cultural or professional elite, and certainly not with those corporate and state elites so omnipresent in Western democratic states. If those who belong to a genuine 'political elite of the people',[46] as Arendt calls it, are self-selected, those who do not are self-excluded. Far from being discriminatory, this self-exclusion would reinforce a freedom *from* politics, a freedom not to participate, that along with the ability to govern oneself must also be part of a genuinely human existence. The freedom from politics deepens the necessary division between private and public, thereby allowing each to shine forth in its particular distinctiveness. In other words, if freedom in a public realm provides for those qualities which can only be expressed among others who share a world in common, freedom from politics allows for the flourishing of intimacy, and the qualities of love and compassion.

Arendt's concept of a political elite, self-chosen from those who care about public freedom and happiness, but in principle open to everybody, stands in stark contrast to so-called elite theories of democracy.[47] Such theories all too accurately describe the anti-political politics of the party systems in Western states, 'where the voter can only consent or refuse to ratify a choice which . . . is made without him,' and where 'the relationship between representative and elector is transformed into that of seller and buyer.'[48] In these systems there is a lack of public spaces which the people could enter and from which could emerge the self-chosen elite. 'The trouble, in other words, is that politics has become a profession and a career, and that the "elite" therefore is being chosen according to standards and criteria which are themselves profoundly unpolitical.'[49]

Nevertheless, the idea of elite domination of the mass fully accords with the reality of modern society where the private has so successfully invaded the public realm. Arendt seems resigned to the fact that our political categories and the practices they shape and illuminate will, at least for the foreseeable future, remain tainted by the triumph of the social. There is no more telling expression of the failure of revolution to find its appropriate institution. The distinctively modern movement for the establishment of freedom has ended up feeding the onslaught of necessity.

Thus Arendt's study of revolution concludes on a note of sadness and melancholy. The spirit of beginning something new appears to have been snuffed out under the impact of increasing worldlessness. For Arendt, there seems little way out of the modern predicament, except for the hope that under as yet unpredictable circumstances some may yet long for the taste of immortality, the splendour that only the public realm can endow.

V

What are we to make of Arendt's striking, if idiosyncratic, account of revolution? No other phenomenon seems to capture so precisely what Arendt means by the idea that we are suspended between past and future, between what has been and is no more, and what might be but is not yet. Revolution is always future-oriented and thus a powerful expression of the historicity of the modern condition, our sense of ourselves as beings who live in time.

Arendt accepts this condition. She does not counsel an impossible and, equally important, undesirable return to a supposedly nobler ancient past. But she also makes clear that what for her is a fundamental dimension of our being located between past and future, namely our ability to, so to speak, leap above the fray, can only take place in thought.[50] Trouble arises when we assume that we can literally and bodily do so. This is what science has tried to do in striving to make literal 'the Archimedean wish for a point outside the earth from which to unhinge the world'. In its experimental and practical activities, it has 'found a way to act on the earth and within terrestrial nature as though we dispose of it from outside.'[51] This is part of what Arendt means by 'world alienation'. To the extent that revolutionary theory and practice emulate this 'leap' from our location between past and future, they contribute to this alienation, a lethal outcome for what is, after all, the attempt to found a public realm.

So we cannot escape our earthly ties, our history. We are bodily and not just intellectually tied to our worldly habitation. But this means that we are dran back to the social question, for, if nothing else, historically evolved physical necessity is a fundamental element of our real location. Can there be in the reality of the social question itself possible sources of what Arendt would consider revolutionary change? Put more broadly, can the realm of necessity ever be shaped according to the demands of freedom? Can the disposition of society's productive resources form the substance of political deliberation and decision? Arendt suggests not, and this is part of the reason for her melancholy in the face of failed revolutions.

But perhaps her own work gives us clues about an alternative. As I argued in chapter 1, there are hints in Arendt's argument that the labour process can harbour the seeds of plurality and inter-subjectivity. More specifically with respect to revolution, she makes clear that liberation from oppression is integral to the realization of freedom in the form of a genuine public life – she even writes of the use of political power to liberate people from necessity in the interests of freedom.[52] Nothing reflects necessity so much as poverty, the social question; to ignore this issue is, from Arendt's own perspective to compromise the possibility of establishing a genuine political community, which requires that all who are to enter the public realm be relieved of the demands of necessity. This is clearly central to Arendt's insight that for Marx poverty not only injures, it silences. In this light even violence, necessity's faithful companion, can have a positive role. It is well to recall that Arendt is no pacifist: violence can help foster political reform, and surely the battle against oppression is at least reformist.

In the end all revolutions have, after all, introduced elements of a genuine public sphere, even if these were ultimately hollowed out, if not destroyed altogether. Perhaps, as Jürgen Habermas has argued, there is no reason why Arendt's interactive and communicative concept of power cannot share common ground with the view that our economic relations can be subjected to conscious direction in a spirit of freedom.[53]

In its very complexity, and even ambivalence, Arendt's understanding of revolution can cast light upon contemporary political developments. Two examples are instructive here. In South Africa the movement away from apartheid, and the efforts by the African National Congress and the existing government to establish a new constitution with new institutions of public life which could lead to majority rule, conform in large measure to what Arendt sees as genuinely revolutionary action. Yet the gnawing presence of the social question – the grinding poverty of the black majority – could substantially diminish the prospects for the successful creation of a realm of freedom.

On the other hand, in Eastern Europe and especially in the republics of the former Soviet Union, things are far less promising. Not only has there been no constitution-building or efforts to establish public spaces, there has also been a perverse attempt to create, in the form of a propertyless mass of people, a social question where one did not exist before. This has ominous implications for the future prospects of freedom and democracy in this region.

Far from being a 'utopian' tract with little historical or practical significance, Arendt's account of revolution provides a realistic, critical framework for exploring political change. Her account suggests that cautious hopefulness is the proper outlook to adopt in the face of efforts to create a new order of things. For a long time I believed that Arendt's position would have been strengthened had she explicitly addressed the issue of ontology, the fact that the demand for a genuine politics poses the problem of what it means to be fully human. What lay behind this criticism was a Marxian-influenced understanding of the human essence as consisting in free, creative activity which, under the proper conditions, could be more or less clearly understood and unproblematically guaranteed. I think now that in fact *On Revolution* is in itself already an ontological account. In its complex interweaving of the relation of private motives to public purposes, and in its treatment of how revolution poses in a dramatic way the relation of political thinking to political acting, Arendt's work illuminates what it is good to be. It has often been noted that Arendt does not give us a historical analysis of revolutions. It has less often been noted that this is in fact intentional. In my view, Arendt gives us instead a historically informed account of the ontology of action: what action has actually meant, and can mean, under certain conditions of lived experience where, by contrast with other human capacities, its peculiar character is most sharply in evidence.

Arendt ends her account of revolution with the words of Sophocles: 'Not to be born prevails over all meaning uttered in words; by far the second-best for life, once it has appeared, is to go as swiftly as possible whence it came.'[54] Only the poets, who stand guard over memory and recollection, can preserve what is in danger of being irretrievably lost: the spirit of freedom. She cites the French writer and Second World War resistance fighter, René Char, on the dilemma facing those confronting the demands of political action without metaphysical guarantees: 'our inheritance was left to us by no testament.' She had cited the same aphorism in introducing her account of the loss of the Western tradition of political thought as a whole. It is in the end the same testament, and the same treasure. It may be that, after all, thinking and acting, philosophy and politics, share something profoundly in common, regardless of the troubled relations historically between them.

In coming to terms with the collapse of our tradition of political thought, Arendt stresses the unavoidable need to engage in 'thinking without a bannister'.[55] Perhaps we have now a similar need to act without a bannister. Can we do so responsibly and with courage? Can we be citizens?

6 What is Thinking Politically?

[I]t took him fourteen years of remembrance and reflection to understand and come to terms with what had happened ... This much time was needed to learn 'simplicity' and to unlearn 'the simplification of abstract thinking,' to become fluent in the art and the language of 'concrete' thoughts and feelings, and thus to comprehend that both abstract notions and abstract emotions are not merely false to what actually happens but are viciously interconnected ... This self-taught concreteness, an unswerving fidelity to the real, as difficult to achieve for the philosopher, whose formal education had been abstract thought, as for the common run of men who indulge in no less abstract feelings and emotions, is the hallmark of this singularly earnest and beautiful book.
Hannah Arendt, Introduction to J. Glenn Gray, *The Warriors*

In her posthumously published *Lectures on Kant's Political Philosophy*, Arendt suggests that the fundamental consideration underlying Kant's largely unwritten, but implied, political philosophy was 'how to reconcile the problem of the organization of the state with his moral philosophy, that is, with the dictates of practical reason.'[1] In the course of dealing with this matter, Kant made a surprising discovery: his moral philosophy was no help. In his explicitly political writings, which Arendt and others find singularly jejeune for a philosopher of his stature, he was forced to fall back upon a post-Hobbesian account of human nature as an explanation for the possibility of politics at all. The right constitution could transform the conflictual strivings of rational, self-seeking beings into proper public conduct, that is, into behaviour consistent with the maintenance of a stable collective organization. Hence Kant concludes that the political problem can be solved 'even for a race of devils', if they are smart enough – a gloomily ironic position for a thinker so committed to the power of human reason and the requirements of human dignity. Little wonder that Kant shared with the Western tradition of political philosophy a tendency to downplay the realm of public affairs as relatively insignificant for the pursuit of distinctively human purposes.

Of course Arendt is dissatisfied with this turn in Kant's thought (as he himself appeared to be). She sought in his writings an alternative basis for his political philosophy, one which would establish that dignity of the public sphere which the demands of his moral philosophy, to say nothing of his enthusiasm for the French Revolution, seemed to require. She thought she found this in his notion of judgement and its capacity to mediate self and the world in light of the reality of human interdependence.

Arendt's desire to tease out a coherent and satisfying political philosophy from the writings of a thinker who exerted a profound influence on her own work suggests yet again the significance the relation of philosophy to politics, theory to practice, for her political thought. As her remarks in the introduction to *The Warriors* indicate, a theoretical attitude towards politics carries always the dangers of a vicious abstractness with concrete implications. In short, it carries the dangers of ideology. As we have seen, Arendt sees the hostility of the philosopher to the domain of public affairs as complicit in this development.

But there is another side to these remarks. Arendt only hints at this in her comment about 'concrete' thoughts. But it has to do with the essential need for concepts which give rational form to experience in ways which allow this experience to speak to beings for whom the capacities for lexis and praxis are fundamental components of their nature. Reason has a vital role in public life, even if the form given it by philosophers has had destructive consequences for the political realm. And this 'public' reason is not some supposedly down-to-earth common sense: the 'common run of men', no less than the philosophers, indulge in abstract thoughts and feelings. Adolf Eichmann was a case in point.

The problem – and the opportunity – is that the concepts of political philosophy and those of political life are the same. This means that the philosopher and the citizen share the same situation, as Plato and Aristotle clearly understood, and as Arendt herself argued in 'Truth and Politics'. But where in particular Plato seemed to believe that this above all posed a threat to the highest sort of human excellence – the life of the mind – and required that the philosopher rule, Arendt believed rather that it pointed to the inescapable need for all to think.[2] (In this respect, she is more closely allied to Kant and the Enlightenment.) Citizenship and reason had somehow to connect, and this connection had to be worked out within the bounds of active citizenship itself. It could not be externally imposed.

In this context, Arendt's criticism of the tradition of Western political philosophy reveals its most provocative quality: this tradition has focused on thinking *about* politics, but not on thinking *as* politics, although its most profound impulses require it to draw upon political life for its self-understanding.[3] Philosophy is a solitary pursuit, but this is a conditioned solitude. The conditioning factor is human plurality, the shared situation: 'we are all the same, that is, human, in such a way that nobody is ever the same as anyone else who ever lived, lives, or will live.'[4] The relation of philosophy and plurality is the backdrop for the tantalizingly ambiguous lines from Cato which conclude *The Human Condition*: 'Never is he more active when he does nothing, never is he less alone than when he is by himself.'[5] This is the point at which the *vita activa* and *vita contemplativa* intersect and interact, the Gordian knot by which they are tied together.

This I think suggests why Arendt's thought has proved so difficult to classify. It draws upon the philosophic tradition, but seeks at the same time to distance itself from this tradition, while continuing to respect its demands and concerns. Philosophy must engage politics, but not subject politics to its claims in the sense that it would rule over public life. Politics must incorporate reason, but at the same time resist the ever-present threat of domination of the particular by and through an abstract universality. In other words, an improperly politicized philosophy risks conversion into its caricature, ideology. An improperly philosophical politics risks becoming *its* distorted mirror image, tyranny.

If it is properly to confront the complex relation of philosophy to politics, theory to practice, political theory must deal not only with the nature of political thinking. It must also inquire what it means to think politically. It must concern itself with the elements of a distinctiely citizen rationality, one which avoids the pitfalls of both abstract philosophy and abstract common sense.

In this chapter, I seek to examine how and to what extent Arendt treats the question of what it means to think politically. Her discussions of modern political forms, genuine and false, of course suggest elements of distinctively political thinking. I wish here to develop these further by focusing on two essays, one relatively well known, the other more obscure, which in my view illuminate her stance. I then conclude with a discussion of judging as the mental faculty most significant for the task of thinking politically. I hope in the end to capture the flavour, and the ambiguit, of her unique theoretical achievement.

In this light, the basis of Arendt's melancholy assessment of revolution and its prospects, and *inter alia* the prospects for political action and citizenship, becomes clearer. This involves more than pessimism in the face of failed revolutions. It also involves the sense that the human situation is such as to render problematic, if not futile, all efforts to make completely coherent and practically effective our best efforts to unify theory and practice, intentions and outcomes, subject and object (take your pick). However, if tradition has disappeared, the ontological issues to which it was directed remain vital.

These ontological concerns are powerfully evident in what Paul Ricoeur calls the peculiar frailty of political action in Arendt's thought. The worldly permanence of action as guaranteed by institutions of remembrance cannot be so permanent after all. People in the best of circumstances may forget, or they may simply remember wrongly; history is a contested terrain, not a fixed datum. (Viewing history as process is one way of dealing with its 'melancholy haphazardness'.) It is powerfully ironic that Hannah Arendt, who as a young woman was forced out of the cloistered pursuit of philosophy and into public life by the rise of Nazism, and who subsequently wrote of the need to recover a truly public world and the joys of public happiness, should near the end of her life leave politics behind and return to philosophy – but now without the assurance that this meant an encounter with things eternal and beyond the world, or that the turn itself was without political consequences, even if this new philosophic thought could not directly address political questions. Politics promised a world it could not deliver. Philosophy assumed a world it could not have, yet had to do so or risk incoherence.

In the end for Arendt how people, in dark times and out, lived these dilemmas with dignity, decency and courage was the most reliable measure of political possibilities in the present era.

I

Although largely hidden in arguments about other issues, there are for Arendt two powerful claims which shape a proper account of citizen rationality. The first emerges, as we have seen, in her treatment of violence and the state. It is the argument that the true citizen does not obey, because the notion of obedience is intimately associated with politics as rulership, a conception Arendt explicitly challenges. The second claim relates to the question of what determined the responses of people to the criminal demands of the Nazi state. This claim holds that the people most willing and able to resist these demands were not necessarily those who had highly developed intelligence or sophistication in moral matters. Rather, it was those able to think and judge for themselves, and thus willing to examine things critically, who most stoutly resisted.[6] These two issues – how people confront the demands of the dominant political and social institutions, and how they consciously live as individuals endowed with certain qualities in the face of their social world – define the texture of Arendt's understanding of what it means to think politically.

Following Kant, Arendt distinguishes between the intellect, which is the source of cognition and thus knowledge, and reason, the urge to think and understand, which by its nature ranges beyond that which can be known. This distinction between thinking and knowing is crucial for Arendt precisely because it carries with it political consequences of which Kant himself seemed unaware. Kant sought to deny knowledge in order to make room again for faith in a scientific era, that is, to reconstruct a systematic metaphysics. For Arendt, on the other hand, the key issue is precisely that knowing is an insufficient basis for genuine action; it is not theory as such which must inform practice, but thinking. Nor is thinking the equivalent of Kant's practical reason, which gives maxims for proper conduct. As the totalitarian experience suggests, neither knowledge, including knowledge of moral standards, nor intelligence necessarily provides a barrier against evil. While he hardly possessed a scintillating intellect, Eichmann was not stupid. Nor was he unaware of the demands of morality. He was thoughtless. It may be that not only was Eichmann's understanding of the categorical imperative flawed. The imperative itself may be problematic.

'Could the activity of thinking as such, the habit of examining whatever happens to come to pass or to attract attention, regardless of results and specific content, could this activity be among the conditions that make men abstain from "evil-doing" or even actually "condition" them against it?'[7] This question emerged from Arendt's encounter with the banal evil of Eichmann, a man who in dealing with reality seemed capable only of clichés and conventional expressions. That how we think, or whether we even think at all, bears some relation to our ability to commit evil suggests that although necessarily a solitary activity, thinking is political and moral at the same time. Even as we withdraw from the world, the company of others, the world can never be far away.

The paradox that while without results in the accepted sense of the term, thinking is nevertheless worldly – that while distinct, the *vita activa* and the *vita contemplativa* are not radically separate – is the starting point for Arendt's two-volume philosophical work, *The Life of the Mind.* But the most lucid statement of the political implications of this paradox is her 1971 essay, 'Thinking and Moral Considerations'.

In 'Thinking and Moral Considerations', Arendt sets out to demonstrate that the activity of thinking is always a kind of political process even if it involves, as it usually does, things which are not political. And it is not just that when we think we rarely focus explicitly on the behaviour of politicians or the meaning of justice. The very act of thinking seems to be 'out of order' in the world for it always involves objects which must be removed from our senses and 're-presented' to us by the imagination before they can function in the thinking process. Objects must dis-appear, become invisible, before they can reappear as thought images, and as Arendt makes clear time and again, appearance is the essence of public life. When one thinks, one has literally left the world of appearances, the only possible home for a public realm.

Nor is this all. Drawing upon the Platonic image of Socrates, the prototypical thinker in our philosophical tradition, as an 'electric ray' which 'paralyzes others only through being paralyzed itself,' Arendt suggests that in thinking we stop what we are doing, as if paralysed, because we are suddenly perplexed about things we had taken for granted, as Socrates himself was perplexed. We may even remain paralysed when we attempt once more to act precisely because we can be 'no longer sure of what had seemed . . . beyond doubt while [we] were unthinkingly engaged in whatever [we] were doing.'[8] Thinking simultaneously causes us to withdraw from the world, and at the same time it challenges and undermines our preconceived notions about the world. (Thus Socrates is not only an electric ray, but also a gadfly.) In both respects it seems to make action highly difficult, if not impossible – and action is, of course, the core element of a genuine politics.

So far, Arendt seems merely to reiterate the age-old notion that philosophy and politics are irrevocably distinct, and that the one has nothing to say to the other. Moreover, since it appears that the pursuit of philosophy, of thinking, is the product of a certain kind of love or desire which cannot reasonably be expected of most people, it seems to be a matter of interest only to a few. By contrast politics is surely an affair of the many. And even for the special few, thinking seems utterly without relevance for the problem of evil because, since the quest for wisdom 'is a kind of love and desire, the objects of thought can only be lovable things – beauty, wisdom, justice . . . Ugliness and evil are excluded by definition from the thinking concern.'[9] The implication of all this seems to be that the few of 'noble nature' (Plato) will go their own way and must be protected from the potential antagonism of the many. And since there can be no solution to the problem of evil given the inability of thinking to confront it, the surest check on it, as Plato argued in the *Republic* and the *Gorgias*, is the myth of heavenly rewards and punishments. In short, political life is necessarily about ruling and being ruled.

But Arendt does not stop here. There are two problems with this implied relation of thinking, or philosophy, to politics. In the first place, the relentlessly destructive quality of the 'dangerous and resultless enterprise' of thinking holds open the prospect that those who pursue it will not be 'content with being taught how to think without a doctrine'. Rather, they will change 'the non-results of the Socratic thinking examination into negative results . . . Such negative results of thinking will then be used as sleepily, with the same unthinking routine, as the old values; the moment they are applied to the realm of human affairs, it is as though they had never gone through the thinking process.'[10] This cynical nihilism, this notion that if a particular norm cannot be sustained then either its opposite, or no norm at all, should be upheld, is the hallmark of Socrates' misguided students, Alcibiades and Critias. It is indeed inherent in the thinking process. But it is not its product. Nihilism is a kind of anti-creed, 'the other side of conventionalism'. It arises not out of 'the Socratic conviction that an unexamined life is not worth living but, on the contrary, out of the desire to find results which would make further thinking unnecessary'.[11] The unwillingness to accept the apparent futility of the thinking process is as likely to arise among those supposedly given over to this process as it is among the non-thinking many. The possession of a 'noble nature' provides no guaranteed barrier against political irresponsibility.

In the second place, the idea, which has been all too often a political reality, that the many cannot (and given its dangers probably should not) think shields people against the need to examine what they believe and do. They are taught to 'hold fast to whatever prescribed rules of conduct may be at a given time in a given society.' They do not examine the content of these rules but use them simply to classify particulars. The rules, in short, exist as external constraints with which people lack a substantial connection. A code of values of this type can be readily shed and replaced with a new one; in fact the 'faster men held to the old code, the more eager will they be to assimilate themselves to the new one . . . How easy it was for the totalitarian rulers to reverse the basic commandments of Western morality – "Thou shalt not kill" in the case of Hitler's Germany, "Thou shalt not bear false testimony against thy neighbour" in the case of Stalin's Russia.'[12] If the urge of the few to think can fail to check the rise of cynicism and nihilism, so too can what we might call strategies of legitimation for the many, which actively discourage people from reflecting on the norms to which they are supposed to be committed, fail to prevent political disaster.

A moment's reflection suggests that for Arendt the two problems are in fact closely interconnected. They both demonstrate an indifference to the world, and to plurality. The cynical anti-creed of the nihilist suggests the zeal of ideology. The rote support of the dominant moral code suggests the mechanical automatism of behaviour. Where thinking and politics go their separate ways, each ends up a distorted mirror image of itself: the pseudo-critical, pseudo-independence of an Alcibiades, and the false communalism of a rule-regulated mass behaviour.

It is here that for Arendt the model of Socrates is decisive for both philosophy and politics. In Arendt's view, Socrates was no 'professional thinker', but rather a representative figure 'who counted himself neither among the many nor among the few.' He was a man 'who did think without becoming a philosopher, a citizen among citizens, doing nothing, claiming nothing that, in his view, every citizen should do and had a right to claim.'[13] His ability to play his representative role, to suggest that the demands of thinking are pressing for all people, hinged on his assumption that a certain sort of experience was in principle possible for all who are in possession of their faculties.

As Arendt sees it, the nature of this experience is best captured by two apparently perplexing Socratic propositions: that it is better for one to be wronged than to commit wrong; and that it is better to be at odds with the multitude of people than, as one, to be out of harmony with oneself. It is this latter proposition, the prerequisite for the first one, which particularly interests Arendt. It suggests that the peculiar oneness of an individual identity incorporates within itself a difference, since at least two elements are needed for there to be harmony, or disharmony. The identity which 'I am', and which must appear to others as truly and absolutely one if I am to be recognized, must for me involve not one element but two. I am both identical and not identical with myself. This identity which is at the same time a non-identity is the basis and outcome of consciousness: 'We call *consciousness* . . . the curious fact that in a sense I also am for myself, though I hardly appear to me . . . I am not only for others but for myself, and in this latter case, I clearly am not just one.'[14] For others, I am one, I am self-identical. For myself, for this ego related to itself, I am inevitably two-in-one.

This reality of human conciousness, obviously shared by all, gives thinking its political character. 'Human consciousness suggests that difference and otherness, which are such outstanding characteristics of the world of appearances as it is given to man as his habitat among a plurality of things, are the very conditions for the existence of man's ego as well.'[15] Consciousness makes thinking possible because the split between me and myself which it incorporates is the essence of that internal dialogue we call thinking: 'What thinking actualizes in its process is the difference given in consciousness.'[16]

It is this ground for thinking which links it with moral considerations, and gives these moral considerations an inherently political quality. As Arendt interprets Socrates, his second proposition suggests that for one who wishes to think, it is vital that the two partners in the thinking process be on good terms. This is why it is better to suffer wrong than to do wrong: one can live with a sufferer, but it is hard to live with a wrong-doer, and virtually impossible to have a dialogue with one.

The two-in-one – consciousness – obviously characterizes all people. But just as the condition of human plurality requires worldly institutions, the structures of a polis, to be actualized and guaranteed, so too in its own way does thinking, the actualization of the difference in consciousness, need its own 'home', its vehicle of remembrance. This 'home' is the solitude in which I have intercourse with myself, the place where I examine things. To return home from the affairs of the external world is to confront a partner, who is sometimes named conscience, before whom I must give an account of myself. It is this partner I fear to contradict, the one who will judge my crimes.

What the Eichmann phenomenon taught Arendt was that world alienation was not just an external, social matter. It had its internal counterpart. There are people, perhaps many, who never go home or have a home to go to, who never stop and think. 'This is not a matter of wickedness or goodness [i.e., conventional morality], as it is not a matter of intelligence or stupidity [i.e., "professional" thinking].' Thinking, a natural human need, 'is not a prerogative of the few, but an everpresent faculty of everybody.' At the same time, 'inability to think is not the "prerogative" of those many who lack brain power but the everpresent possibility for everybody – scientists, scholars, and other specialists in mental enterprises not excluded – to shun the intercourse with oneself whose possibility and importance Socrates first discovered.'[17] Those unable to examine what they say and do will not mind, or even necessarily notice, that they contradict themselves. Nor will they mind committing a crime because it will almost immediately be forgotten. They will in short without the least hesitation be able to commit evil with no particular motive for doing so.

Somehow the overcoming of both forms of world alienation, internal and external, must go together. The capacity of all to think, as opposed to the ability to acquire knowledge, is critical. Of course, Arendt does not intend to substitute thinking for acting: the two are necessarily distinct. Acting depends as much on knowing as it does on thinking, although knowing is by itself insufficient, and 'thinking as such does society little good, much less than the thirst for knowledge in which it is used as an instrument for other purposes. It does not create values, it will not find out, once and for all, what "the good" is, and it does not confirm but rather dissolves accepted rules of conduct.'[18] In fact its full political and moral meaning is evident only in extreme times: 'When everybody is swept away unthinkingly by what everybody else does and believes in, those who think are drawn out of hiding because their refusal to join is conspicuous and thereby becomes a kind of action.'[19]

To be sure, these moments of crisis, 'when', as she put it, 'the chips are down', may be more numerous than one might suspect; in any event they rarely announce themselves as such and could easily lurk in the apparently everyday and normal routines of social life. Regardless, whenever these moments come up, it is not thinking as such, with its resultlessness, which becomes manifest in the action of those who think against the grain. It is something else, the ability to say 'this is wrong' or 'this is beautiful.' It is judging, the faculty which allows us to rule on particulars without subsuming them under general standards which can be taught and learned by rote. Thus if 'thinking, the two-in-one of the soundless dialogue, actualizes the difference within our identity as given in consciousness and thereby results in conscience as its by-product, then judging, the by-product of the liberating effect of thinking, realizes thinking, makes it manifest in the world of appearances . . . The manifestation of thought is no knowledge; it is the ability to tell right from wrong, beautiful from ugly.'[20]

It is because judging manifests thinking in the world of appearances that it is for Arendt the most explicitly political of our mental faculties. It will attempt to provide a fuller treatment of it later in this chapter. For the moment, the important point to note is that citizen rationality, the capacity to think politically, requires the establishment of conditions under which people can be 'at home' with themselves, able to engage in that dialogue of the two-in-one by means of which they can examine what they say and do.[21]

Yet thinking is not only 'a marginal affair for society at large except in emergencies'.[22] It is also and necessarily individualistic. It equips us for collective life, renders us able to judge collective phenomena (or individual phenomena in the light of their collective significance). But there is a moment of collective life in the polis – the moment of solidarity, of what Arendt calls being 'with' as opposed to being 'for' or 'against' someone – that thinking as Arendt views it cannot by itself inform. For this, something else, related to thinking but distinct from it, seems necessary. This 'something else', I suggest, is what Arendt calls 'understanding'.

II

The need for solidarity as a central element of a genuine politics points to questions of how people get on and make sense together, reach agreements (or have comprehensible disagreements); in short, define their situation as a common situation, or fail to do so. In other words, solidarity involves a hermeneutic moment: how it is possible for people to express and interpret their own intentions and those of others in a world that is irreducibly plural and thus poses for its constituents problems of practical life, that is, problems of binding social and political norms that can only be solved through discussion and agreement that presupposes conscious and distinctively human purposes. Is there a hermeneutic dimension to Arendt's work which not only casts light on questions of living together, but also suggests how we might go about doing so?

'Understanding and Politics' is a passionate, haunting and allusive essay which suggests that Arendt's work does indeed posses such a dimension. Published in 1953, the essay stands where her specifically philosophic concerns intersect with her more recently developed political ones; indeed the need to make sense of totalitarianism provides the context, and much of the content, of this piece. As its title suggests, the article demonstrates that the structures of the *vita activa* and the *vita contemplativa*, even before Arendt had explicitly formulated them in this fashion, are linked together in complex ways. She leaves no doubt that whether politics is approached from the standpoint of philosophy, or philosophy from that of politics, the task which confronts us in the current, post-totalitarian situation could not be more elemental: it is to determine what 'makes it bearable for us to live with other people, strangers forever, in the same world, and makes it possible for them to bear with us.'[23] 'Understanding' is somehow central to this task.

A sense of urgency suffuses the essay as Arendt seeks to spell out as lucidly as possible a comprehensive account of our current dilemmas. Like thinking, '[u]nderstanding, as distinguished from correct information and scientific knowledge, is a complicated process which never produces unequivocal results. It is an unending activity by which, in constant change and variation, we come to terms with, reconcile ourselves to reality, that is, try to be at home in the world.' Quite simply, understanding 'is the specifically human way of being alive, for every single person needs to be reconciled to a world into which he was born a stranger and in which, to the extent of his distinct uniqueness, he always remains a stranger.'[24] Understanding and worldliness are intimately linked together and make possible the generation of meaning. The contemporary crisis of meaning, which Arendt eloquently describes in her accounts of history and science, is in a fundamental sense a crisis of understanding. Scientific knowledge, to which we have turned for illumination of practical matters, is incapable of providing such meaning and indeed, to be meaningful itself, must return to what Arendt calls 'preliminary understanding': 'those judgements and prejudices which preceded and guided the strictly scientific inquiry . . .,' and which 'permeates as a matter of course, but not with critical insight, [scientific inquiry's] whole terminology and vocabulary.'[25] Understanding, arising out of our living in the world with others, thus both precedes and succeeds knowledge.

To be sure, knowledge cannot be reduced to understanding. And understanding requires knowledge, scientific knowledge especially, if it is be not merely preliminary, but, rather, 'true', that is, critical, self-reflexive understanding. However, science is indissolubly linked with the 'stringent logicality' that has come to predominate in virtually all areas of social life. Logicality operates independently of the world and lived experience, for the internally consistent 'truths' it produces need no human, social confirmation. Thought reduced to the operations of logic loses all contact with meaningful reality and becomes static, empty. Of course thought as mere logicality has a close affinity with ideology.

Yet it is apparent why the failure of meaning has triggered the substitution of logic for common sense as the vehicle for its search. The ability to use logic is common to us all. But precisely because it is exclusively an internal operation of the individual mind, logic is unworldly and as such cannot serve to generate meaning. The pursuit of meaning is frustrated by the very means used for the purpose; this is why science by itself cannot resolve the crisis of understanding.

Only in conditions where the common realm *between* men is destroyed and the only reliability left consists in the meaningless tautologies of the self-evident, can this capacity become 'productive', develop its own lines of thought whose chief political characteristic is that they always carry with them a compulsory power of persuasion. To equate thought with these logical operations means to level down the capacity for thought, which for thousands of years has been deemed to be the highest capacity of man, to its lowest common denominator where no difference in actual existence count any longer, not even the qualitative difference between the essence of God and man.[26]

Arendt does not believe that the accepted categories of understanding can any longer permit us to deal sensibly with reality once they have been stripped of their illuminating power; this in part is what she means by the decline of tradition. While she discusses the failure of such categories with specific reference to the wholly novel problem of totalitarianism and attempts to grasp its elements by such traditional notions as 'tyranny' and 'conspiracy', she makes clear that this failure is not restricted to our perplexity about the total state. It is not our inability to grasp the essential nature of this or that political question, but our ability to think and act politically itself which is at risk. And the crisis of understanding points in the same direction as do the demands of thinking: it points towards judging. Thus: 'Is not understanding so closely related to and intersected with judging that one must describe both as the subsumption of something particular under a universal rule which according to Kant is the very definition of judgement, whose absence he so magnificently defined as "stupidity", an "infirmity beyond remedy"?'[27]

Although understanding and thinking clearly stem from a common source – the need for us to reconcile ourselves to a world which we create but do not absolutely control – they differ subtly but significantly in their relation to action. While thinking shapes the conditions under which action takes place, understanding is a kind of thinking-in-action. As Arendt puts it: 'If the essence of all, and in particular of political, action is to make a new beginning, then understanding becomes the other side of action, namely that form of cognition, in distinction from many others, by which acting men . . . eventually can come to terms with what irrevocably happened and be reconciled with what unavoidably exists.'[28] If thinking suggests the dimensions of a subjective objectivity – how as conscious individuals we require a worldly solitude for our unique two-in-one dialogues – then understanding points towards the elements of an objective subjectivity: the ways in which as embodied individuals we engage others who are like us in their very distinctiveness. Thinking involves the world which must be present (or more accurately re-presented) in its absence. Understanding involves engagement with the world without submersion in it, which would come about if individuals were merely exemplifiers of those trends which contemplative philosophies of history and statistical analyses consider them to be.[29] Both are crucial for citizen rationality.

The contours of understanding, this distanced engagement with the world, brings to mind for Arendt what philosophers call the hermeneutic circle, the claim that when we confront the demands of practical life, '[u]nderstanding and consent [of and to one's life situation] are not only in question . . . they are also underlying elements.'[30] As Arendt puts it, 'understanding is a strange enterprise. In the end, it may do no more than articulate and confirm what preliminary understanding, which always consciously or unconsciously is directly engaged in action, sensed to begin with. It will not shy away from this circle but on the contrary be aware that any other results would be so far removed from action, of which it is only the other side, that they could not possibly be true.' She goes on to suggest how thinking and understanding are intimately connected, even given their differences, for in its apparently 'vicious' circularity, understanding 'may . . . even somewhat resemble philosophy whose great thoughts always turn around in circles, engaging the human mind in nothing less than an interminable dialogue between itself and the essence of everything that is.'[31]

Given the peculiar character of understanding, which involves returning to a starting point we have never really left without at the same time simply regaining this point as if we had not taken a journey, understanding requires a distinctive quality. According to Arendt, this quality is to be found in the uniquely human gift of the 'understanding heart'. This gift, as 'far removed from sentimentality as it is from paperwork', and neither 'mere reflection nor mere feeling' (and thus the opposite of revolutionary pity) is nothing less than the faculty of imagination which, to borrow from Wordsworth, as Arendt does, is reason in its most exalted mood. Imagination allows us both to put 'distance' between ourselves and things which would otherwise be too closely at hand for us to grasp their significance, and to bridge the abyss between phenomena whose remoteness from each other obscures their underlying relationship. As Arendt sees it, this distancing of some things and bridging the abyss to others 'is part of the dialogue of understanding for whose purposes direct experience establishes too close a contact and mere knowledge erects artificial barriers.'[32]

And the possibility of imagination becoming an effective force in the world has an ontological foundation: 'Even though we have lost yardsticks by which to measure, and rules under which to subsume the particular, a being whose essence is beginning may have enough of origin within himself to understand without preconceived categories.'[33] This 'being' is in fact a multiplicity of 'beings', 'contemporaries' in the world. But our ability to live as contemporaries, that is, in solidarity, is not guaranteed. 'We are contemporaries only so far as our understanding reaches. If we want to be at home on this earth, even at the price of being at home in this century, we must take part in the interminable dialogue with its essence.'[34] Like the capacity to think, the ability to understand is a given of the human situation whose actualization is always in doubt. Both point to the possibility of humans actively creating a world within which their capacities can be denied, a world of false politics.

III

The complex character of politically grounded thinking, a distinctive citizen rationality, is evident in Arendt's accounts of thinking and understanding. This rationality must be both subjective and objective, a matter of both inner and outer experience. It must partake of both solitude and community; it must make it possible for me to be for myself while being with others, indeed to be for myself *because* I am with others. Hannah Arendt considers judging the most explicitly political of our mental faculties because it actualizes in the realm of appearances what it means to think politically. It is judging's peculiar quality that it involves both thinking in the stead of another (and thus requires the presence of others) and the capacity to determine 'right' and 'wrong', the 'beautiful' and the 'ugly', which are distinctive hallmarks of the 'who' one shows oneself to be in appearing before others in a public space.

As noted in chapter 3, the concept of judgement plays an important part in Arendt's accounts of the crisis in culture and the politics of lying, where it is seen to be the quality which allows us to rule about the things in our world, while at the same time respecting the existence of this world as a domain we cannot will out of existence through acts of sovereign creativity. Judgement was there identified with an 'enlarged mentality', the capacity to put oneself in the place of another, to engage in 'representative thinking'. In 'Thinking and Moral Considerations' and in the volume *Thinking* in *The Life of the Mind*, judging involves the ability to make moral and aesthetic distinctions in a way that could condition against the commission of evil; this is also the role judging plays for Arendt in the context of the Eichmann trial. And in the *Lectures on Kant's Political Philosophy*, judging entails in addition to these the evaluation by the spectator of events going on around him or her (in Kant's own case, the French Revolution).

Arendt did not live to write the volume on judging which would have formed the third part of *The Life of the Mind*. But those elements of what she had to say on the matter which do exist, most notably the lectures on Kant's political philosophy and the abbreviated version of them which was added as an appendix to the volume on willing in the *The Life of the Mind*, are sufficient to support the view that it is this quality which both allows us to think politically, and expresses our ability actually to do so. The different meanings of judging can be seen not as radically distinct forms of it, but rather as different aspects of the same complex phenomenon which is both philosophical and political, individual and collective, at one and the same time.[35]

Although she gave in her later treatment of it a more specifically individualistic and philosophic twist, Arendt always presupposed the existence of an enlarged mentality as the ground upon which judgement could be exercised. Unlike thoughts or cognitions, judgements are always public. To claim that something is right or wrong, or beautiful or ugly, is to presuppose the presence of others who will assent to or challenge the claim. Because of this indispensable element of publicity, judgements do not only assert. They also seek to persuade, although this element of persuasion may be hidden by the apparent demand of a judgement to be absolutely binding.[36]

For judgements to be both assertive and persuasive, or persuasive in their assertiveness, certain conditions must be realized. It is these conditions which Arendt seeks to articulate in her use of the Kantian notion of the enlarged mentality, or the 'enlargement of the mind'.[37] This enlargement is achieved by 'comparing our judgement with the possible rather than the actual judgements of others, and by putting ourselves in the place of any other man.'[38] Only in this way can our judgements possess the genuinely persuasive power that comes from participation in a common situation, a 'common sense'.

The faculty which allows us to put ourselves in the place of another is the imagination, the very gift of an 'understanding heart' which Arendt considers so vital to rational understanding. The 'force of the imagination' makes other people present and 'thus moves in a space that is potentially public, open to all sides; in other words, it adopts the position of Kant's world citizen.' Hence: 'To think with an enlarged mentality means that one trains one's imagination to go visiting.'[39] To be able to 'visit' – to be at home in the world – requires the ability to move outside of the singularity of one's own conscious experience and develop empathy with others.

But Arendt does not assume that the enlarged mentality involves simple replication in the mind of one person of what is found in the mind of another. (Although her critique of behaviourism certainly suggests that to the extent that action is displaced by behaviour, such replication may become a literal fact.) Rather, '[t]o think, according to Kant's understanding of enlightenment, means *SELBSTDENKEN*, to think for oneself, "which is the maxim of a never-passive reason. To be given to such passivity is called prejudice." ' She goes on to claim that to accept 'what goes on in the minds of those whose "standpoint" (actually, the place where they stand, the conditions they are subject to, which always differ from one individual to the next, from one class or group as compared to another) is not my own would mean no more than passively to accept their thought, that is, to exchange their prejudices for the prejudices proper to my own station.'[40] The key is consciously to transcend the limits of self-interest, and to do so not by simply adopting the self-interested position of another. What is required is to think in terms of the world and not life.

Because the central element of the enlarged mentality is the ability to incorporate the standpoints of others in one's thinking without simply adopting them in place of one's own, the achievement of the enlarged mentality involves, according to Kant, the assumption of the role of the impartial spectator, the 'viewpoint from which to look upon, to watch, to from judgements, or, as Kant says, to reflect upon human affairs'. For Kant, such spectatorship is from the standpoint of political action, purely passive: 'Kant does tell one how to take others into account; he does not tell one how to combine with them in order to act.'[41]

It is at this point that, in my view, Arendt parts company with Kant and stakes out her own position on the political implications of judging. From Arendt's perspective, judging as spectatorship only seems passive. To adopt the standpoint of another without attempting to replicate what is in that person's mind is to take the place of another without taking it over. It is to let others 'be', while reaffirming that we all 'be' together; it involves a certain sort of 'receptivity' to others.[42] At the same time, not to replicate what is in the mind of another allows one to criticize what is there. In other words: judgement as spectatorship, the enlarged mentality, seeks to go beyond the dilemma of 'imputed' versus 'empirical' consciousness. (To this extent, judging avoids the pitfalls of ideology, with obvious implications particularly for a progressive politics too often haunted by the lure of vanguardism.)

All this is not without consequences for those dimensions of judgement which at first glance appear apolitical. Kant himself seemed to recognize this in his distinction between genius and taste, and the consequent relation between the artist and the audience. At stake is the status of beauty: whether it inheres in an object exclusively or whether it involves the relation of this object to a collective milieu, that is, whether it is a matter of reception. Kant leaves no doubt it is the latter. As he puts it: 'Abundance and originality of ideas are less necessary to beauty than the accordance of the imagination in its freedom with the conformity to the law of the understanding [which is called taste].'[43] The use of the term 'law', so prevalent throughout Kant's philosophy, already suggests a political context. This is affirmed in Kant's argument that while genius, the unteachable ability to give form in a unique way to ideas, is essential to artistic creation, its primary task is to make 'generally communicable' ideas which only the artist can make visible, but which we are all capable of sharing. According to Arendt, the 'faculty that guides this communicability is taste, and taste or judgement is not the privilege of genius.' As Arendt indicates in 'The Crisis in Culture', both political action and beautiful objects are meant to appear; both require a public space. She notes: 'The condition *sine qua non* for the existence of beautiful objects is communicability; the judgement of the spectator creates the space without which no such objects could appear at all. The public realm is constituted by the critics and the spectators, not by the actors or the makers. And this critic and spectator sits in every actor and fabricator; without this critical, judging faculty the doer or maker would be so isolated from the spectator that he would not even be perceived. Or, to put it another way, still in Kantian terms: the very originality of the artist (or the very novelty of the actor) depends on his making himself understood by those who are not artists (or actors). And while one can speak of genius in the singular . . . [s]pectators exist only in the plural.'[44] What spectators have in common with one another, and this includes the maker or the doer to the extent that she is necessarily also a spectator, is judgement.

It is here that the importance of common sense, *sensus communis*, becomes evident. This sense is both the ground of judging and is reconstituted by judgements themselves to the extent that these judgements exhibit the existence of an enlarged mentality. Again, Arendt cites Kant: '[U]nder the *sensus communis* we must include the idea of a sense *common to all*, i.e. a faculty of judgement which, in its reflection, takes into account (a priori) of the mode of representation of all other men in thought, in order, *as it were*, to compare its judgement with the collective reason of humanity.'[45] The political significance here is that common sense is the ground of aesthetic and moral judgements which appear to be without political content. As

Arendt puts it, the 'it-pleases-or-displeases-me, which as a feeling seems so utterly private and noncommunicative, is actually rooted in this community sense and is therefore open to communication once it has been transformed by reflection, which takes all others and their feelings into account . . . In other words, when one judges, one judges as a member of a community.'[46] All judging is political, although not all judgements are (or should be) political judgements. The ability to say 'this is right' or 'this is beautiful' is closely connected with the possession of an enlarged mentality, while evidence of this mentality is provided by the character of such judgements.

Arendt derives this account from Kant's writings. For her, judgement is at the core of his submerged political philosophy. And this is the rub: while Arendt's account takes Kant's views in a direction strongly suggested by these views, it is not a direction Kant himself took. That she does so is not merely a question of coming to terms with an important philosophical influence. It also involves the dilemmas and tensions of political philosophy, and the way in which these provide clues to the status of political action, and thus what it means to think politically, in the contemporary era.

The nature of these dilemmas can best be gleaned through an examination of two tensions or contradictions Arendt finds in Kant's work. Both of them suggest why his explicitly political reflections are peculiarly detached from, and inferior to, his philosophic insights. The first of these relates to the position of the spectator in political affairs. As is well known, Kant as a spectator himself enthusiastically approved of the French Revolution, even as he strongly condemned the actions of those who brought it about as being in conflict with the demands of right and the moral law. This is because the spectator 'can perceive [the] design of providence or nature, which is hidden from the actor . . . In the context of the French Revolution, it seemed to Kant that the spectator's view carried the ultimate meaning of the event, although this view yielded no maxim for action.'[47] However wrong the actions of the revolutionaries themselves, the historical judgement rendered by the spectator indicates that the revolution accorded with the hidden design of nature, or providence; it was a step on the road to the universal kingdom of ends, a cosmopolitan world. In this case, morally wrong actions produced historically beneficial, even necessary, results.

In this context, although Kant's position may be ironic, it does not necessarily involve a dilemma. It rather points to the gulf between the moral philosopher and the political actor (or even the political theorist). It suggests that politics and morality are at odds – which of course is a common view of the matter in any case. If Kant had stopped here, nothing much more would need to be said, save perhaps to counter Kant's position with that of, for example, Machiavelli (Arendt's own choice) and his very different conception of the relations of means to ends, good to evil.

But Kant did not stop here. According to Arendt, he deals with a situation that is the opposite of the French Revolution, and in so doing reveals more explictly the dilemma of spectatorship and a more problematic relation between morality and politics. This is 'a situation where the single events offer a spectacle that is "sublime", and so do the actors, and where, moreover, the sublimity may well coincide with the hidden design of nature; and still reason, which yields our maxims, categorically forbids us to engage in this "sublime" act.'[48] The issue at hand is Kant's position on war and his maxim that people are morally obligated to pursue peace.

For Kant, moral-practical reason demands that there shall be no war. It is our moral duty to act as if perpetual peace could really come about, even in the face of all evidence to the contrary. Yet at the same time, Kant, the spectator exercising historical judgement, views war as essential to human progress. The act of war, in its revelation of courage, is a sublime act. 'On the other hand, a long peace generally brings about a predominant commercial spirit and, along with it, low selfishness, cowardice, and effeminacy, and debases the disposition of the people.'[49] By stirring up human passions and prodding people to develop their capacities to the fullest, conflict among nations serves nature's ends.

Arendt expresses the tension in this way: 'Even though Kant would always have acted for peace, he knew and kept in mind his judgement. Had he acted on the knowledge he had gained as a spectator, he would, in his own mind, have been criminal. Had he forgotten, because of his "moral duty", his insights as a spectator, he would have become what so many good men, involved and engaged in public affairs, tend to be – an idealistic fool.'[50] The significance of the political philosophy, based on judgement, that Kant did not write becomes evident here. For what Kant does not see is the possibility that the gulf between the spectator and the actor could be bridged precisely by means of a capacity to judge which is grounded in the *sensus communis*. The relation of the individual, who as Arendt points out stands at the centre of Kant's moral philosophy, and 'the human race' in its progress, which is at the centre of his philosophy of history, can be rendered less obscure and more meaningful to individuals themselves.

The need to reconcile the individual and species, being and history, which a clearly developed and articulated political philosophy might have done, is evident in the second tension or contradiction that Arendt identifies: that between Kant's doctrine of human progress and his commitment to human dignity. As Arendt puts it: 'Infinite Progress is the law of the human species; at the same time, man's dignity demands that he be seen (every single one of us) in his particularity and, as such, be seen – but without any comparison and independent of time – as reflecting mankind in general. In other words, the very idea of progress – if it is more that a change in circumstances and an improvement of the world – contradicts Kant's notion of man's dignity.'[51] If an individual is judged by the moral content of his or her actions, what meaning can this have if the standard by which humanity as a whole is judged cannot be the basis of moral actions and indeed, to the extent that they are actors and not spectators, cannot even be recognized by individuals themselves?

Here, too, Arendt finds a potential solution to this contradiction in Kant's understanding of judging, and in particular his conception of those judgements which are exemplary: an 'exemplar is and remains a particular that in its very particularity reveals the generality that otherwise could not be defined.'[52] The particular which is a generality in its very particularity promises a more substantially grounded and accessible relation of the individual to the whole, a more recognizably human link, mandated by Kant's very philosophy itself, between past and future.

Given that Kant's account of judging pointed towards a political basis for this faculty, and a political character to its exercise, why did he not follow up on these intimations? Why, in other words, did he not write his political philosophy? The answer is not simply that Kant has the philosopher's contempt for politics. As Arendt points out, reason itself is for Kant a communal quality.[53] The answer lies rather in the peculiarly persuasive quality of judging itself, a quality which Kant clearly recognized. Judgement is closely intertwined with the *sensus communis*, and this common sense for Kant involved certain maxims of conduct: the maxims of enlightenment, of enlarged mentality, of consistency. As Arendt notes, such maxims 'are not matters of cognition; truth compels, one doesn't need any "maxims". Maxims apply and are needed only for matters of opinion and in judgements [i.e., in politics]. And just as, in moral matters, one's maxim of conduct testifies to the quality of one's will, so the maxims of judgement testify to one's "turn of thought" (*Denkungsart*) in the worldly matters that are ruled by the community sense.'[54] The inability of judgements to possess the compelling power of truth made it difficult for Kant, who sought after all to restore the lost lustre of metaphysics, to accept that they could adequately ground a political philosophy (or, if you prefer, a political metaphysic). And given what Arendt sees as Kant's Sophoclean melancholy about life – a 'time of probation' he called it – it is also evident that from Arendt's point of view there is in Kant's philosophy some of the disdain for the world that she finds to be the unfortunate hallmark of modern thought as a whole.[55]

To put it another way: Kant's hope for the human race was by and large detached from his pessimism about human affairs. He saw no way of reconciling them except by resort to the ruse of nature. As Arendt sees it, a theory of progress is not optimistic about human prospects, even if it professes such optimism. It is fearful, if not dismissive, of them.[56] Only that perspective which reconciles hope and pessimism can be genuinely optimistic – precisely the perspective Arendt sought to articulate in *Eichmann in Jerusalem*. The life of the citizen, a life of reason and publicity (two concepts also critical for Kant), is a necessary forum in which this reconciliation can be actualized, although there is no guarantee that this will come about. Accepting the necessary frailty of the public realm means accepting the frailty of judging, a frailty which, to use the words of Paul Ricoeur, is more powerful and secure than any metaphysical guarantee.

In Kant's work itself there are hints about how, through judgement, this reconciliation could be brought about. For one thing, the 'critic and spectator sits in every actor and fabricator,' not only in the few. For another, Kant's concept of common sense calls to mind Cicero's claim that it is truly marvellous and remarkable 'how little difference there is between the learned and the ignorant in judging.'[57] That all, or almost all, people have these capabilities suggests that in spite of the evidence suggesting otherwise, surprisingly great things, political things involving the many and not just the few, could always come into being. Revolutions have until now failed. They may or may not ever succeed in their task of constituting a genuine space of appearance. But attempts to create this space can never be ruled out; no philosophy of history, Kantian, Marxian or otherwise – nor any anti-philosophy of history – can truly grasp if, when or where these might take place.[58] For political theorists as well as other citizens, thinking politically, and not just political thinking, is vital.

That the capacity to judge is in fact available to all suggests that there are in principle no limits to who can be an 'exemplar', one able to crystallize the promises, fears, hopes and prospects of collective life. In this respect perhaps the clearest and certainly the most moving statement of Hannah Arendt's own hopes for public life was written during the darkest days of the Second World War. Fittingly, it is devoted to the work of Franz Kafka:

[Kafka] wanted to build up a world in accordance with human needs and human dignities, a world where man's actions are determined by himself and which is ruled by his laws and not by mysterious forces emanating from above or from below . . . In order to become part of such a world . . . he first had to anticipate the destruction of a misconstructed world. Through this anticipated destruction he carried the image, the supreme figure of man as a model of good will, of man the *fabricator mundi*, the world-builder who can get rid of misconstructions and reconstruct his world. And since these heroes are only models of good will and left in anonymity, the abstractness of the general, shown only in the very function good will may have in this world of ours, his novels seem to have a singular appeal as though he wanted to say: This man may be anybody and everybody, perhaps even you and me.[59]

It is this '*fabricator mundi*' who has the ability to, and the need to, ask: 'what kind of world am I creating by my actions, and would I want to live in it were someone else creating it?'

Conclusion: Whither Political Theory?

What is the use of political theory? In the Introduction to this book, I suggested that the recent explosion of academic political theory has gone hand in hand with the apparently diminishing ability of people to control their own affairs directly and meaningfully. I further suggested that we needed a new sense of the nature of the political and its role in human society. This would allow us rationally to assess current political prospects, while keeping in touch with the lived experience of individuals and their real, as opposed to imagined or fetishized, capacities to participate in public life.

While at one level my intention involves bridging the gap between theory and practice, at another it is rather more modest than this: to draw upon and reinforce the ability of people to reflect upon their shared bonds, whether of conflict or co-operation, in a manner which could allow them to judge what they and others do. My hope was to find a way by which we would be encouraged, ultimately by ourselves, to 'think what we are doing'.

I have argued that Hannah Arendt provides us with a unique and powerful contribution to this task. To be sure, her work is political theory (how *academic* it might be is an interesting subject for discussion) and draws upon the specialized language of this intellectual pursuit. But I hope that my treatment of her ideas has at least suggested that such language need not, current depressing tendencies notwithstanding, remain foreign to the everyday concerns of potentially responsible citizens, at least as these involve matters that can be objects of the kind of reflection that results in judgements. There is a conversational quality to Arendt's writings, even her more specifically philosophical ones, an invitation to think with her that could reach a larger audience than scholars or academics or intellectuals alone. In other words, Arendt writes for a public sphere that is 'not yet' but some day 'may be'.

To claim that Arendt's writings have this quality is I think to claim something else as well: that her work has a distinctively personal character. In my view the term 'personal', indeed the notion of the 'person', has been denied a meaningful role in most dominant currents of political thought. Here it is possible to understand in a particularly illuminating way Arendt's concern about the potentially corrosive effects of philosophy on politics. Our theoretical language of politics (in some respects, Arendt's included) treats 'subjects' and 'individuals'. From Arendt's perspective, both can become philosophical abstractions which represent sovereign vantage points on the world, conceptually and politically. By contrast, the notion of the 'person' entails the idea of reciprocity and hence the condition of plurality whereby distinct biological beings are nevertheless bound together such that the recognition of each is made possible by the recognition of others.

The qualities of persons in this sense are expressed by and through those distinctive characteristics Arendt associates with free action in a public realm: the revelation of one's 'who', the capacity to forgive, the ability to make and keep promises.[1] The modes of thinking which both develop with the personal and allow us to grasp it theoretically in the sense I mean it here are understanding and judging. Since, taken together, these constitute what are for Arendt genuine political thinking and political acting, in a powerful sense the personal is truly the political.

This is *not* to say that the *private* is the political. Arendt's argument is that this relation of personal to political requires not the obliteration but the preservation of the distinction between private and public spheres, at least in so far as the private involves those qualities of personal intimacy that cannot stand the glare of publicity. Indeed this distinction must be *deepened*. 'A life spent entirely in public, in the presence of others, becomes, as we would say, shallow. While it retains its visibility, it loses the quality of rising into sight from some darker ground which must remain hidden if it is not to lose its depth in a very real, non-subjective sense.'[2]

To see the personal as the political and, just as important, the political as a constitutive element of the personal, is to acknowledge a kind of connectedness, a solidarity, with others. Arendt calls this connectedness the web of relationships. This is an 'in-between' among people who share the capacities for speech and action, and can thus disclose 'who' they are. The web is intangible but none the less real because 'the physical worldly in-between along with its interests is overlaid and, as it were, overgrown with an altogether different in-between which consists of deeds and words and owes its origins exclusively to men's acting and speaking directly *to* one another.'[3] The particular quality of this web is that it is both context and creation. Acting individuals, embedded within an existing web shaped by the actions of others with whose life trajectories one necessarily comes into contact, initiate processes which alter the shape of this web, and affect other life stories in unpredictable ways.

Of course it is precisely in order to deal with the unpredictable consequences of such action that Arendt emphasizes the capacities for forgiveness, and for making and keeping promises. And it is in this context that the significance of her critical analysis of sovereignty comes clearly into focus. Sovereignty is the futile attempt to escape the web of relationships which can only therefore be an assault on the capacities for speech and action. But I wish here to examine two other implications of the relation of the personal to the political in Arendt's work.

In the first place, Arendt's resort to metaphor as the only mode of expression that can capture the intangible reality of the web of relationships gives a powerful aesthetic cast to her fundamental political ideas. Specifically, it points to the importance of a common life of action in a worldly place, a public realm. As we saw in chapter 1, stories in the sense of the accounts of actions with identifiable agents or protagonists, but not authors, provide the stuff of a genuine history – the need for stories and the necessity of history imply each other. What is important about stories and persons is that stories can make the consequences of actions both comprehensible and bearable. Borrowing from Isak Dinesen, Arendt argues that almost anything can be borne if put into a story and shared with others.[4] In a very powerful and non-trivial sense, stories are consoling. In this respect they are the counterpart to ideology in the same way that action is the counterpart to labour.

Understanding the importance of this aesthetic dimension for a genuine politics answers one question – how one can 'know' and deal with the consequences of action – while raising another one: what is the relation of this 'personal' politics to political institutions more generally and conventionally understood? In these reflections on personal revelation we seem far removed from politics at the level of the state. Yet perhaps not. Clearly one aspect of Arendt's position is her evident preference for small-scale republican forms like the revolutionary councils and town-hall meetings over large-scale, impersonal (in both the conventional and Arendtian senses), representative and bureaucratic institutions.

But there is something else as well. That action undertaken in a web of relationships produces unintended consequences, indeed that it is because actors are embedded in a web of relationships that action generates consequences, means that our intentions can never be fully realized in the world. In fact our actions can boomerang, their consequences neither desired nor desirable. We can have a difficult time living with things that with all the good will in the world we could not or did not prevent. To life in a plural world there is thus a tragic dimension.

However, to say that life has a tragic dimension is *not* to claim that life itself is tragedy, much less that Arendt has a tragic vision of things. Although Arendt's thought has an aesthetic dimension, politics is not art, the actor is not an artist. The plight of the artist *as* artist is different from the situation of a person (including the artist in so far as she acts) as actor. The actor encounters not human and non-human material as means of artistic expression, but other actors. She thus encounters the prospect of solidarity, a milieu within which precisely the ability to make and keep promises, and to forgive and be forgiven, is possible. Where this is possible, people can bear suffering as beings who both initiate and undergo the consequences of actions. Tragedy can be met by reconciliation. Art can facilitate but not displace this reconciliation.[5]

While it might be clear that the personal and the political are connected in a unique way for Arendt, it still might be wondered how the political in this sense relates to the existing world of states and governments, corporations and public bureaucracies, political parties and interest groups. Is there a gap between politics (including politics as economics in the form of a corporate-directed economy) and the distinctively political? Ultimately, even though Arendt writes of momentous historical phenomena such as totalitarianism and revolution, and discusses existing institutions such as courts and juries, one must acknowledge that there is a gap. Moreover, because these institutions are very much the products of and implicated in the rise of the social realm, there seems as little prospect that they can be made authentically political as there is for the abolition of the social realm itself.[6] In these circumstances it seems unlikely that existing institutions can be in any way relevant to Arendt's concerns. Whether or not one accepts her account of the political, one must look elsewhere for practical insights about political change.

I do not believe this to be the case. The demand for public space could conceivably be pressed within the framework of existing institutions. In chapter 2, I pointed out recent examples of this. It is possible, in other words, at least to envisage elementary republics emerging in the present.[7] And as I suggested in my discussions of Marx and of revolution, it is even possible within Arendt's own framework to open up social matters to political determination. In other words, even if modern states must remain, and corporate capitalism will be with us for the foreseeable future, there is in principle the prospect of limiting their capacity to render people passive objects of forces beyond their control.

Even more significantly than this, however, is that the personal qualities required for acting and judging are highly relevant to existing as well as prospective institutions. Like Aristotle, Arendt wrote her 'ethics' at least alongside, if not before, her 'politics'. Moreover, and this is a very powerful current in Arendt's work, the capacities needed for this are potentially well within the range of almost everyone. By contrast, Karl Marx, who makes rather heroic demands of the working class if it is to emancipate society, is for this reason much more likely to breed deep pessimism about human prospects than is Arendt (as witnessed by Lefort, Castoriadis and Heller).

So I would argue that Arendt can tell us much about how we can think and act in the present situation. It all depends upon what you are looking for. In search of the knowledge that can make things right, harmonious, tidy, transparent, we are all the 'sufferers' of sovereignty. Arendt asks us to resist this, without at the same time claiming that this resistance itself transforms things or, on the other side, that one should be politically quiescent. To 'think what we are doing' has consequences.

But it is still thinking, and it will not fully resolve ambiguities about what to do. To the extent, however, and this is one of the lessons of Arendt's treatment of Socrates, that one can live with oneself, then one can live with others. But both forms of living together are always achievements, never givens. Can we come to terms with this without succumbing either to a kind of decisionism or to tragic despair?

I want to conclude this book by dealing with three essays which show how Arendt's account can make clear the relation of the personal to the political, and therefore suggest how her political theory is a unique source of insights into our situation. The first of these essays is an exercise in 'conventional' political theory by a thinker strongly influenced by Arendt. The other two are by Arendt herself and are 'personal' reflections on her two main mentors, Karl Jaspers and Martin Heidegger, studies that powerfully demonstrate how 'the personal is the political.' In effect these latter essays demonstrate what it means to judge, and are judgements themselves.

I

Several years ago, in a remarkable essay, Paul Kress, an American political theorist, argued that we could more clearly understand the problem of political action and valuation, or the problem of thinking and acting, in terms of two metaphors of 'reason and value': the web and the tree. As a conception of human action, the tree metaphor accords fully with the utilitarian view of action as instrumental, rational-purposive behaviour, which attempts to marshal the most appropriate means for the realization of given ends. At the level of values, the metaphor provides an analytic scheme by means of which the immediate values or preferences that justify group or individual behaviour, or policy choices, can in turn be traced back through the branches of the tree to the trunk – the fundamental value beyond which no further justification can be offered.

The tree metaphor has the virtue of clarity. A systematic classification scheme plus an empirical theory of causal relationships can lay the basis for the formal derivation of policy consequences from the root value. But the root value, the ultimate justification, cannot itself be ultimately justified. In a policy context, the determination of values or ends is a product of pure decisionism, a prerogative of the decision-maker or sovereign (recall Arendt's critique of sovereignty). 'The political scientist, qua citizen, may decline to implement certain public values, but this opposition must be understood as *his* ultimate value preference and not as an imperative of science, reason, or his profession.'[8]

On the other hand, the metaphor of the web suggests a far less ordered arrangement of value preferences and motives for action. It envisages a value system as a set of webs stretched across the ground of experience, with the strands of the webs representing logical and empirical connections among phenomena, and the intersections or terminations of strands representing values. Some peripheral and internal strands, although not necessarily those that terminate in the most important values, are anchored to the ground and represent the most specific applications of values to experience. Changes in the content and scope of experience alter the shape of the web and its capacity to handle stress and strain. The fundamental idea is that the relation of values to experience is more fluid, far less analytically precise, than the metaphor of the tree, or utilitarianism, suggests. The web can develop asymmetrically in response to the changing character of experience, with the centre of the web, its core values, shifting accordingly; it is difficult to imagine the trunk of the tree being so altered. Thus the web metaphor conveys the idea of systemic interdependence, and thus of functional interrelation. It suggests an openness to modification through experience that seems characteristic of the human organism . . . [And] while the connections which obtain among trunk, branch, twig, and leaf are highly structured, indeed invariant – that is, from any leaf there is one direct path to the roots – the knots or ties of the web have multi-level, multi-path interconnections.[9]

In suggesting that the metaphor of the web is truer to actual experience than is the metaphor of the tree – in Arendt's terms, that political action is not work – Kress is claiming that the tree metaphor fundamentally misrepresents the nature of moral-practical choices that emerge in the course of everyday life in a plural world of 'systemic interdependence and functional interrelation'. He notes that the utilitarian view of individual action and the character of the rational actor misses 'the intricate and trans-individual network of collective values that structure, support and inhibit individual choice and behaviour'. He stresses that 'the values of this contextual setting include "non-logical" (traditional, religious, habitual) imperatives as well as their instrumental efficacy.'[10] Moreover, even the most resolutely utilitarian individualism must concede the existence of some shared context, some 'idea of fundamental principles or constitutional laws which are prior and superior to the pursuit of interest and the conduct of politics.'[11]

In the end, the metaphor of the web shows clearly that in the public realm, 'a desired state of affairs is less an isolable "object" than a particular configuration of values.'[12] Kress concludes from this that political theory and political science should not seek the rigorous 'precision' of economic theory or natural science, and that the model of the rational actor most appropriate to political theory is not the scientist, as it is for utilitarianism, but the (classical) politician. Ultimately Kress seeks to vindicate the classical doctrine of politics, 'the Platonic lesson that knowledge yields not only power but virtue'.[13]

While Arendt might have had reservations about the classical doctrine of politics, I think she would have accepted Kress's conclusions. She would have also agreed with what Kress implies: that virtue is not conformity of action with dogmatically stated norms, but rather a quality of lived experience situated within the web, the 'intricate and trans-individual network of collective values'. That 'virtue' has this quality, and can show itself in surprising ways as a result, is evident from her essays on Jaspers and Heidegger.

II

In a collection of personal portraits called *Men in Dark Times*, Arendt writes of men and women who have played for us the role of 'exemplars'. Such people reveal to us in a profound way the character and limits of public life in particular historical periods. In a century of 'dark times', when the light which the public realm casts on human affairs has been extinguished by everything from 'credibility gaps' to 'invisible governments', we have gained illumination from individuals who have made our situation comprehensible to us. They have left us with the sense that, however grim things are or have been, they could be otherwise. They have done so not because they have reflected the 'trends' of the time, but because they have largely stood against them.

Arendt's reflections here suggest that, alongside Marx and Kant, there stands a third figure of crucial importance for her political thought. This figure is Machiavelli, a thinker who also viewed the personal as an indispensable moment of the public realm. Machiavelli saw in history exemplars of his own who showed what could be done when all seemed resistant to change, individuals who, in Arendt's terms, thrust themselves through word and deed into the glare of public life.

The Machiavellian 'moment' in Arendt's thought has for the most part gone unnoticed, largely because she nowhere provides a systematic account of his work. But the frequent inability of analysts to grasp the essential elements of Arendt's account of the public realm in part reflects this lack of sensitivity to the importance of Machiavelli for her thought. And both are frequently subjected to similarly misleading criticisms. For example, both are seen to have effected an absolute rupture between morality and politics. Yet moral considerations are clearly decisive for Arendt's work, and for Machiavelli's too. After all, he neither calls vice virtue nor argues that the prince should not be moral. What both Arendt and Machiavelli argue against is a certain sort of public morality that, in its profession of virtue, in fact sustains the opposite. As Maurice Merleau-Ponty brilliantly points out, 'What is a goodness incapable of harshness? What is a goodness which wants to be goodness? A meek way of ignoring others and ultimately despising them.'[14] The Machiavelli who exerts a powerful influence on Arendt is the Machiavelli, neither a cynic nor an innocent, who is aware of 'that knot of collective life in which pure morality can be cruel and pure politics requires something like a morality'.[15] This is the Machiavelli who also knows the difference between the subject and the person, who understands that people 'judge by their eyes rather than by their hands; because everyone is in a position to watch, few are in a position to come in close touch with you.'[16] It is the Machiavelli who counsels political responsibility and demands that political actors know what they are doing, even if and indeed because they cannot know what their actions might ultimately bring about.

Because Machiavelli believed politics the highest human calling and the world its forum, he sought to challenge those who brought unworldly concerns into the public realm and so threatened to destroy it. Among his targets were the learned men of religion. Arendt, too, wants to preserve the world, and among the targets of her critical account are the successors to the medieval theologians: the philosophers and intellectuals who destroy their own thinking in the false politicization of it, very much as for Machiavelli the Church destroyed itself in its acquisition of a falsely political role.

These concerns set the context within which Hannah Arendt addresses the political legacy of Karl Jaspers and Martin Heidegger. What she says about each gives a clear sense of how Arendt thought politically about people and issues that mattered to her in profound ways.

While making a thinker stand for a concept is from Arendt's perspective a dubious exercise, it still may be suggestive to see Jaspers as the embodiment of the achievements of judging, while Heidegger represents the dilemmas of thinking and the potential perils of philosophy. Karl Jaspers, who sought in his thought to articulate and defend the notions of universal humanity and world citizenship, in a world notably hostile to both, provides for Arendt a model of the truly *political* philosopher. He worked on the assumption that 'both philosophy and politics concern everyone,' that philosophy is an element of a public realm 'which extends far beyond what we ordinarily mean by political life.'[17] This successor to Kant embodied Kant's 'enlarged mentality' because he was always at home in the world, be it the world of public affairs or the 'world in miniature' he and his wife shared together, where he 'unfolded and practised his incomparable faculty for dialogue, the splendid precision of his way of listening, the constant readiness to give a candid account of himself, the patience to linger over a matter under discussion, and above all the ability to lure what is otherwise passed over in silence into the area of discourse, to make it worth talking about.'[18] Jaspers' thought is worldly, spatial, because it 'forever remains in reference to the world and the people in it ... Thought of this sort, always "related closely to the thoughts of others", is bound to be political, even when it deals with things that are not in the least political.'[19]

Philosophy is a public thing, a matter for everyone, because its essence is communication. Truth is what binds us, living and dead, past, present and future, together. This truth 'itself is communicative, it disappears and cannot be conceived outside communication; within the "existential" realm, truth and communication are the same.' The notion of 'limitless communication' suggests that philosophy has in Jaspers' hands 'left the proverbial ivory tower of mere contemplation. Thinking becomes practical, though not pragmatic; it is a kind of practice between men, not a performance of one individual in his self-chosen solitude.' Thinking of this kind can provide a foundation of world citizenship, human unity, because it 'signifies the faith in the comprehensibility of all truths *and* the good will to reveal and to listen as the primary condition of all human intercourse.'[20]

And since the communicative dialogue that is thinking require a plurality of individuals if there is to be harmony or unity, the unity of humankind, its 'solidarity', cannot 'consist in a universal agreement upon one religion, or one philosophy, or one form of government, but in the faith that the manifold points to a Oneness which diversity reveals and conceals at the same time.'[21] The realization of humanity would not see the end of political action as history to which Kant's notion of 'mankind' points. Nor would it involve the Hegelian realization of the Absolute as World History or Spirit which, because it does not involve the factual emergence of a unified humanity, has 'hardly any political connotations in Hegel's work, despite the strong political impulses of the young Hegel'.[22] Jaspers' notion of a united humanity is both more historical than Kant's and more political than Hegel's, while at the same time combining 'the depth of Hegel's historical experience with Kant's great political wisdom'.[23]

Yet because he accepted neither Kant's view of the 'melancholy haphazardness' of history nor Hegel's sense of a 'cunning of reason', Jaspers broke with 'both the despair and consolation of German idealism in philosophy'.[24] Philosophy is an indispensable guide to political action because it inheres in the situation of beings who communicate together. It indicates 'a realm of the spirit where all are contemporaries', a 'realm of *humanitas*, which everyone can come to out of his own origins'.[25] This *humanitas* is a product and presupposition of a public realm to which therefore all in principle have access. Its presence would indicate a philosophy which 'has lost both its humility before theology and its arrogance toward the common life of man.'[26]

The case of Martin Heidegger is very different indeed. Not least because of his immense influence upon contemporary currents of thought, from the hermeneutics of Gadamer to the deconstructionism of Derrida, Heidegger's philosophy and his political involvement with the Nazi regime remain matters of intense controversy.[27] For her part, Arendt's contribution to a *Festschrift* commemorating Heidegger's eightieth birthday is scrupulously circumspect. It points to the master's undeniable philosophical achievements and it downplays Heidegger's involvement with the Nazis by arguing that this involvement was brief, that he recognized his error and that he took politically dangerous risks in university and literary circles during the Nazi period. Thus Arendt emphasizes the power of Heidegger as a teacher whose reputation had been secure even before the publication of *Being and Time*. She seeks to show how in his work and life, thinking was 'pure activity', a passionate pursuit by means of which he 'laid down a vast network of thought-paths' which, when trod by those able to do so, 'caused the edifice of traditional metaphysics . . . to collapse, just as underground tunnels and subversive burrowings cause the collapse of structures whose foundations are not deeply enough secured.' His thought seems not of this century, but like that of Plato, which still sweeps over us like a powerful wind long after his time, 'comes from the primeval, and what it leaves behind is something perfect, something which, like everything perfect (in Rilke's words), falls back to where it came from.'[28]

Yet a tone of ironic detachment in the essay suggests a much more critical perspective than might at first glance seem apparent. Whatever else might be said about it, Heidegger's power as a teacher, his ability to attract those dissatisfied with prevailing currents of thought, is clearly not a matter for the many; it is no public affair. And a thought which 'does not spring from the century he happens to live in' is by no means an unmixed blessing in a century so in need of enlightenment about its own situation. Heidegger's power and profundity as a thinker is self-evident, but from Arendt's perspective his philosophy could hardly be said to have 'lost both its humility before theology and its arrogance toward the common life of man.'

Beyond this, how Heidegger understood the thinking process pointed away from those qualities that give thinking its genuine, and genuinely political, character, and thus its sense of responsibility. Annihilating the self of consciousness, one's 'character', the passion of thinking shapes a thinking 'I' which, for Heidegger is without qualities and exists in utter solitude. In this solitude, wherein lived Heidegger's thinking 'I', there always reverberated 'something "unutterable" which cannot be brought fully to sound through language and articulated in speech, and which, therefore, is not communicable,

not to others and not to the thinker himself.'[29] In its restless destruc-
tiveness, Heidegger's thinking was a constant effort to begin *ex nihilo*,
to undo what had before been done: 'Each of Heidegger's writings,
despite occasional references to what was already published, reads as
though he were starting from the beginning and only from time to
time taking over the language coined by him.'[30]

We are obviously very far from truth as communicability which
Jaspers considers the essence of philosophy. We are far from life in
a world in which it is impossible, and self-defeating, to start from
scratch every day, a world in which indeed Heidegger, the thinker,
saw himself as having no part. His unconditioned solitude is very
different from the conditioned solitude Arendt defends, with consequences which Arendt tactfully hints at: 'One could well imagine
that – though this is hardly the case with Heidegger – the passion of
thinking might suddenly beset the most gregarious man and, in
consequence of the solitude it requires, ruin him.'[31]

What sort of public world is entailed by Heidegger's philosophy,
beyond the obvious fact of his involvement with the Nazis? Arendt
refers to the story, from Plato's *Theaetetus*, of the Thracian peasant
girl, 'who, watching the "wise man" glance upward in order to
observe the stars only to fall into the well, laughed that someone who
wants to know the sky should be so ignorant of what lies at his
feet.'[32] From Plato to Hegel, the Thracian girl, who of course wrote
no books, represented for philosophers the common person's indifference to the 'higher things'. For Plato, who sought to banish
laughter from the ranks of the guardian class in his ideal polis, the
girl's laughter expressed more than indifference, was more threatening
than overt hostility. It expressed the common view that philosophy
was useless. To challenge this view, Plato advised the tyrant of
Syracuse on the proper conditions of philosophic rule – which, 'seen
from the peasant girl's perspective, looks considerably more comical
than Thales' mishap.'[33]

The peasant girl might well have seen the comedy in Plato's attempt
to set the tyrant right. But philosophers generally have not. 'Men
have obviously not yet discovered what laughter is good for – perhaps
because their thinkers, who have always been ill-disposed toward
laughter, have let them down in this respect, even though a few of
them have racked their brains over the question of what makes us
laugh.'[34]

Philosophers may not have discovered what laughter is good for.
But the peasant girl seems to know. She may tell us more about
philosophy than the philosophers. Yet in whose world would she be
welcome? Plato's? Karl Jaspers'? Martin Heidegger's?

In respect to these matters, Arendt gives us at the conclusion of 'The Crisis in Culture' a brief statement about the meaning of solidarity as *humanitas*, the spiritual (but not immaterial) realm where all are contemporaries. To be cultured in the sense of having *humanitas* is to be able to know 'how to reply to those who so frequently tell us that Plato or some other great author of the past has been superseded; we shall be able to understand that even if all criticism of Plato is right, Plato may still be better company than his critics.' A truly cultivated person is 'one who knows how to choose his company among men, among things, among thoughts, in the present as well as in the past'.[35]

Both Plato and the Thracian girl are good company. So is Hannah Arendt.

Notes

Introduction

1 For a good treatment of these issues, see D. Held, *Political Theory and the Modern State* (Stanford: Standford University Press, 1989).

2 See C. Lefort, *Democracy and Political Theory* trans. D. Maley (Minneapolis: University of Minnesota Press, 1988), especially ch. 3: 'Hannah Arendt and the Question of the Political'.

3 For an excellent account of the importance of these two themes for Arendt's political thought, see L. Bradshaw, *Acting and Thinking: The Political Thought of Hannah Arendt* (Toronto: University of Toronto Press, 1989).

4 H. Arendt, *The Human Condition* (Chicago: University of Chicago Press, 1959), p. 10.

5 See 'Theory and Politics: A Discussion with Herbert Marcuse, Juergen Habermas, Heinz Lubasz and Telman Spengler' trans. L. Adelson et al., *Telos* vol. 11, no. 3 (winter 1978–79), pp. 124–53. For a good account of the dilemmas which arise from the disavowal of ontology, see A. Kontos, 'Through a Glass Darkly: Ontology and False Needs', *Canadian Journal of Political and Social Theory* vol. 3, no. 1 (winter 1979–80), pp. 25–45.

6 Cf. G. Kateb, 'Freedom and Worldliness in the Thought of Hannah Arendt', *Political Theory* vol. 5, no. 2 (May 1977), pp. 141–82 and his *Hannah Arendt: Politics, Conscience, Evil* (Totowa, N.J.: Rowman and Allenheld, 1983).

7 Cf. R. Jacoby, *Social Amnesia* (Boston: Beacon Press, 1975), pp. 5–6.

8 'A Letter by Professor Hans-Georg Gadamer', in R. J. Bernstein, *Beyond Objectivism and Relativism* (Philadelphia: University of Pennsylvania Press, 1985), p. 264.

9 Cf. S. Draenos, 'The Totalitarian Theme in the Work of Max Horkheimer and Hannah Arendt', (paper presented at the State University of New York, Albany, 6 Feb. 1980).

Chapter 1

1 According to Elisabeth Young-Bruehl, *The Human Condition, Between Past and Future* and *On Revolution* all emerged from research for a book Arendt intended to write on Marxism, but never completed. See E. Young-Bruehl, *Hannah Arendt: For Love of the World* (New Haven and London: Yale University Press, 1982), pp. 278–9.

2 Arendt, 'Tradition and the Modern Age', in *Between Past and Future* enlarged edition (New York: Penguin Books, 1977), pp. 17–40.

3 Arendt was particularly hostile to the Freudian-influenced Marxism of the Frankfort School. See, for example, Arendt, 'On Hannah Arendt', in M. Hill (ed.), *Hannah Arendt: The Recovery of the Public World* (New York: St. Martin's Press, 1979), p. 326. She also believed that Engels interpreted Marx correctly (Arendt, 'Tradition and the Modern Age', loc. cit.).

4 Arendt, *The Human Condition*, pp. 106, 105.

5 Arendt, 'Tradition and the Modern Age', p. 21.

6 ibid.

7 Arendt, 'The Concept of History', in *Between Past and Future*, p. 42.

8 Arendt, 'Understanding and Politics', *Partisan Review* XX 4 (July-August 1953), p. 389.

9 Arendt, 'The Concept of History', p. 42.

10 ibid., p. 45.

11 Cf. A. Kontos, 'Domination: Metaphor and Political Reality', in Kontos (ed.), *Domination* (Toronto: University of Toronto Press, 1975), pp. 222ff.

12 Arendt, 'Bertolt Brecht: 1888–1956', in *Men in Dark Times* (New York: Harcourt, Brace and World, 1968), pp. 238–9.

13 Cf. G. Grant, 'The Computer Does Not Impose On Us the Ways It Should Be Used', in A. Rotstein (ed.), *Beyond Industrial Growth* (Toronto: University of Toronto Press, 1976), pp. 117–32.

14 Arendt, 'The Concept of History', p. 55.

15 ibid., pp. 55–6.

16 ibid., p. 60.

17 ibid., p. 58.

18 ibid., p. 59.

19 ibid., p. 79.

20 ibid., p. 81. Cf. Arendt, 'Dilthey as Philosopher and Historian', *Partisan Review* XII/3 (summer 1945), pp. 404–6.

21 ibid., p. 73.

22 J. Habermas, 'The Classical Doctrine of Politics', in *Theory and Practice* trans. J. Viertel (Boston: Beacon Press, 1973), pp. 44–5.

23 Arendt, 'The Concept of History', pp. 85–6.

24 ibid., p. 88.

25 ibid.

26 Cf. A. Megill, 'Martin Heidegger and the Metapolitics of Crisis', in J. S. Nelson (ed.), *What Should Political Theory Be Now?* (Albany, N.Y.: State University of New York Press, 1983), pp. 264–324.

27 'The Social Bond is linguistic, but it is not woven with a single thread. It is the fabric formed by the intersection of at least two (and in reality an indeterminate number of) language games, obeying different rules . . . We may have a pessimistic impression of this splintering, nobody speaks all of these languages, they have no universal metalanguage, the prospect of the system-subject is a failure, the goal of emancipation has nothing to do with science, we are all stuck in the position of this or that discipline of learning, the learned scholars have turned into scientists, the diminished tasks of research have become compartmentalized and no one can master them all. Speculative or humanistic philosophy is forced to relinquish its legitimation duties, which explains why philosophy is facing a crisis wherever it persists in arrogating such functions and is reduced to the study of systems of logic or the history of ideas where it has been realistic enough to surrender them.' J. F. Lyotard, *The Post-modern Condition: A Report on Knowledge* trans. G. Bennington and B. Massumi (Minneapolis: University of Minnesota Press, 1984), p. 41.

28 Although this is not generally seen. Cf. Megill, loc. cit.

29 This is the main theme of *The Origins of Totalitarianism*. See chapter 4 below.

30 On this issue, see, for example, P. Dews, *Logics of Disintegration* (London: Verso, 1987); J. Keane, 'Democracy, Ideology, Relativism', in his *Democracy and Civil Society* (London and New York: Verso, 1988), esp. pp. 23ff.; D. Kellner, 'Postmodernism as Social Theory: Some Challenges and Problems', *Theory, Culture and Society* vol. 5, nos 2–3 (June 1988), pp. 239–69. For an account of Richard Rorty's position, see R. Comay, 'Interrupting the Conversation: Notes on Rorty', *Telos* vol. 19, no. 3 (fall 1986), pp. 119–30 and G. Warnke, *Gadamer: Hermeneutics, Tradition and Reason* (Cambridge: Polity Press, 1987), ch. 5.

31 Arendt, 'The Concept of History', pp. 63–4.

32 ibid. p. 81.

33 Arendt, *The Origins of Totlitarianism* second edn (Cleveland and New York: Meridian Books, 1958), pp. 34ff.

34 Arendt, *The Human Condition*, p. 88.

35 ibid., p. 121.

36 ibid., p. 101.

37 K. Marx, *Das Kapital*, III, 783; cited in Arendt, *The Human Condition*, p. 104.

38 Arendt, *The Human Condition*, p. 105.

39 ibid., p. 133.

40 ibid., p. 117.

41 ibid.

42 ibid., p. 133.

43 See, for example, J. Baudrillard, *The Mirror of Production* trans. M.

Poster (St Louis, Mo.: Telos Press, 1975); J. Cohen *Class and Civil Society: The Limits of Marxian Critical Theory* (Amherst, Mass.: University of Massachusetts Press, 1982); A. Wellmer, *Critical Theory of Society* trans. J. Cumming (New York: Seabury Press, 1974).

44 See, for example, A. Gorz, *Farewell to the Working Class* trans. M. Sonenscher (Boston: South End Press, 1982); J. Keane and J. Owens, *After Full Employment* (London: Hutchinson, 1986); C. Mouffe and C. Laclau, *Hegemony and Socialist Strategy* (London: Verso, 1985). Of course the two streams of critical analysis are not necessarily mutually exclusive. For an example of a vital analysis with elements of both, see S. Bowles and H. Gintis, *Democracy and Capitalism* (New York: Basic Books, 1986).

45 Arendt, *The Human Condition*, pp. 105–6.

46 ibid., pp. 79–80.

47 'I do not share Marx's great enthusiasm about capitalism. If you read the first pages of the *Communist Manifesto* it is the greatest praise of capitalism you ever saw and this at a time when capitalism was already under sharp attack especially from the so-called right . . . Also the cruelty of capitalism in the seventeenth, eighteenth, and nineteenth centuries was, of course, overwhelming. And this you have to keep in mind if you read Marx's great praise of capitalism. He was surrounded by the most hideous consequences of this system and nevertheless thought this was a great business. He was, of course, Hegelian and believed in the power of the negative. Well I *don't* believe in the power of the negative, of the negation, if it is the terrible misfortune of other people.' Arendt, 'On Hannah Arendt', in Hill (ed.), op. cit., pp. 334–5.

48 Arendt, *The Human Condition*, p. 99.

49 This is of course a central theme in Marx, 'Economic and Philosophic Manuscripts' (1844), in Marx and Engels, *Collected Works* vol. 3 (London: Laurence and Wishart, 1975).

50 See, for example, A. Heller, *The Theory of Need in Marx* (London: Allison and Busby, 1976); W. Leiss, *The Limits to Satisfaction* revised edition (Toronto: University of Toronto Press, 1979) and 'Marx and Macpherson: Needs, Utilities and Self-Development', in A. Kontos (ed.), *Power, Possessions, and Freedom* (Toronto: University of Toronto Press, 1979), pp. 119–38; C. B. Macpherson, 'Needs and Wants: An Ontological or Historical Problem?' in R. Fitzgerald (ed.), *Human Needs and Politics* (Sydney, Australia: Macmillan, 1977), pp. 26–35. A recent study which draws on both this work and that of Arendt is S. Benhabib, *Critique, Norm and Utopia* (New York: Columbia University Press, 1986). Nancy Fraser has related the question of needs to the insights of contemporary feminist theory. See her 'Struggle Over Needs: Outline for a Socialist-Feminist Theory of Late Capitalist Political Culture; in her *Unruly Practices: Power, Discourse and Gender in Contemporary Social Theory* (Minneapolis: University of Minnesota Press, 1989), pp. 161–87. Fraser acknowledges the importance of feminism's insights into the contest-

ability of concepts, including any notion of 'true' versus 'false' needs, while defending the possibility of distinguishing between 'better' and 'worse' interpretations of needs as an important element of a political theory committed to social change.

51 Cf. Leiss, *The Limits to Satisfaction*, part I.

52 See, for example, J. Keane, *Public Life and Late Capitalism* (London: Cambridge University Press, 1984), esp. ch. 6.

53 See especially Heller, op. cit. To be sure, Heller agrees that Marx himself did not refer often to class questions, although his successors did. In any case, Marxists could learn from Arendt in this respect because her categories are potentially sensitive to this distinction.

54 Cf. Arendt, 'What is Freedom?', in *Between Past and Future*, pp. 143–71. Arendt also links the question of needs to the historical development of the quest for wordly immortality, the individual search for social status and the advent of monetary reward as the primary social criterion of memorability. See Arendt, *The Human Condition*, pp. 51ff.

55 A prime example of this is J. Bernauer, 'On Reading and Misreading Hannah Arendt', *Philosophy and Social Criticism* vol. 11, no. 1 (summer 1985), pp. 1–34. Bernauer and others tend to overdraw the distinction in Arendt's work between the social/economic and the political, and, less visibly, between thinking and doing.

56 Arendt, *The Human Condition*, p. 123.

57 For an account of the growing, if ambiguous, relationship between the ecology and labour movements, see, for example, L. E. Adkin and C. Alpaugh, 'Labour, Ecology, and the Politics of Convergence', *Socialist Studies* 4 (1988), pp. 48–73. The question of industrial conversion is crucial here as well. See, for example, H. Wainwright and D. Elliot, *The Lucas Plan: A New Trade Unionism in the Making* (New York: Pluto Press, 1982); D. Wells, 'Politics and the Economic Conversion of Military Production in Canada', *Studies in Political Economy* 27 (August 1988), pp. 113–36.

58 For a powerful account of the role of popular neighbourhood associations in the conflict over efforts to achieve the racial desegration of schools in Boston, Massachusetts, see J. A. Lukas, *Common Ground* (New York: Vintage Books, 1986).

59 Arendt argues that humans need entertainment and diversion as a release from worldly cares. See Arendt, 'The Crisis in Culture', in *Between Past and Future*, pp. 197–226.

60 Arendt, *The Human Condition*, p. 133.

61 This was a fundamental issue in recent debates about the nature of the German peace movement. See the various contributions in *Telos* vol. 15, no. 1 (spring 1982), pp. 32ff. and vol. 15, no. 2 (summer 1982), pp. 5–40, 99–128, 190–3.

62 Arendt, *The Human Condition*, p. 179.

63 ibid.

64 ibid., p. 180.

65 I. Kant, 'Idea for a Universal History with a Cosmopolitan Purpose', in H. Reiss (ed.), *Kant's Political Writings* trans. H. B. Nisbet, second, enlarged edn (Cambridge: Cambridge University Press, 1991), p. 44.

66 Cf. Arendt, *The Human Condition*, pp. 180–1.

67 This is compatible with Arendt's emphasis on the importance of perspectivalism in Kant's *Critique of Judgment*. See chapter 6 below. Arendt herself advances a comparable claim in her analysis of those who resisted the 'lawful' demands of the Nazi state. See Arendt, 'Personal Responsibility Under Dictatorship', *Listener*, 6 August 1964, p. 205.

68 In this respect, Arendt's position is similar to that of the French social theorist, Alain Touraine. See his *The Self-Production of Society* (Chicago: University of Chicago Press, 1977), p. 15, and the application of this analysis to social movements in *The Voice and the Eye: An Analysis of Social Movements* trans. A. Duff (New York: Cambridge University Press, 1981).

69 Arendt, 'What is Freedom?', in *Between Past and Future*, p. 152.

Chapter 2

1 Arendt, *The Human Condition*, p. 7.

2 See Arendt, *On Revolution* (New York: Viking Press, 1965) and 'Thoughts on Politics and Revolution', in *Crises of the Republic* (New York: Harcourt Brace Jovanovich, 1972), pp. 199–233.

3 Arendt, *The Human Condition*, pp. 23ff., 77–8.

4 ibid., p. 37.

5 Arendt, 'What is Freedom?', in *Between Past and Future*, pp. 146, 153.

6 ibid., p. 162.

7 ibid., p. 163.

8 ibid., p. 164.

9 ibid. Arendt also makes the point that the identification of freedom with sovereignty entails 'the ideal of a free will independent from others and eventually prevailing against them' (ibid., p. 163).

10 ibid., p. 165.

11 ibid., p. 155. As will be seen in chapter 4, this theme is central to Arendt's brilliant analysis of Thomas Hobbes in *The Origins of Totalitarianism*.

12 This is a central element of George Kateb's criticism of Arendt's political thought, as I attempt to demonstrate below.

13 'What is Freedom?', p. 169.

14 ibid., p. 171. Cf. 'The Conquest of Space and the Stature of Man', in *Between Past and Future*, pp. 279–80.

15 ibid., pp. 154–5.

16 ibid., p. 151.

17 ibid., p. 152.

18 ibid.

19   Arendt, 'Lying in Politics: Reflections on the Pentagon Papers', in *Crises of the Republic*, pp. 3–47.
20   Arendt, *The Jew as Pariah* R. H. Feldman (ed.) (New York: Grove Press, 1978), part III.
21   Arendt, *The Human Condition*, p. 244.
22   ibid.
23   ibid., p. 237.
24   ibid., p. 243.
25   Of course this is the central theme of Hill (ed.), *Hannah Arendt: The Recovery of the Public World*.
26   Arendt, *The Human Condition*, p. 50.
27   Cf. S. Wolin, *Politics and Vision* (Boston: Little, Brown and Company, 1960), ch. 1, especially the discussion of the concepts of 'political time' and 'political space'. In this regard, see as well W. Magnusson and R. Walker, 'Decentring the State', *Studies in Political Economy* 26 (summer 1988), pp. 37–71.
28   Arendt, *The Human Condition*, p. 58.
29   'Unlike the *animal laborans*, whose social life is worldless and herdlike and who therefore is incapable of building or inhabiting a public, worldly realm, *homo faber* is fully capable of having a public realm of his own, even though it may not be a political realm, properly speaking . . . Historically, the last public realm, the last meeting place which is at least connected with the activity of *homo faber*, is the exchange market on which products are *displayed*.' (ibid., pp. 160–2).
30   ibid., p. 52.
31   ibid., p. 53.
32   ibid., p. 182. George Orwell's haunting description in *Nineteen Eighty-Four* of Winston Smith's encounter with a London that had lost its history, that is, its durability as a place in the world and not just a domain of physical objects, provides a strikingly similar vision of 'worldliness' and the consequences of its loss. I attempt to deal with the relation of Arendt's thought to Orwell's position in ' "When men are different from one another and do not live alone": Orwell and Arendt on Total Control and Ontology', in H. Chorney and P. Hansen, *Toward a Humanist Political Economy* (Montreal: Black Rose Books, 1992) pp. 161ff.
33   In this light, the influence of Marx on Arendt is once again evident. Marx's work may be seen as an attempt to state the necessary conditions for the development and expression of our nature as potentially communal beings, and that foremost among these conditions is something like the ability to appear as genuine actors on the stage of history. Indeed, Arendt seems to view this as a vital element of Marx's revolutionary theory. Thus in discussing the importance of what she calls 'the social question' – poverty – for modern revolutionary movements, she suggests perceptively that 'the conviction that darkness rather than want is the curse of poverty is extremely rare in the literature of the modern age, although one may suspect that Marx's effort to rewrite history in

terms of class struggle was partially at least inspired by the desire to rehabilitate posthumously those to whose injured lives history has added the insult of oblivion' (*On Revolution*, p. 64). Arendt sees Marx speaking out, angrily and eloquently, on behalf of those who from the outset of the modern age have been denied voices of their own. This denial corresponds in Arendt's terms to the withering away of the space of appearance and, although she does not put it explicitly in this way, is an assault on the human nature of those affected, their capacity to live as political beings.

34 'Commercial society, or capitalism in its earliest stages when it was still possessed by a fiercely competitive and acquisitive spirit, is still ruled by the standards of *homo faber*' (Arendt, *The Human Condition*, p. 163).

35 Arendt uses this point to make an interesting comment on the source of the division of labour in modern industrial societies. Distinguishing between division of labour and 'specialization of work', which 'have in common only the general principle of organization, which itself has nothing to do with either work or labor but owes its origin to the strictly political sphere of life, to the fact of man's capacity to act and act together and in concert,' Arendt suggests that division of labour 'presupposes the qualitative equivalence of all single activities for which no special skill is required, and these activities have no end in themselves, but actually represent only certain amounts of labor power which are added together in a purely quantitative way. Division of labor is based on the fact that two men can put their labor power together and "behave toward each other as though they were one". This one-ness is the exact opposite of co-operation, it indicates the unity of the species with regard to which every singly member is the same and exchangeable' (*The Human Condition*, p. 125). Prefiguring the work of analysts such as Harry Braverman, Arendt attributes the degradation of work to the application of the division of labour to the processes of work such that the production of use objects assumes the character of the perishable, consummable products of labour. The result: 'the objective difference between use and consumption, between the relative durability of use objects and the swift coming and going of consumer goods dwindles to insignificance' (*The Human Condition*, p. 125). Again, it should be noted that Arendt sees labour as a natural phenomenon of human existence. Its modern manifestation as wage labour simply intensifies the impact of its 'permanent' features. However questionable her assumption of labour's a historical character might be, Arendt nevertheless provides important insights into how a specific kind of human production process moulds the human material comprising it. As we shall see below, these insights are particularly important as a basis for Arendt's distinction between 'behavior' and 'action'.

36 Arendt, *The Human Condition*, p. 145.

37 ibid., p. 71.

38 ibid., p. 110.

39 ibid., p. 69.

40 Orwell, *Nineteen Eighty-Four* (Harmondsworth: Penguin, 1975), p. 26.

41 Arendt, *On Revolution*, and 'Thoughts on Politics and Revolution', in *Crises of the Republic*.

42 A. Heller, 'The Great Republic', in F. Feher and A. Heller, *Eastern Left, Western Left* (Cambridge: Polity Press, 1987), pp. 188ff. However as I argue in chapter 4, Heller's account of the relation of Arendt's work to this tradition is not without problems.

43 K. Frampton, 'The Status of Man and the Status of his Objects: A Reading of *The Human Condition*', in Hill (ed.), *Hannah Arendt: The Recovery of the Public World*, p. 117. This essay relates Arendt's distinction between labour and work to the transformation of architecture and urban form under the impact of an expanding industrial (and increasingly post-industrial) capitalism.

44 Before the emergence of more affirmative, 'post-modern' analyses of urban form, thinkers such as Henri Lefebvre and the French Situationists developed a critical theory of urban life which sought to pinpoint the nature and consequences of the 'meanings' created by and through instrumental strategies of spatial construction. More particularly, they addressed the consequences of the ability of bureaucratic organizations, private and public, to 'package' history as a disposable commodity, in the process reinforcing the social amnesia and fragmentation said to characterize contemporary urban experience. This account bears clear parallels to that of Arendt; in a sense, from Lefebvre's perspective, Arendt's worst fears about the consequences of history understood as the product of *homo faber* have been realized.

For Lefebvre's position, see, for example, *The Survival of Capitalism* trans. F. Bryant (London: Allison and Busby, 1976). The dilemmas of a Marxian account of the urban are evident in the work of Manuel Castells. Compare his *The Urban Question* (London: Arnold, 1977) with *The City and the Grass Roots* (Berkeley and Los Angeles: University of California Press, 1983). Positive accounts of post-modernism and its implications both for critical thinking generally and urban form in particular include M. Ryan, *Marxism and Deconstruction* (Baltimore and London: The Johns Hopkins University Press, 1982) and F. Jamieson, 'Postmodernism, or the Cultural Logic of Late Capitalism', *New Left Review* no. 146 (July-Aug. 1984), pp. 53–92. For a more critical view, see M. Davis, 'Urban Renaissance and the Spirit of Post Modernism', *New Left Review* no. 154 (May-June 1985), pp. 106–13. Davis suggests that a 'profoundly anti-urban impulse inspired by unfettered financial forces and a Hausmannian logic of social control seem to me to constitute the real *Zeitgeist* of postmodernism' (p. 113). A powerful account of the impact of the urban experience upon social theory generally is H. Chorney, *City of Dreams: Social Theory and the Urban Experience* (Scarborough, Ont.: Nelson, 1990).

45 See, for example, A. Kernohan, 'Democratic Socialism and Private

Property', *Studies in Political Economy* 22 (spring 1987), pp. 145–66. This essay argues for a more favourable consideration of private property from a democratic socialist point of view. Such reflections form an element of the current reconsideration of the economic and political meaning of socialism in the current era. A notable example of this is A. Nove, *The Economics of Feasible Socialism* (Boston and Sydney: George Allen and Unwin, 1983).

46 Arendt, 'Lying in Politics'.

47 Arendt, 'Walter Benjamin: 1892–1940', in *Men in Dark Times*, p. 153.

48 Arendt, 'Tradition and the Modern Age' and 'The Crisis in Education', in *Between Past and Future*, pp. 17–40 and 173–96.

49 Arendt's analysis here seems to indicate a subtle but important shift in her understanding of thinking and action, philosophy and politics. In *The Human Condition*, for example, she saw philosophy as exercising a baleful influence on politics. Near the end of her life, however, she appeared to see philosophy, or thinking, as increasingly important and necessary when the possibilities for action were threatened. If the conditions of action were to be restored, thinking needed to play a crucial role. The antagonism between philosophy and politics was not so deep or enduring.

The turning point in Arendt's understanding of this matter was the Eichmann controversy and is most clearly represented by the essay 'Truth and Politics', where Arendt interprets the relation of truth to public life much more positively than is usually recognized. This shift is also *inter alia* central to the argument of the *Life of the Mind*. Of course while from the vantage point of politics she viewed thought more favourably, at no time did Arendt substitute theory for politics, as various contemporary thinkers have been wont to do.

50 Arendt, 'Truth and Politics', in *Between Past and Future*, p. 227.

51 These are the words of historian Michael Sturmer, an adviser to German chancellor Helmut Kohl and a participant in the dispute. They are cited in G. Craig, 'Facing Up to the Nazis' *The New York Review of Books* vol. XXXVI, no. 1 (Feb. 2 1989), p. 15.

52 For a good account of the controversy and its implications, see 'Special Issue on the *Historikerstreit*', *New German Critique* 44 (spring-summer 1988). That people are situated in the 'gap' between past and future was made explicit by Michael Sturmer: 'in a country without history, he who fills the memory, defines the concepts and interprets the past, wins the future.' Sturmer, 'Suche nache der verborenen Erinnerung', *Das Parlament*, 17–24 May 1986, cited in J. Habermas, 'A Kind of Settlement of Damages (Apologetic Tendencies)', *New German Critique* 49 (spring-summer 1988), p. 28.

53 See in this respect the contribution by Habermas in *New German Critique*.

54 Thus, writing from a perspective strongly influenced by both Marxist structuralism and Arendt's own work, Samuel Bowles and Herbert Gintis argue for a comprehensive definition of politics which sees it as inherent

in contestation over 'rules' which govern specific 'practices' (appropriative, distributive, political, cultural) undertaken at various social 'sites' (economy, state, family). It is the relation of the meaning-constituting rules to different practices, and not whether a specific question concerns that particular site called the state, which defines the political content of a social relationship or action. See Bowles and Gintis, *Democracy and Capitalism* (New York: Basic Books, 1986).

55 C. Lasch, 'Introduction', *Salmagundi* no. 60 (spring-summer 1983), pp. iv, v.

56 'Freedom and Worldliness in the Thought of Hannah Arendt', *Political Theory* vol. 5, no. 2 (May 1977), pp. 141–82; *Hannah Arendt: Politics, Conscience, Evil* (Totowa, N.J.: Rowman and Allenheld, 1983); 'Arendt and Representative Democracy', *Salmagundi* no. 60 (spring-summer 1983), pp. 20–59.

57 Kateb, 'Arendt and Representative Democracy', p. 126. Kateb has in mind in particular Arendt's account of the limits of representation and her enthusiastic approval of popular councils in *On Revolution*. I discuss this more fully in chapter 5.

58 ibid., p. 27.

59 ibid., p. 30.

60 ibid., pp. 30–1.

61 ibid., p. 41.

62 ibid.

63 Cf. Kateb, 'Freedom and Worldliness in the Thought of Hannah Arendt'.

64 Notable in this respect is Carl Schmitt's *The Crisis of Parliamentary Democracy* trans. E. Kennedy (Cambridge, Mass.: The MIT Press, 1988). On Schmitt's ideas and the resurgence of interest in them, see 'Special Issue on Carl Schmitt', *Telos* vol. 20, no. 2 (summer 1987) and J. Keane, 'Dictatorship and the Decline of Parliament. Carl's Schmitt's Theory of Political Sovereignty', in *Democracy and Civil Society*, pp. 153–89.

65 For an examination of these forces, see F. Fox-Piven and R. A. Cloward, *Why Americans Don't Vote* (New York: Pantheon, 1988).

66 For a subtle appreciation of Arendt's sense of the potential frailty of political life, see P. Ricoeur, 'Action, Story and History: On Re-reading *The Human Condition*', *Salmagundi* no. 60 (spring-summer 1983), pp. 60–72. Ricoeur's argument turns on the distinction in Arendt's work between 'immortality' and 'eternity'. The permanence of immortality is what mortal humans seek through political action. But as thinking beings, we necessarily think from the standpoint of the eternal. Working within a phenomenological and hermeneutical framework similar to Arendt's own, Ricoeur sees the dilemma of political thinking and political acting in the unavoidable presence of thought – for action can only be truly such when worked into a story, made the stuff of history – in action. The quest for immortality is shaped fundamentally by the consideration of eternity: universalist claims about human good which can never be fully realized, nor even unambiguously recognized, in political

action, and which always require a story or metaphor for their preservation. Hence the frailty of action.

This is not a question of an ostensibly dualist human nature. Rather, it involves the density of that collective life, 'the web of human relationships', within which humans are born as new beginnings, and within which human action is marked by unpredictability and irreversibility.

That we seek to immortalize ourselves from the standpoint of an eternity which we cannot (and, for Arendt, must not, even if we could) achieve is the basis of 'both the greatness and illusion of the whole human enterprise'. As Ricoeur puts it, 'Hannah Arendt, as one who *thinks* the political status of man without being herself a political actor (except by accident and by necessity), consistently refused to despise this greatness in spite of its vanity – or to conceal this illusion for the sake of its greatness' (pp. 62–3).

67   M. O'Brien, *The Politics of Reproduction* (London: Routledge and Kegan Paul, 1981), p. 100.

68   ibid., p. 115.

69   ibid., p. 103.

70   ibid., pp. 105–6. O'Brien further suggests that 'family and economics played a large part in the public life of the polis. Thucydides noted the value of reproduction. Economic concerns were also of public import, but Arendt's view of the glamour of political action excludes such commonplaces as collecting and spending taxes, of which the necessity to finance public works, such as fortifications and harbour facilities for the visible, physical protection of the polis, were but one instance.'

71   ibid., p. 110.

72   ibid., pp. 109–10.

73   ibid., pp. 102, 100. Of course O'Brien finds inadequate Arendt's treatment of activity, a central phenomenological theme.

74   See A. Muszynski, 'What is Patriarchy?' *Socialist Studies* 5 (1989), pp. 65–86. I have been strongly influence by Dr Muszynski's thinking about the issues of 'public', 'private' and 'patriarchy'. I am grateful to her for sharing her ideas with me.

75   Of course Arendt does argue that the relation of humans to nature has an element of antagonism. Freedom lies in the rational mastery of necessity; nature must be 'made over' or 'worked up' by humans. O'Brien needs to be more specific about the content of an integrative relation with nature.

76   C. Pateman, 'Feminist Critiques of the Public/Private Dichotomy', in S. I. Benn and G. F. Gaus (eds), *Public and Private in Social Life* (London and Canberra: Croom Helm, 1983), pp. 281–303.

77   ibid., p. 299.

78   This is also the position of Ann Lane. See 'The Feminism of Hannah Arendt', *Democracy* vol. 3, no. 3 (summer, 1983), pp. 107–17. For fuller accounts of the relation of feminism to questions of public life, see, for

example, S. Benhabib and D. Cornell (eds), *Feminism as Critique* (Minneapolis: University of Minnesota Press, 1987).

79 O'Brien, op. cit., p. 113.

Chapter 3

1 One such effort is N. O'Sullivan, 'Hannah Arendt: Hellenic Nostalgia and Industrial Society' in A. deCrespigny and K. Minogue (eds), *Contemporary Political Philosophers* (New York: Dodd, Mead and Company, 1975), pp. 228–51.

2 H. Pachter, *Weimer Etudes* (New York: Columbia University Press, 1982), esp. chs 3, 12. *The Politics of Cultural Despair* is the title of a well-known study of the cultural origins of National Socialism by Franz Stern.

3 Arendt, 'The Crisis in Culture', in *Between Past and Future*, p. 219.

4 ibid., p. 199.

5 'Mass society . . . wants not culture but entertainment, and the wares offered by the entertainment industry are indeed consumed by society just like any other consumer product' (ibid., p. 205).

6 ibid., p. 204.

7 ibid., p. 202.

8 ibid., p. 204. Cf. Arendt, *The Origins of Totalitarianism* second enlarged edn (Cleveland and New York: Meridian Books, 1958), pp. 338ff.

9 Cf. E. M. Wood, *Mind and Politics* (Los Angeles: University of California Press, 1972) and H. Arvon, *Marxist Esthetics* trans. H. Lane (Ithaca, N.Y.: Cornell University Press, 1973), ch. 3.

10 Arendt, 'The Crisis in Culture', p. 208.

11 Arendt, *The Human Condition*, p. 168.

12 ibid., pp. 172–3.

13 ibid., p. 168.

14 Arendt, 'The Crisis in Culture', p. 217.

15 ibid., p. 215.

16 ibid., p. 223.

17 ibid., p. 221. Cf. Habermas, 'Arendt's Communications Concept of Power', *Social Research* 44:1 (spring 1977), pp. 3–24.

18 I am indebted to Alicja Muszynski for suggesting the importance of this issue for Arendt's account of art and culture.

19 Arendt, 'The Crisis in Culture', p. 214.

20 ibid., p. 224.

21 With respect to this issue, see the analysis of Arendt's work in S. Dossa, *The Public Realm and the Public Self* (Waterloo, Ont.: Wilfrid Laurier Press, 1989).

22 Arendt, 'The Crisis in Culture', p. 200; see also Arendt, *On Revolution*, pp. 15, 16.

23 One analyst who does accord an important role to 'The Crisis in Culture'

is Ronald Beiner. See his 'Interpretative Essay', in Arendt, *Lectures in Kant's Political Philosophy* ed. R. Beiner (Chicago: University of Chicago Press, 1982), pp. 102ff.

24 W. Benjamin, 'The Work of Art in the Age of Mechanical Reproduction', in Arendt (ed.), *Illuminations* trans. H. Zohn (New York: Schocken Books, 1969), p. 251.

25 Arendt, 'Truth and Politics', in *Between Past and Future*, p. 250.

26 Arendt, 'Lying in Politics', in *Crises of the Republic*, p. 5.

27 ibid., p. 6.

28 Arendt, 'Truth and Politics', p. 242.

29 ibid., pp. 236–7.

30 Although there may well be proto-deconstructionist elements in her work, Arendt would part company with certain strains of deconstructionism, or post-modernism, for whom the malleability of 'facts' seems to be a given. This question, which from the perspective of Arendt's argument here reflects precisely those developments which she sought to address, have become important in the debate over the behaviour of the writer and literary theorist Paul de Man in Belgium during the Second World War. See W. Hamacher et al. (eds), *Paul de Man's Wartime Journalism, 1939–1943* (Lincoln, Neb.: University of Nebraska Press, 1988).

31 Arendt, 'Truth and Politics', p. 249.

32 Hence Arendt makes the point that 'All these lies, whether their authors know it or not, harbor an element of violence; organized lying always tends to destroy whatever it has decided to negate, although only totalitarian governments have consciously adopted lying as the first step to murder. When Trotsky learned that he had never played a role in the Russian Revolution, he must have known that his death warrant had been signed. Clearly, it is easier to eliminate a public figure from the record of history if at the same time he can be eliminated from the world of the living' (ibid., pp. 252–3).

33 ibid., p. 254.

34 ibid., p. 258.

35 ibid., p. 256.

36 Arendt, 'Lying in Politics', pp. 7, 36.

37 Arendt, 'Truth and Politics', p. 262. This theme is echoed in Arendt's account of the life and work of Isak Dinesen in *Men in Dark Times*, pp. 95–109.

38 ibid., p. 259.

39 *The Origins of Totalitarianism* can plausibly be seen as such a theory of the state – which, given the nature of Arendt's analysis, must also and necessarily be seen as a theory of the *breakdown* of the modern state, its disintegration under the impact of a complex set of historical developments. I discuss this more fully in chapter 4.

40 A still useful collection of essays on this theme is C. McCoy and J. Playford (eds), *Apolitical Politics* (New York: Thomas A. Crowell, 1967). This sort of critique is clearly presupposed by Habermas in his account

of the dilemmas inherent in the rationalization of the 'lifeworld'. See Habermas, *The Theory of Communicative Action Volume Two: Lifeworld and System: a Critique of Functionalist Reason*, trans. T. McCarthy (Boston: Beacon Press, 1987). The critique itself has older origins. See, for example, R. Lynd, *Knowledge for What?* (1939) (New York: Grove Press, 1964) for a pioneering statement of it. To be sure, this critique reached a peak of sorts during the political ferment of 1960s and has in recent years been to some some extent eclipsed, even in ostensibly radical thought. It would be interesting to examine how the theme of the 'death' of the subject, presupposed by structuralist antecedents of certain currents of contemporary radical thought, unwittingly reinforces behaviourist assumptions and practices.

41 Arendt, *The Human Condition*, pp. 28–9, 254.
42 ibid., p. 40.
43 ibid., p. 43.
44 Arendt, 'The Concept of History', p. 87.
45 Arendt, *The Origins of Totalitarianism*, p. 468.
46 Arendt, 'Personal Responsibility under Dictatorship' *The Listener* (6 Aug. 1964), pp. 185–7, 205.
47 See, generally, the work of John Thompson, notably *Studies in the Theory of Ideology* (Berkeley and Los Angeles: University of California Press, 1984) and *Ideology and Modern Culture* (Cambridge: Polity Press, 1990).
48 See, 'Ideology', in Frankfurt Institute of Social Research (ed.), *Aspects of Sociology* trans. J. Viertel (Boston: Beacon Press, 1972), pp. 182–205.
49 C. Lefort, *The Political Forms of Modern Society* ed. J. Thompson (Cambridge: Polity Press, 1986), esp. ch. 6.
50 Arendt, *The Human Condition*, p. 200.
51 ibid., p. 201.
52 ibid., p. 200.
53 See Habermas, *The Theory of Communicative Action Volume Two*.
54 See Arendt, 'What is Authority?', in *Between Past and Future*, pp. 91–141.
55 Arendt, 'On Violence', in *Crises of the Republic*, pp. 151, 155.
56 ibid., p. 105.
57 With respect to Polish Solidarity in particular, see S. Persky, *At the Lenin Shipyard* (Vancouver: New Star Books, 1981) and A. Touraine et al., *Solidarity The Analysis of a Social Movement: Poland 1980–1981* trans. D. Denby (Cambridge: Cambridge University Press, 1983).
58 Arendt, 'On Violence', p. 161.
59 ibid., p. 163.
60 ibid., p. 161.
61 ibid., pp. 183–4.

Chapter 4

1 Comparisons of totalitarian and non-totalitarian states suffuse the entire account offered by *The Origins of Totalitarianism* and provide the unstated premise of Arendt's response to criticisms of her position. See, for example, *Eichmann in Jerusalem* (New York: Viking Press, 1965) and *The Jew as Pariah*, pp. 240–79. The argument that Hitler and Stalin were 'non-persons' is made most explicitly in 'Rosa Luxemburg', in *Men in Dark Times*, pp. 33–4, but it is also of obvious significance for Arendt's treatment of Eichmann. The general influence of Bertolt Brecht is clearly visible here as well. On this, see Young-Bruehl, *Hannah Arendt: For Love of the World*, pp. 330–1.

2 To avoid any misunderstanding: when I say that totalitarianism 'makes sense' or is 'justified' in as much as it meets human needs, albeit in a perverse way, I certainly do not mean that totalitarianism is 'rational' in terms of everyday practical rationality and epistemology. The point is that the tendency to see totalitarianism as inexplicable in some fundamental respect blocks proper analysis of it. Although she does argue that totalitarianism explodes our 'normal' categories of political thought, in my view Arendt does not mean that this explosion of traditional categories does away with the normative dimensions of those concepts. Only in light of these dimensions can totalitarianism be shown for what it is, its historical roots unearthed.

3 See Arendt's response to Eric Voegelin's review of *The Origins of Totalitarianism*, in *Review of Politics* XV/1 (January 1953), pp. 76–85.

4 M. Canovan, *The Political Thought of Hannah Arendt* (London: J. M. Dent and Sons, 1974), p. 47.

5 A. Heller, 'An Imaginary Preface to the 1984 Edition of Hannah Arendt's *The Origins of Totalitarianism*', in F. Feher and A. Heller, *Eastern Left, Western Left* (Cambridge: Polity Press, 1987), p. 243.

6 A recent example of such criticisms of Arendt can be found in R. D'Amico, 'The Myth of the Totally Administered Society', *Telos* vol. 24, no. 2 (summer 1991), pp. 84ff.

7 Arendt, *The Origins of Totalitarianism*, p. 80.

8 ibid., pp. 133ff., pp. 186ff.

9 ibid., p. 131. Arendt here cites Lord Cromer, a British colonial administrator.

10 This seems as well to be one of the implications of Arendt's analysis of American foreign policy in 'Lying in Politics'. What effect such an implication might have had on Arendt's generally favourable view of American institutions is an interesting matter for speculation. Her increasing fear about the future of the American state suggests that it may have been considerable.

11 ibid., pp. 147, 148.

12 ibid., p. 157.

13   ibid., p. 155.

14   I do not mean to suggest that political life before the nineteenth century represented a golden age of politics, to which we should attempt to return. As Rousseau so brilliantly reminds us, those social and political structures were clearly built on oppression and domination. There was no shortage of what Max Horkheimer once called murder with and without due process, and as Herbert Marcuse suggests at the conclusion of *Eros and Civilization*, there can be no redemption of those who died in pain, even if this pain was 'necessary' because of the haunting presence of scarcity. Nevertheless, those structures did hold out the prospect of an organization of life more consistent with the demands of the human essence. As Marcuse also points out, the early development of the bourgeois state had a progressive character because bourgeois rationality and critical rationality coincided. By the end of the nineteenth century, this was no longer true. Bourgeois values had turned on themselves.

Nor does Arendt herself pine for a golden age. In this respect, her comments on slavery, certainly an institution widely prevalent throughout history (including of course in ancient Greece) are worth noting: 'Slavery's crime against humanity did not begin when one people defeated and enslaved its enemies (though of course this was bad enough), but when slavery became an institution in which some men were "born" free and others slave, when it was forgotten that it was man who had deprived his fellow men of freedom and when the sanction for the crime was attributed to nature' (*The Origins of Totalitarianism*, p. 297).

15   ibid., pp. 300, 297.

16   ibid., p. 54.

17   The complex character of the relation of the Jews to post-Enlightenment European culture and society is a central theme in Arendt's study, *Rahel Vernhagen: The Life of a Jewish Woman* revised edn (New York and London: Harcourt Brace Jovanovich, 1974).

18   Arendt, *The Origins of Totalitarianism*, p. 478.

19   ibid., p. 311.

20   ibid., p. 338.

21   ibid., p. 362.

22   ibid., pp. 305ff.

23   ibid., p. 374.

24   ibid., p. 325.

25   Paul Piccone criticizes the use made of the 'totalitarianism' thesis by most analysts to explain the political dynamics of the former Soviet Union precisely on the grounds that this seriously underestimates the importance of leadership, not just in a contemporary context but historically as well. P. Piccone, 'Paradoxes of *Perestroika*', *Telos* vol. 23, no. 2 (summer 1990), p. 9.

26   Arendt, *The Origins of Totalitarianism*, p. 419.

27   ibid., p. 427.

28 ibid., p. 445.

29 For an example of the criticisms, see M. Canovan, op. cit. Bernard Crick outlines some of the major criticisms and offers his own positive assessment in 'On Rereading *The Origins of Totalitarianism*', in Hill (ed.), *Hannah Arendt: The Recovery of the Public World*, pp. 27–47. An interesting general treatment of Arendt's account is S. J. Whitfield, *Into the Dark: Hannah Arendt and Totalitarianism* (Philadelphia: Temple University Press, 1980).

30 This term provides the title for a masterful novel by the Czech-Canadian writer, Joseph Svorecky.

31 For an analysis of the intellectual foundations of the so-called New Right, particularly in the United States, see H. Chorney, M. Mendell and P. Hansen, 'Les sources de la Nouvelle Droite americaine', in L. Jalbert and L. Beaudry (sous la direction de), *Les Métamorphoses de la Pensée Libérale* (Sillery, Que.: Presses de l'Université du Quebéc, 1987), pp. 87–123. A good general treatment of American neo-conservatism in particular is P. Steinfels, *The Neo-Conservatives* (New York: Simon and Schuster, 1979).

32 The best-known statement of the 'ungovernability' thesis is M. J. Crozier et al. *The Crisis of Democracy: Report on the Governability of Democracies to the Trilateral Commission* (New York: New York University Press, 1975).

33 A recent example of this questioning of the modern Enlightenment is A. Heller, *Can Modernity Survive?* (Berkeley: University of California Press, 1990).

34 C. Lefort, 'Hannah Arendt and the Question of the Political', p. 55. In the context of this claim, Lefort, misleadingly in my view, links Arendt to Martin Heidegger and Leo Strauss.

35 Arendt, *The Origins of Totalitarianism*, p. 142.

36 As I hope should be clear throughout this book, this is *not* to claim that other elements of the modern project are unproblematic. Arendt *is* critical of modernity as such in many respects. As I argued in chapter 1, this is one significant difference she has with Marx. Nevertheless, it is true that she indicts bourgeois modernity as particularly culpable in the rise of totalitarianism. And it should be remembered that, as important as it is to her thought and to twentieth-century life, totalitarianism is only one feature of the modern world. Put otherwise, Arendt is no theorist of a Weberian 'iron cage' or a Marcusean 'one-dimensionality' – and such perspectives tend to go hand in hand with indictments of modernity as such.

37 ibid., pp. 34ff.

38 ibid., p. 238.

39 ibid., pp. 458, 454.

40 For Lefort, Marx himself provided an exemplary, if frequently self-contradictory, figure, a thinker for whom the 'social imaginary' – images and visions of lived experience not capturable exactly by the logic of

historical materialism – was vital. A domain beyond thought, but only accessible through thought, played a critical role in his reflections. See Lefort, 'Marx: One Vision of History to Another', in *The Political Forms of Modern Society*, pp. 139–80.

41 Lefort, 'Reversibility', *Telos* vol. 18, no. 1 (spring 1985), pp. 106–20.

42 Lefort, 'The Logic of Totalitarianism', in *The Political Forms of Modern Society*, p. 279.

43 ibid., pp. 279–80.

44 Lefort, 'Hannah Arendt and the Question of the Political', p. 55.

45 An excellent example of this is 'From Marx to Aristotle, From Aristotle to Us', *Social Research* 45:4 (winter 1978), pp. 667–739.

46 C. Castoriadis, 'The Destinies of Totalitarianism', *Salmagundi* no. 60 (spring-summer 1983), pp. 107–22.

47 ibid., p. 119. For a brief account of this new regime, see Castoriadis, 'Facing the War', *Telos* vol. 13, no. 4 (winter 1980–81), pp. 43–61. According to Castoriadis, Marxists cannot understand this new regime because Brute Force destroys the rationality of history.

48 Castoriadis, 'The Destinies of Totalitarianism', pp. 119, 120.

49 'The slogans [of the peace movement] apparently most "serious and political" – the de-nuclearization of Europe from Poland to Portugal – are politically weak and morally untenable. What does it matter that the Russians and Americans annihilate one another with atomic weapons, so long as we Europeans survive! Everything takes place as if for people of Western society there is nothing left worth paying for, paying with one's person, risking one's life' (Castoriadis and P. Thibault, 'The Toughest and Most Fragile of Regimes', *Telos* vol. 15, no. 1 (spring 1982), p. 182). For more general reflections on the cultural content of these developments, see Castoriadis, 'The Crisis of Western Societies', *Telos* vol. 15, no. 3 (fall 1982), pp. 17–28.

50 A. Heller, 'An Imaginary Preface to the 1984 Edition of Hannah Arendt's *The Origins of Totalitarianism*', p. 250.

51 ibid., p. 258.

52 ibid., pp. 250ff.

53 ibid., pp. 257–8.

54 ibid., p. 244.

55 This does not even begin, of course, to take into account Mary O'Brien's criticisms of the 'male-stream' character of this heritage.

56 He is not of course alone in this on the left or near-left. See, for example, J. Herf, 'Western Society and Public Discussion: The "Double Decision" Makes Sense', *Telos* vol. 15, no. 2 (summer 1982), pp. 114–28 and 'The "Double Decision" Still Makes Sense: A Response to My Critics', *Telos* vol. 16, no. 2 (summer 1983), pp. 156–71. Those advocates of a resurgent 'civil society' who still see themselves on the left have not been immune to similar perspectives, even if they have not gone quite as far as Herf has in defending the new Cold War. These advocates include Agnes Heller, Jean Cohen and Andrew Arato, among others. For a representative

collection of their views, particularly as these relate to the Soviet experience, see F. Feher and A. Arato (eds), *Gorbachev: The Debate* (New York: Humanities Press, 1989).

57 Heller, 'An Imaginary Preface', p. 244.

58 Heller, 'The Great Republic', in Feher and Heller, op. cit. pp. 187–200.

59 Positions taken years ago in this controversy have in many cases remained virtually unshaken. Thus a recent article by one of the original critics of Arendt's account claims flatly that, according to *Eichmann in Jerusalem*, 'the organizer of the final solution was a normal man without fanatical hatred of Jews, while Jewish leaders were his accomplices' (G. Ezorsky, 'Hannah Arendt's View of Totalitarianism and the Holocaust', *The Philosophical Forum* vol. XVI, nos 1–2 (winter 1984–85, p. 63). Unlike other critics, Ezorsky sees the connection between *Eichmann in Jerusalem* and *The Origins of Totalitarianism*, but then misrepresents the argument of the latter work by claiming that Arendt's account of how totalitarianism meets human needs in a distorted way is equivalent to arguing that people under totalitarian rule willingly co-operated in their own oppression, and that totalitarianism was politically invincible. Such claims are patently false, as the conclusion of *The Origins of Totalitarianism* makes clear. Hence Ezorsky's criticism that 'Arendt's notion of people gladly conforming to terror is contrary to democratic hopes that are pinned on the desire to be free' (p. 80) is in every respect gratiutous. The first part is as wrong about Arendt's argument as the last reflects her own aspirations.

Ezorsky's arguments provide a good summary of the essential elements of the hostile attacks on *Eichmann in Jerusalem*. A significant exception to this general line of criticism, one which does take Arendt's theoretical claims seriously, is N. Fruchter, 'Arendt's Eichmann and Jewish Identity', *Studies on the Left* vol. 5, no. 2 (winter 1965).

60 If, as Norman Fruchter suggested, the debate posed the question of the nature of the American state and the potential for reaction found there in light of the forces identified at work in Nazi Germany, then there may be a connection between hostile responses to Arendt's argument in the 1960s, and the emergence of neo-conservate opposition to the attack of the new left and the counterculture on the American state and society in the context of the war in Vietnam in the 1970s and 1980s. Fruchter, himself, presciently identified and critically examined those forces at work among American Jewish intellectuals which would later induce many of them to embrace neo-conservative ideas. He also anticipated what these ideas would involve: an exaggerated sense of American patriotism and an inflated, personalistic religiosity.

A prime example of the kind of intellectual Fruchter had in mind is Norman Podhoretz. Podhoretz strongly criticized Arendt's interpretation of Eichmann when it first appeared, and subsequently opened up the pages of *Commentary*, the journal he has long edited, to neo-conservative ideas, while at the same time developing his own. See, for example, *Why We Were in Vietnam* (New York: Simon and Schuster, 1982).

One neo-conservative thinker who draws a explicit connection between Arendt's ideas and those of the New Left, and thus links her to what he views as the political irresponsibility of the 1960s, is Peter Berger. See 'A Woman of This Century', *New York Times Book Review*, April 1982, pp. 1, 20–1. (This is a review of Young-Bruehl's biography.) Berger sees Arendt and the New Left as sharing a romantic, anti-bourgeois tradition of revolutionary eschatology. Cf. A. McKenna, 'Bannisterless Politics: Hannah Arendt and her Children', *History of Political Thought* 5(2) (summer 1984), pp. 333–60.

61 This proposal calls for a new international order and penal code that could deal with the new crime of genocide, the unfortunately enduring legacy of totalitarianism. See Arendt, *Eichmann in Jerusalem* (New York: The Viking Press, 1965), *passim* and Epilog.

62 ibid., p. 289.

63 ibid., p. 296.

64 ibid., p. 136.

65 Arendt, *The Life of the Mind Volume I: Thinking* (New York and London: Harcourt Brace Jovanovich, 1978), pp. 3ff.

66 Arendt, *Eichmann in Jerusalem*, p. 137.

67 ibid., p. 150.

68 See C. S. Maier, *The Unmasterable Past: History, Holocaust, and German National Identity* (Cambridge, Mass. and London: Harvard University Press, 1988).

69 C. Taylor, *Sources of the Self* (Cambridge, Mass.: Harvard Unversity Press, 1989), p. 3.

Chapter 5

1 Jaspers to Arendt, 5 May 1963; cited in Young-Bruehl, *Hannah Arendt: For Love of the World*, p. 404.

2 Arendt, *On Revolution* (New York: The Viking Press, 1965), p. 21.

3 ibid., pp. 26–7. Emphasis mine.

4 ibid., p. 35.

5 ibid., p. 25.

6 ibid.

7 Arendt's support for the American Revolution was not in this respect unqualified, however. The 'social question' in the form of slavery did exist and was ultimately to become a cancer in the American body politic. See ibid., p. 65. Cf. Arendt, 'Civil Disobedience', in *Crises of the Republic*, pp. 51–102.

8 Arendt, *On Revolution*, p. 54.

9 ibid., pp. 56–7.

10 ibid., p. 64.

11 ibid., p. 60.
12 ibid., p. 69.
13 See J. Miller, *Rousseau Dreamer of Democracy* (New Haven and London: Yale University Press, 1984), esp. ch. 6.
14 Arendt, *On Revolution*, p. 74. As Arendt was aware, Rousseau's influence on Kant's conception of 'duty' was considerable – a main reason why she parted company with Kant on some crucial matters, even in the face of his otherwise considerable influence on her thinking.
15 ibid., p. 91.
16 For a treatment of Rousseau which is sensitive to this dimension of his position, see A. Horowitz, *Rousseau, Nature, and History* (Toronto: University of Toronto Press, 1987).
17 Arendt, *On Revolution*, pp. 81–2.
18 ibid., p. 83.
19 ibid., p. 84.
20 ibid., p. 91.
21 ibid., pp. 91–3.
22 ibid., p. 134.
23 ibid., p. 222.
24 ibid., p. 176.
25 Arendt, 'The Conquest of Space and the Stature of Man', in *Between Past and Future*, p. 267.
26 ibid., p. 274.
27 Arendt, *On Revolution*, pp. 234–5.
28 See, again, 'Civil Disobedience'.
29 This is, of course, a main concern of 'Lying in Politics'. See also Arendt, 'Home to Roost', in S. B. Warner (ed.), *The American Experiment* (Boston: Houghton, Mifflin, 1976), pp. 61–77.
30 Arendt, 'Civil Disobedience' and 'On Violence'.
31 For a similar critical account of the American experience, one explicitly indebted to Arendt, see N. Jacobson, 'Parable and Paradox: In Response to Arendt's *On Revolution*', *Salmagundi* no. 60 (spring-summer 1983), pp. 123–39. Jacobson sees the American revolutionary spirit carried forward under the Articles of Confederation, and then snuffed out by the Constitution.

   The considerations raised by Arendt and Jacobson seem noticeably absent from Castoriadis' assessment of the democratic heritage (of which the United States must *inter alia* be thought a bearer). They are also missing from a recent attempt by Ferenc Feher to apply Arendt's ostensible lessons about the American Revolution counterfactually to its French counterpart. See Feher, 'Freedom and the "Social Question" (Hannah Arendt's Theory of the French Revolution)', *Philosophy and Social Criticism* vol. 12, no. 1 (spring 1987), pp. 1–30. To be sure, Feher places his remarks in the context of an interesting argument about Arendt's failure to develop what is immanent in her work: a generalized theory of modernity.

32 Arendt, *On Revolution*, p. 225.
33 J. Habermas, 'The Public Sphere: An Encyclopedia Article', in S. E. Bronner and D. M. Kellner (eds), *Critical Theory and Society: A Reader* (New York and London: Routledge, 1989), pp. 136, 139.
34 Arendt, *On Revolution*, p. 272.
35 ibid., p. 231.
36 Sheldon Wolin brilliantly explores this paradox in his *Politics and Vision* (Boston: Little, Brown and Company, 1960), ch. 8.
37 Arendt, *On Revolution*, p. 221.
38 ibid., pp. 258–9.
39 ibid., p. 238.
40 ibid., p. 256. An important American critic of this historical dynamic was the late William Appleman Williams. See in particular *The Great Evasion* (Chicago: Quadrangle Books, 1964), *The Contours of American History* (Chicago: Quadrangle Books, 1966) and *Empire As A Way of Life* (New York: Oxford University Press, 1980).
      A number of studies which adopt a perspective on the question of civic culture similar to Arendt's have recently appeared. Especially noteworthy are R. N. Bellah et al., *Habits of the Heart: Individualism and Commitment in American Life* (New York: Harper and Row, 1985) and W. M. Sullivan, *Reconstructing Public Philosophy* (Berkeley and Los Angeles: University of California Press, 1986).
41 Arendt, *On Revolution*, p. 252.
42 ibid., p. 260.
43 ibid., p. 267. Arendt here cites the work of the Austrian socialist, Max Adler. For further considerations of this theme, see Arendt, 'Thoughts on Politics and Revolution', in *Crises of the Republic*, pp. 201–33.
44 ibid., p. 268.
45 ibid., p. 278.
46 ibid., p. 284.
47 ibid. Elsewhere, Arendt makes the following argument: 'By no means every resident of a country needs to be a member in such councils. Not everyone wants to or has to concern himself with public affairs. In this fashion a self-selective process is possible that would draw together a true political elite in a country. Anyone who is not interested in public affairs will simply have to be satisfied with their being decided without him. But each person must be given the opportunity' (Arendt, 'Thoughts on Politics and Revolution', p. 233).
48 ibid., pp. 280–1. For a lucid account of these theories, see C. B. Macpherson, *The Life and Times of Liberal Democracy* (Oxford: Oxford University Press, 1977), ch. 4.
49 ibid.
50 Arendt, 'Preface: The Gap Between Past and Future', in *Between Past and Future*, pp. 11ff.
51 Arendt, *The Human Condition*, p. 262.
52 Arendt, *On Revolution*, pp. 61ff.

53 Habermas, 'Hannah Arendt's Communications Concept of Power' *Social Research* vol. 44, no. 1 (spring 1977).
54 Arendt, *On Revolution*, p. 285.
55 Arendt, 'On Hannah Arendt', in Hill (ed.), *Hannah Arendt: The Recovery of the Public World*, p. 336.

Chapter 6

1 Arendt, *Lectures on Kant's Political Philosophy* ed. R. Beiner (Chicago: University of Chicago Press, 1982), p. 17.
2 I leave aside here the question whether Plato was being deliberately ironic in proposing that the philosopher rule, and that his real purpose was to argue *against* this. For her part, Arendt does not question Plato's expressed position.

  For a sensitive and subtle treatment of the meaning of Plato's political solution, see the work of Alkis Kontos, particularly 'Domination: Metaphor and Political Reality', in Kontos (ed.), *Domination* (Toronto: University of Toronto Press, 1975), pp. 211–28, and 'The Intellectual Life', *Canadian Journal of Political and Social Theory*, vol. 1, no. 3 (fall 1977), pp. 59–70.
3 'The whole history of philosophy . . . tells us so much about the objects of thought and so little about the process of thinking itself' Arendt, 'Thinking and Moral Considerations: A Lecture', *Social Research* 38:3 (autumn 1971) pp. 424–5.
4 Arendt, *The Human Condition*, p. 8.
5 ibid., p. 325.
6 Arendt, 'Personal Responsibility Under Dictatorship'.
7 Arendt, *The Life of the Mind: Thinking* (New York: Harcourt Brace Jovanowich, 1978), p. 5.
8 Arendt, 'Thinking and Moral Considerations', p. 434.
9 ibid., p. 437.
10 ibid., pp. 434–5.
11 ibid., p. 435.
12 ibid., p. 436.
13 ibid., p. 427. Arendt makes clear that it is not the historical figure of Socrates, but the model of the Socratic thinker which interests her in these reflections. Of course by no means is Socrates the only figure so treated. We have seen already her account of Robespierre in the French Revolution. And about Marx, Arendt notes that in an attempt to discredit his ideas, 'professional anti-Marxists' had 'even discovered that Karl Marx himself was unable to make a living, forgetting for a moment the generations of authors whom he has "supported" ' (*The Human Condition*, p. 71). The role that an image or model of a person plays in history may be more significant than the historical facts of the person's

life. In any event the facts themselves do not exhaust the meaning of a life.

14 Arendt, 'Thinking and Moral Considerations', p. 441.
15 ibid., p. 442.
16 ibid.
17 ibid., pp. 444, 445.
18 ibid., p. 445.
19 ibid., pp. 445–6.
20 ibid., p. 446.
21 A primary purpose of Arendt's treatment of modern education is to indicate how this vital institution fails to equip children for the world. See 'The Crisis in Education', in *Between Past and Future*, pp. 173–96.
22 Arendt, 'Thinking and Moral Considerations', p. 445.
23 Arendt, 'Understanding and Politics', *Partisan Review* XX/4 (July-Aug. 1953), p. 391.
24 ibid., p. 377.
25 ibid., p. 380.
26 ibid., p. 387.
27 ibid., p. 383.
28 ibid., p. 391.
29 Submergence in the world, in the sense meant here, also seems the hallmark of political decisionism. This appears to provide further evidence against Martin Jay's assessment of Arendt as a proto-political decisionist. See Jay, *Permanent Exiles: Essays on the Intellectual Migration from Europe to America* (New York: Columbia University Press, 1985), pp. 237–56.
30 D. Misgeld, 'Critical Theory and Hermeneutics: The Debate between Habermas and Gadamer', in J. O'Neill (ed.), *On Critical Theory* (New York: The Seabury Press, 1976), p. 176. Cf. H.-G. Gadamer, *Truth and Method* (New York: The Crossroad Publishing Co., 1984), p. 261.
31 Arendt, 'Understanding and Politics', p. 391.
32 ibid., pp. 391, 392.
33 ibid., p. 391.
34 ibid., p. 392.
35 Cf. R. Beiner, 'Preface' to Arendt, *Lectures on Kant's Political Philosophy*. I disagree with Beiner's claim in his interpretive essay on this work (p. 91) that there are in Arendt's writings two theories of judging, an 'early' and a 'late' theory, with the first considering it from the point of view of the *vita activa* and the second from the vantage point of the *vita contemplativa*. My claim is that in Arendt's work, judging is *both* at the same time because the separation of the two domains is not as complete as is often thought.

For an account of judging which shares common ground with the one I am suggesting here, see E. Young-Bruehl 'Reflections on Hannah Arendt's *The Life of the Mind* [New York, 1978]', *Political Theory* vol. 10, no. 2 (May 1982), pp. 277–305.

36 Obviously official legal judgements do more than persuade. They compel. Yet their compulsion is different from force, although of course force stands behind legal judgements. The persuasive character of legal judgements resembles what Habermas calls the peculiarly 'forceless force' of the better argument. Indeed this quality of legal judging may be thought the basis of the acceptance of actual force as the means of ensuring that judgements are carried out.

    Needless to say, this conception of judging, like Habermas' conception of the ideal speech situation (which itself reflects the significance of the tradition of public law for his own political theory) is counterfactual. That is, it involves a socio-political phenomenon which is only partially realized in actual social life, or realized in distorted ways, or in ways which, because of the prevailing social structure, produce undesirable unintended consequences. The persuasive force of legal judgements is more the product of the political authoritativeness of those judging than of the intrinsic properties of the judging process itself. Enforcement is secured through citizen obedience and not (rational) citizen consent.

    In this light, the crisis of authority in Arendt's terms is also a crisis of judging, something which totalitarianism and the Eichmann case seemed to suggest. The attempt to undo the facts which Arendt identifies with the politics of lying may be seen as an ironic and distorted attempt to reaffirm the capacity to judge in the face of a seemingly intractable and undesirable reality.

37 Arendt, *The Life of the Mind: Willing*, p. 257.
38 Kant, *Critique of Judgement*, no. 40; cited in Arendt, *Lectures on Kant's Political Philosophy*, p. 43.
39 Arendt, *Lectures*, p. 43.
40 ibid.
41 ibid., p. 44.
42 Fred Dallmayr, whose work is strongly influenced by Arendt, is particularly insightful on this question of receptivity. See his *Polis and Praxis* (Cambridge, Mass: M.I.T. Press, 1984).
43 Arendt, *Lectures*, p. 62. She cites here Kant, *Critique of Judgement*, no. 50.
44 ibid., p. 63.
45 Kant, *Critique of Judgement* no. 40; cited in Arendt, *Lectures*, p. 71.
46 ibid., p. 72.
47 ibid., p. 52.
48 ibid.
49 Kant, *Critique of Judgement*, no. 28; cited in Arendt, *Lectures*, p. 53.
50 Arendt, *Lectures*, p. 54.
51 ibid., p. 77.
52 ibid.
53 ibid., p. 40.
54 ibid., p. 71.
55 Cf. ibid., pp. 22ff.

56 It may be that reason itself is undermined by this split between hope and pessimism which seems to inform Kant's thought. This is perhaps why Eichmann could with no apparent sense of contradiction or unease uphold the categorical imperative.

57 Cicero, *On the Orator* 3:197; cited in Arendt, *Lectures*, p. 64.

58 It would have been interesting in this light to have Arendt's assessment of contemporary developments in Eastern Europe.

59 Arendt, 'Franz Kafka: A Revaluation', *Partisan Review*, X/4 (fall 1944), p. 422.

Conclusion

1 Arendt tended to shy away from self-categorization, but she did allow that she was a phenomenologist of sorts. These concerns suggest the extent to which this was so. In this respect her earlier writings on the German philosophic tradition, far less well known than her later ones, take on new significance.

2 Arendt, *The Human Condition*, p. 71.

3 ibid., p. 182.

4 ibid., p. 175.

5 That there is a powerful need for this reconciliation is one of the great insights of Orwell's *Nineteen Eighty-Four*. The scene involving the discredited former revolutionaries at the Chestnut Tree Cafe is critical here. The totalitarian state forces one to undertake unconscionable acts, binds him or her to it by virtue of complicity with it in such acts and forgives the person – only to continually repeat the cycle as a means of reinforcing submission to its dictates. I consider this aspect of Orwell's novel, and relate it to Arendt's concerns, in my ' "when men [*sic*] are different from one another and do not, live alone": Orwell and Arendt on Total Control and Ontology', in Chorney and Hansen, *Toward a Humanist Political Economy*.

6 Given that there are two dimensions to the private realm – the economic and the intimate – the 'abolition' of the social would entail a return to craftwork in terms of which people could invest their products with emotional resonance. This is unlikely on a mass scale, but might be possible in certain contexts in which small-scale production could be undertaken. It would be interesting to see if new microtechnologies could contribute to this.

7 The notion of an 'elementary republic' seems implicit in recent attempts to develop a theoretical account of a new federalism as an alternative to the traditional nation-state. In this respect, see, for example, recent issues of the journal *Telos*, particularly its special issue on federalism, vol. 25, no. 1 (spring 1992).

8 P. Kress, 'The Web and the Tree: Metaphors of Reason and Value', *Midwest Journal of Political Science* vol. 13, no. 3 (August 1969), p. 398.

9 ibid., p. 399.
10 ibid., p. 408.
11 ibid., p. 410.
12 ibid., p. 412.
13 ibid., p. 414.
14 M. Merleau-Ponty, 'A Note on Machiavelli', in *Signs* trans. R. C. McClearly (Evanston, Ill.: Northwestern University Press, 1964), p. 217. This issue is highly relevant to Arendt's distinction between the individual (subject) and the person. The self-consciously and deliberately 'moral' individual is very much the subject who seeks to control the person revealed in the public sphere and, as Arendt sees it, '[a]nyone who consciously tries to intrude his personality into his work is play-acting, and in so doing he throws away the real opportunity that publication means for himself and others' (Arendt, *Men in Dark Times*, p. 73). Arendt's analysis of Herman Melville's *Billy Budd* may also be understood in this light.
15 ibid., p. 211.
16 Machiavelli, *The Prince* trans. G. Bull (London: Penguin Books, 1981), p. 101.
17 Arendt, *Men in Dark Times*, pp. 74, 73.
18 ibid., p. 78.
19 ibid., p. 79.
20 ibid., pp. 85, 86.
21 ibid., p. 90.
22 ibid., p. 92.
23 ibid., p. 93.
24 ibid.
25 ibid., pp. 85, 80.
26 ibid., p. 86.
27 See for example R. A. Berman and P. Piccone, 'Hidden Agendas: The Young Heidegger and the Post-Modern Debate', *Telos* vol. 21, no. 3 (fall 1988), pp. 117–27 and G. Steiner, 'Heidegger's Silence', in *George Steiner: A Reader* (New York: Oxford University Press, 1984), pp. 258–65. The controversy has recently been renewed further with the publication of Victor Farias' *Heidegger and Nazism* trans. P. Burrell (Philadelphia: Temple University Press, 1989).
28 Arendt, 'Heidegger and Modern Philosophy', in M. Murray (ed.), *Heidegger and Modern Philosophy* (New Haven and London: Yale University Press, 1978), pp. 296, 303. This essay was originally published in 1969.
29 ibid., pp. 298–9. Arendt does not deny the authenticity of this thinking experience. What she seems to question are its implications.
30 ibid., p. 298.
31 ibid., p. 299.
32 ibid., p. 301.
33 ibid.
34 ibid. Although Arendt does not write from a consciously feminist per-

spective, it is no accident that the Thracian episode involves a peasant 'girl' challenging male 'wisdom'. The perspective of a victim of generic oppression can lead to the articulation of a powerful critique of 'malestream' traditions of thought and political practice.

35 Arendt, 'The Crisis in Culture', pp. 225–6.

Index